P9-CMC-695

ENTREPRENEURSHIP EDUCATION AND TRAINING

Entrepreneurship Education and Training

COLETTE HENRY
Centre for Entrepreneurship Research,
Dundalk Institute of Technology

FRANCES HILL
School of Management and Economics
Queen's University, Belfast

CLAIRE LEITCH
School of Management and Economics
Queen's University, Belfast

ASHGATE

© Colette Henry, Frances Hill and Claire Leitch 2003

All rights reserved. No part of this publication may be reproduced, stored in a retrieval system or transmitted in any form or by any means, electronic, mechanical, photocopying, recording or otherwise without the prior permission of the publisher.

Colette Henry, Frances Hill and Claire Leitch have asserted their right under the Copyright, Designs and Patents Act, 1988, to be identified as authors of this work.

Published by
Ashgate Publishing Limited
Gower House
Croft Road
Aldershot
Hants GU11 3HR
England

Ashgate Publishing Company
Suite 420
101 Cherry Street
Burlington, VT 05401-4405
USA

Ashgate website: http://www.ashgate.com

British Library Cataloguing in Publication Data
Henry, Colette
    Entrepreneurship education and training
    1. Entrepreneurship - Great Britain 2. Occupational training
    - Great Britain 3. Small business - Great Britain
    I. Title II. Hill, Frances III. Leitch, Claire
    338'.04

Library of Congress Cataloging-in-Publication Data
Henry, Colette.
    Entrepreneurship education and training / Colette Henry,
  Frances Hill, and Claire Leitch.
      p. cm.
    Includes bibliographical references and index.
    ISBN 0-7546-3215-6
    1. Small business--Management--Study and teaching. 2. Entrepreneurship--Study and teaching. I. Hill, Frances, 1951- II. Leitch, Claire. III. Title.

  HD62.7.H4745 2003
  658.02'2'071--dc21

2003042195

ISBN 0 7546 3215 6

Printed and bound in Great Britain by Biddles Ltd *www.biddles.co.uk*

Contents

PART I: THEORETICAL FOUNDATION

PART II: A STUDY OF EFFECTIVENESS

List of Figures

List of Tables

Preface

In the OECD's[1] Bologna Charter on SME Policies it is recognised that SMEs are increasingly important in 'economic growth, job creation, regional and local development, and social cohesion', that 'entrepreneurship and a dynamic SME sector are important for restructuring economies and combating poverty', that 'globalisation, the acceleration of technological change and innovation create opportunities for SMEs but also involve transition costs and new challenges', and that 'SME policies need to be tailored to the circumstances and priorities of individual countries and sectors, while contributing to sustainable development and progress'.

Furthermore, the Bologna Charter identifies a number of contributors to enhanced SME competitiveness. First, 'a regulatory environment which does not impose undue burdens on SMEs and is conducive to entrepreneurship, innovation and growth'. Second, 'education and human resource management policies that: foster an innovative and entrepreneurial culture, including continuous training and lifelong learning; encourage mobility of human resources; and reduce skill disparities by improving the match between education and labour market demand'. Third, 'effective access to financial services, particularly to seed, working and development capital, including innovative financial instruments to reduce the risks and transactions costs of lending to SMEs'. Fourth, 'an environment that supports the development and diffusion of new technologies by and for SMEs to take advantage of the knowledge-based economy'. Fifth, 'strengthening public-private partnerships and political and social dialogue involving territorial and institutional actors as a tool for exchange of information, utilisation of knowledge and elaboration of policy'. Finally, 'ensuring the cost-effectiveness of SME policies and their consistency with other national policies, as well as with existing international programmes'.

Many of these areas have been, and continue to be, the subject of extensive academic research and debate. For example, there is now an extensive literature on the contribution of SMEs to innovation, *vis a vis* the role of large firms, both as innovators and as adopters of innovation, and much of this research has examined specifically the emergence, role and characteristics of the new (or high) technology-based firm. Equally, the operation of the capital markets and the flow of finance into the SME sector has been the focus of considerable research, which has examined the operation of the banking system, the provision of venture capital and, more recently, the operation and development of the business angel, or informal venture capital, market. The growth of interest in the economic (and

---

[1] OECD (2000) The Bologna Charter on SME Policies, pp. 247-250 OECD (2000), The Bologna Charter on SME Policies, pp. 247-250 in OECD (2001) *Enhancing SME Competitiveness: The OECD Bologna Ministerial Conference.*

social) contribution of the SME sector to job generation, innovation, economic development and social inclusion has also been reflected in an increased level and variety of public and private sector policy initiatives at local, regional, national and supranational scales to stimulate and support the development of the sector. This in turn has stimulated a growing body of academic research and literature evaluating the impact of these initiatives.

The result of this accumulated research evidence is that we now know much more about how the SME sector operates, its role in the development of economies at a range of scales, the issues that affect the future development of the sector, and the constraints that limit its development. Within this, however, there remain significant areas that have not yet been subject to the same level of debate and formal analysis, where we remain less knowledgeable than is appropriate about how the SME sector performs. In particular, to date the issue of human capital formation in an entrepreneurial and SME context, in its broadest sense, has been an under-researched and under-discussed field. This is not because issues of education and human resource management policies, the fostering of an innovative and entrepreneurial culture, continuous training and lifelong learning, the mobility of human resources, and skill disparities (in OECD's terms) are unimportant.

Indeed, the opposite is the case: attempts to improve the innovation performance and capability of the SME sector (and in particular to increase the absorptive capacity of the sector) or to improve the flow of finance into SMEs and entrepreneurial firms will be improved if the owners and managers of these firms have the aptitude, capability and skills to take or create the opportunities for the development of their businesses. In a very real sense, achievement of the goals of other policy initiatives (to improve access to finance, to increase innovation, to reduce the regulatory burden to allow SMEs to develop, and so on) requires increased levels of human capital in the sector, and without this, other interventions and support mechanisms will be less successful in meeting their goals. Equally, initiatives to increase the overall level of new firm formation (by encouraging the development of a more entrepreneurial culture, publicising effective and successful role models, addressing the stigma of failure, introducing education and awareness initiatives in schools and higher education institutions, removing the actual and perceived barriers to entry to an entrepreneurial career), as well as initiatives to support the survival and growth of those firms which do start, require effective mechanisms to support human capital formation.

This is an area where academic research has tended to lag behind practice. There have been studies of the impact of investment in training in SMEs, mostly using cross-sectional panel data rather than longitudinal process-based data, which have suggested that there are few identifiable returns to training. Yet most researchers and policy makers – if not SME owner/managers – continue to believe (rightly in my view) that effective and appropriate training can and should make a difference to firm performance. There is growing interest in the phenomenon of 'entrepreneurial learning', much of the literature on which consists of little more than accounts of training and learning interventions and programmes within SMEs or among collectives of SMEs. However, such literature is at least redirecting attention to the need to formally consider and address the issues of what training (by which I include by extension education and learning needs) should be provided, by whom, using what delivery channels, to what client bases and with what effect. Nevertheless, in entrepreneurship, as in other areas of management studies, issues of education and training remain something of a Cinderella activity, which is only now beginning to come out of the shadows. What we need more of, therefore, are robust studies and evaluations of entrepreneurship education and training initiatives across the full range of provision, and across national boundaries (to reflect variations in priorities and circumstances), because what works and is appropriate at the pre-start stage, for example, will not necessarily be appropriate for the established business. Only then will we begin to fully understand how to meet the challenge of maximising the contribution of entrepreneurial activity to local, regional and national economic development.

Richard T Harrison
Dixons Chair of Entrepreneurship and Innovation
University of Edinburgh Management School

November 2002

Acknowledgements

The authors wish to express their gratitude to all those who participated in this study. In addition, the advice and guidance of Professor Richard Harrison in developing the original outline for this monograph is fully appreciated.

The authors are particularly grateful to Professor Barra Ó Cinnéide for his contribution to the final structuring and editing process. His constructive comments on the content and presentation of the research findings have proved invaluable in the completion of this monograph.

Sincere thanks are also due to Gerry Carroll and Helen McKeown for their input as critical readers.

PART I
THEORETICAL FOUNDATION

Chapter 1

Entrepreneurship and Economic Development

Introduction

The importance of entrepreneurship and new business creation to the economy has been the subject of increased attention in recent years. Historically, economists have associated entrepreneurship with profit orientation, capital investment and risk (Cantillon, 1755; Say, 1803; Schumpeter, 1934), supporting the view that it is responsible for economic expansion (Weber, 1930; Schumpeter, 1965; Cole, 1965). In modern society, however, the role of entrepreneurship seems to have become even more important, with entrepreneurial activities viewed as having the potential to positively affect the economy of an area by building a strong economic base and creating jobs (Hisrich and Peters, 1998, p. 17).

For many, the power of entrepreneurship, and its importance in maintaining a growing and thriving economy, is unquestionable. In a significant proportion of the literature, entrepreneurship is seen as the 'engine' driving the economy of most nations, creating new industries, employment and wealth (Keats and Abercombie, 1991; Gorman et al., 1997; Jack and Anderson, 1998). Indeed, it has been argued that new business creation holds the key to economic regeneration (Musson and Cohen, 1996; Jack and Anderson, 1998) as it is through the process of entrepreneurship that industrial bases are renewed and economic structures are maintained. Thus, it is vitally important that entrepreneurship and new business creation are encouraged so that economies can continue to grow and prosper.

Aims of the Study

The study presented in this monograph explores entrepreneurship from an intervention perspective. Essentially, the study is an investigation into the nature and effectiveness of entrepreneurship education and training programmes. In particular, the principal aim of the study is to make a valuable contribution in the area of entrepreneurship training. In this context, the first main objective of the study is to contribute to the intervention debate by emphasising the importance of entrepreneurship to the economy and reviewing the various arguments both for and against intervention. Such issues are mainly dealt with in this introductory chapter.

The second objective is to make a useful contribution to existing entrepreneurship theory by reviewing the traditional approaches to considering the entrepreneurial personality, setting these in context alongside new and emerging theories, and thus facilitating a better understanding of the process of entrepreneurship. This leads to the study's third main objective, which is to make an important contribution to understanding the nature of entrepreneurship education and training programmes, and to this end, a review of other studies of effectiveness conducted to date is also included.

The fourth objective of the study is to significantly enhance understanding of the nature of *aspiring entrepreneurs*. For the purposes of this study, aspiring entrepreneurs are defined as 'individuals who are considering starting their own business, and who may be at different stages of the preparation and early stage development process'. Participants of entrepreneurship programmes have been chosen to represent aspiring entrepreneurs in this study. Providing a profile of the aspiring entrepreneur in this way not only updates previous profiles, but also serves to highlight the range of characteristic variables that need to be considered in entrepreneurship programme provision.

Another key objective of the study is to contribute significantly to the effectiveness debate by comparing the various inputs and outputs of a number of entrepreneurship training programmes in operation in Europe. However, the main contribution of the study to effectiveness is represented by a focused longitudinal study where both the tangible and intangible outcomes of a particular entrepreneurship training programme are examined. An aspect which enhances the findings of this study is the use of control and comparator groups which, given the nature of the field, are becoming more and more difficult to find. Other studies of effectiveness in this field have tended to focus on either qualitative or quantitative outputs, often utilising a restricted range of methodologies, each with their own difficulties and drawbacks. This study, however, has utilised a combination of methodologies, including qualitative and quantitative techniques, which has helped to facilitate the analysis of both tangible and intangible outcomes. In this regard, one of the main aims of the study is to portray the views of actual programme participants.

Finally, the ultimate objective of this study is to highlight key considerations for programme design and delivery, and to offer some practical suggestions for improving overall programme effectiveness. The study, therefore, concludes with a framework for entrepreneurship programme design, presented in the form of a set of guidelines and recommendations which are based on the findings from the authors' study and which are intended to have wide ranging applicability. In this respect, this book is expected to be of interest to an international audience which includes academic researchers, as well as lecturers and fellow scholars in the field of Entrepreneurship. In addition, the implications of the empirical work will be of particular interest to policy makers and those involved in entrepreneurship education and training design, provision and funding.

This monograph comprises two substantive sections. Part I – chapters 1 to 4, lay the theoretical foundation for the empirical work by reviewing the origins of the field in an attempt to clarify the reader's understanding of the process of entrepreneurship. The various traditional approaches to studying the entrepreneur are examined, and new and emerging approaches are also explored. The issues involved in starting a new business are considered, as are the educational and training needs of aspiring and established entrepreneurs. The differences between entrepreneurship education and training are highlighted, and emphasis is placed on the need for entrepreneurship educators and trainers to abandon traditional teaching methods in favour of learning approaches more akin to real life situations.

In part II – chapters 5 to 9, the focus shifts to consider entrepreneurship training in practice. The objectives, structure, content and outputs of various European entrepreneurship programmes are compared, and the various characteristics of aspiring entrepreneurs are examined. The issue of effectiveness is further examined through a small, focused longitudinal study, which tracks a group of programme participants over a three-year period, and considers their particular views and experiences. The book concludes by using the findings of the authors' study to highlight the key considerations for designers, providers and funders of entrepreneurship training programmes, and offers some practical suggestions to improve programme effectiveness. Finally, additional issues in the field of entrepreneurship training that the authors feel require further investigation, are identified.

This introductory chapter examines the contribution of entrepreneurship to the economy and to society, and leads to a discussion on the need for and benefits of, supportive, structured interventions. The growth of the small firms sector is also discussed, and some of the reasons behind this growth are examined. The economic debate surrounding intervention in the development of new business creation is presented, and the various arguments both for and against structured interventions are considered. This is followed by a consideration of the various types of intervention strategy and the general enterprise policies in operation in the USA, Europe, the UK and Ireland.

The Importance of Entrepreneurship to the Economy

Fiet (2000b, p. 102) believes that the sustained interest in entrepreneurship is more than just a fad; rather it reflects an 'emerging economic environment created by the confluence of changes in the corporate world, new technology and emerging world markets'. Indeed, academics, politicians and policy-makers now accept the potential contribution that entrepreneurship can make to an economy (Bruyat and Julien, 2000). They recognise the very positive impact that new business creation can have on employment levels, as well as the competitive advantages that small firms can have over large firms (Scase, 2000).

From the literature, there appears to be some agreement that entrepreneurship is both beneficial and necessary for a healthy economy (Bolton, 1971; Keats and Abercombie, 1991; Hisrich and Peters, 1998; Gorman et al., 1997; Jack and Anderson, 1998). Indeed, the role of entrepreneurship in sustaining economies and producing prosperity is now widely recognised (Musson and Cohen, 1996; Jack and Anderson, 1998). For instance, Bruyat and Julien (2000), with particular reference to the US, have observed that 'the field of entrepreneurship is recognised as being of fundamental importance for our economy'. Alongside this, it has been strongly suggested that high levels of entrepreneurship create jobs and encourage growth (Economist, 1998), with some evidence that, in the USA, a rise in business birth rates tends to be directly followed by periods of economic growth (IPPR, 1998). A study by the job creation agency, Scottish Enterprise (1993), supports this point, and the conclusion is drawn that a high birth rate for businesses is a necessary condition for a healthy economy (Economist, 1998, p. 29). This view is supported by others who have found that virtually all new jobs created in the US, UK and Europe tend to be generated by either newly formed businesses or expanding firms (Daly, 1991; Timmons, 1994; Storey, 1994). In addition, Deakins (1999) notes that the share of total employment in the small business sector has increased steadily since the early 1980s. In particular, there has been a significant growth in the importance of the micro firm, i.e. a firm employing less than 10 people. The number of these firms appears to have almost doubled in the 1980s, and their volume continues to grow.

In the UK, start-up and micro businesses together create almost two-thirds of all new jobs (Daly, 1991), and there are now approximately 3.6 million small businesses in comparison to just over one million in 1979 (Johnson et al., 2000). The next section looks at this growth trend in more detail and considers some of the reasons behind it. Firstly, however, it is important to define the term 'small firm'.

Defining the Small Firm

There have been some difficulties with defining the small firm and this causes obvious problems for statistical analysis or international comparisons. Over the years, a number of different definitions have been used. The Bolton Committee (1971), for example, adopted a range of size definitions for the small firm, depending on the particular industry sector. Their definitions included a mixture of different turnover and employment statistics, such as, a maximum of 200 employees in the manufacturing sector and £50,000 turnover in retailing. According to Bridge et al. (1998, p. 101), the UK's DTI (Department of Trade and Industry) uses the following definitions for small businesses:

- 1 – 9 employees   micro
- 10 – 49 employees   small
- 50 – 249 employees   medium
- 250+ employees   large

The US Small Business Administration sets the limit for small and medium sized enterprises (SMEs) at under 500 employees, while, in the past, the

EC has used the figure of 250 employees to define an SME, with firms employing more than this categorised as larger businesses. More recently, the EC (2001) has defined the small enterprise as one that has less than 100 employees (Storey, 1994), and has also started using the term 'micro' enterprise, which is a firm employing fewer than 10 people. Thus, revised definitions for the firms in the SME sector suggest slightly different size categories, as follows:

- 1 – 10 employees   micro
- 11 – 50 employees   small (with a turnover of not more than €7 million)
- 51 – 250 employees   medium (with a turnover of not more than €40 million)
- 251+ employees   large (with a turnover of more than €40 million)

Some researchers prefer to use what is known as a *grounded* definition for the small firm. This is where representatives of the particular industry sector under research are asked for their definition of small, based on the prevailing industry structure and in relation to the economic activities in which the firms are involved. However, the revised EC definitions (1996) mentioned above would now appear to be the most readily accepted and most commonly used size categories for the small firms sector.

The Growth in the Small Firms Sector

The importance of new business creation to both the economy and society has been the focus of much attention since the Bolton Report (1971), which predicted the demise of the small firm in the UK:

> The contribution of the small firm to national output and employment is declining in the long term not only in this country (UK), but also in all the other developed countries. The number of small firms in existence in the United Kingdom is also decreasing. Behind these statistics lie a number of factors which amount to an increasingly hostile environment for the small firm. Indeed, we have found it extremely difficult to identify any factors working strongly in favour of the small firm (Bolton, 1971, p. 75).

The Bolton Report questioned the role of small firms in economic development and concluded that the contribution of such firms was in decline. Overall, the report showed that, although small firms appeared to be surviving, their share in economic activity on an international basis was declining and that this decline was more advanced in the UK than elsewhere.

Ironically, the decline of the UK small firms sector had actually come to an end in the late 1960s and early 1970s when there was a significant turnaround in the trend in small firms' share of manufacturing employment. Figures quoted by Stanworth and Gray (1991, pp. 4-5) show that the number employed in small manufacturing enterprises in the UK rose from 1,421,000 in 1968 to 1,565,000 in

1971, indicating that, in the manufacturing sector, the small firms' share of employment had risen from 19.2 per cent to 21.0 per cent. The number of new small firms in the UK manufacturing sector had also increased from 58,000 in 1968 to 71,000 in 1971. However, as mentioned above, this turnaround in the small firms sector did not become apparent until several years later; indeed, after the publication of the Bolton Report.

Stanworth and Gray (1991) refer to Bannock and Daly's (1990) study that reported a significant increase in the number of small businesses, as well as their share of employment, in the private sector for the period 1979 – 1986. During this period, the number of small businesses rose from 1.79 million to 2.47 million. As Table 1.1 shows, the number of firms in most size categories rose by between 18.6 per cent and 42.7 per cent, with the exception of the 100-199 and 1000+ categories.

Table 1.1 Growth in the UK Small Firms Sector between 1979 and 1986

Size Band (employees)	Number of Firms 1979	1986	Change (Per cent)	Percentage of Total Employment 1979	1986
1-10	1,596,677	2,241,683	+ 40.4	19.2	25.9
11-49	155,064	183,857	+ 18.6	14.5	16.8
50-99	15,585	19,732	+ 26.6	5.3	6.9
100-199	14,865	14,066	- 5.3	10.2	9.9
200-499	5,365	7,657	+ 42.7	8.1	11.9
500-999	2,169	2,974	+ 37.1	7.5	10.5
1000+	1,774	892	- 49.7	35.3	18.2
Totals	**1,791,499**	**2,470,861**	**+37.92**	**100**	**100**

(Adapted from Stanworth and Gray, 1991, p. 6).

Of significant importance is the marked increase in the number of very small or micro firms. This category of business increased significantly, with a substantial growth in the number of firms in every size category under 99 employees. In contrast, during the same period, the number of very large firms, i.e. those employing more than 1000, was reduced by almost half. In addition, the share of total employment increased in the smaller firms but decreased in the very large firms, again emphasising the growing importance of the small firms sector.

Deakins (1999) notes that the growth in the small firms sector has not been confined to the UK. Throughout the European Union (EU) there has been a significant increase in the number of small firms employing less than 100 people, with over three million jobs created in this sector between 1988 and 1993 (European Observatory for SMEs, 1994). Deakins (1999), concluding that the growth in the small firms sector was European wide, suggests that this growth was due to the following combination of factors:

- the decline of the UK's manufacturing sector and the growth of the service sector which favoured the smaller firm;
- smaller firms' suitability to smaller-scale production leading to a greater flexibility and a quicker market response time;
- changes in macro-economic and government policy in favour of small firms;
- private sector initiatives which encouraged enterprise;
- high unemployment rates in the 1980s.

Storey (1994), while agreeing that the 1980s witnessed a growth in the small firms sector in most developed countries, suggests that this was most apparent in the UK. He attributes this growth to *supply* and *demand* factors. On the supply side, Storey lists technological changes, cost advantages, unemployment, government policies and prices; while on the demand side, he lists structural changes, macro-economic conditions and economic development (p. 35).

Garavan et al. (1997) note that, since the 1970s, small businesses have become a net creator of jobs, while large businesses have become a net shedder (p. 11). Studies supporting this point include that of the European Observatory for SMEs (1993), which stated that 75 per cent of jobs created in the non-primary sector were in small and medium sized businesses. A study by Birch (1994) indicated that businesses with less than 20 employees were responsible for over two thirds of the net growth in employment in the United States during the period 1969 and 1979, while the larger businesses shed over 2.5 million jobs during the same period. Others (Fothergill and Gudgin, 1979; Storey and Johnson, 1987; Daly, 1991) have supported the significant job creation trend of the small firms sector, and some (Gallagher and Miller, 1991) have shown this trend to continue up to the end of the 1980s. According to the European Commission's (EC) report on 'Creating an Entrepreneurial Europe' (2001), more than 99 per cent of the 18 million EU enterprises in the non-agricultural market sectors are SMEs. They account for more than 66 per cent of total employment and 55 per cent of total business turnover in the EU (p. 17).

Why Intervene? – The Economic Debate

According to Hisrich and Ó Cinnéide (1985), while entrepreneurship is essential in any country for birthing new ideas, creating new enterprises and nurturing the economy, it is particularly important in areas where there is high unemployment and a small base of indigenous manufacturing companies (p. 1). Shapero (1982) agrees, supporting the view that entrepreneurs are critical to a growing economic environment. His model of the entrepreneurial event, which will be discussed in the next chapter, requires the presence of 'potential', i.e. a preparedness to accept opportunities, plus something which 'triggers' the decision to act. As Kruegel and Brazeal (1994) explain, the model assumes that inertia guides human behaviour until something interrupts or displaces that inertia, and this displacement can be positive or negative. The entrepreneurial event requires the potential to start a business to exist prior to the displacement. Resilience is the key for Shapero, since this is what characterises successful communities and organisations. It is, therefore, critical that a steady supply of potential entrepreneurs is identified and encouraged. However, as some researchers have pointed out (Caird, 1989; Storey, 1994; Deakins, 1999), discussions surrounding the role and importance of entrepreneurship for the health and growth of the economy, have not been without some controversy. According to Cole (1965) and Schumpeter (1965), enterprise can only exist in societies where there has been a considerable decentralisation of economic power, yet, at the same time, enterprise must be present in all developing economies (Aitken, 1965; Kirzner, 1978).

Thus, there is a question as to whether or not enterprise, and the small business sector in particular, should be deliberately encouraged and supported. The following sections will consider the arguments both in favour of, and against, intervention.

Arguments in Favour of Intervention

Entrepreneurship is seen to bring benefits at both the macro and micro levels of economic development. On the one hand, entrepreneurship provides benefits in terms of social and economic growth and, on the other, it provides benefits in terms of individual self-fulfilment, with the entrepreneur breaking through the barriers of class, race and gender (Stanworth and Curran, 1971). Gibb and Cotton (1998) support the idea of a macro-micro spectrum of benefits which can be gained from entrepreneurship, and illustrate these in terms of the various changes and pressures at the global, societal, organisational and individual levels (see Figure 1.1).

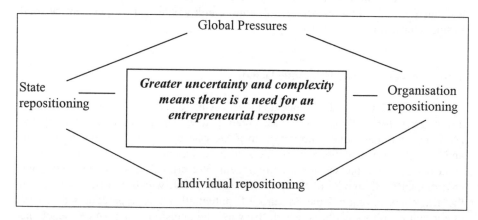

(Adapted from Gibb and Cotton, 1998, p. 8).

Figure 1.1 Entrepreneurship Education and the Changing World

At the global level, the reduction of trade barriers and the reality of the Euro currency, together with the advancements in telecommunications, technology and transportation, all combine to provide more opportunities as well as more uncertainty in the world. At the societal level, privatisation, deregulation, new forms of governance, mounting environmental concerns and the growing rights of minority groups are all presenting society with greater complexity and uncertainty.

At the organisational level, decentralisation, downsizing, re-engineering, strategic alliances, mergers and the growing demand for flexibility in the workforce, all contribute to an uncertain climate. Finally, at the Individual Level the individual is now faced with a wider variety of employment options, the probability of ending up with a portfolio of jobs, more responsibility at work and more stress. In addition, on a personal level, today's individual may be a single parent with more responsibility for managing credit and securing finances for their future (Gibb and Cotton, 1998, pp. 8-9).

Given the above, it is apparent that, at all levels, there will be a greater need for people to have entrepreneurial skills and abilities to enable them to deal with life's current challenges and an uncertain future. Furthermore, whatever their career choice or personal situation, individuals will be able to benefit from learning an innovative approach to problem solving; adapting more readily to change; becoming more self-reliant and developing their creativity through the study of entrepreneurship. There is no doubt that in any economic climate such learning could have far reaching benefits for society. It could be argued, therefore, that the need for entrepreneurship education and training has never been greater.

In addition to the above, there seems to be a belief that entrepreneurship can be developed and fostered by governmental action so that even the most economically deprived regions can be developed. Hisrich and Peters (1998) see the role of entrepreneurship in economic development as 'more than just increasing per capita output and income; it involves initiating and constituting change in the structure of business and society' (p. 14). They emphasise the need for an understanding of the product-evolution process where the focus is on innovation that is commercialised through entrepreneurial activity. For Hisrich and Peters, the product-evolution process begins with knowledge in the areas of science, thermodynamics, fluid mechanics, electronics and technology, with marketable products and services as the end result. It is when this knowledge meets a recognised social need that the product development phase really begins, with the government, intrapreneur or entrepreneur acting as the catalyst (pp. 14-16). However, Hisrich and Peters also point out that the government lacks the relevant business skills for successful commercialisation and is often too bureaucratic to become effectively involved in business (p. 16). In addition, even though entrepreneurship is the most effective method for commercialising new products and services, the new entrepreneur often lacks the required experience, skills and resources to do so (p. 17). Some intervention or support is, therefore, required.

In many countries, entrepreneurship is seen as the answer to economic recession and rising unemployment rates as well as a recipe for economic prosperity (Garavan and Ó Cinnéide, 1994). There is, therefore, an obvious need to increase the supply of entrepreneurial talent to create and grow new businesses that will generate employment and create wealth for the local economy. Developing entrepreneurship education and training initiatives is one way of helping to achieve this goal. Even at a very early stage, entrepreneurship education programmes delivered as part of wider curricula, play a very important role in raising awareness about self employment as a viable career option. Even purely academic entrepreneurship modules can have a significant impact on students' attitudes towards setting up their own business and helping them to develop important new skills (Henry, et al., 2001). Furthermore, entrepreneurship training can complement the early stage awareness raising function of entrepreneurship education, as it provides the more practical skills that entrepreneurs require when they are ready to set up their business.

In setting out the case in favour of intervention to support the start-up process in the UK, Atherton et al. (1997) present a practical framework of arguments for debate and discussion. The key arguments they identify include:

- the need to increase the national stock of small businesses in line with other European countries;
- the contribution of start-ups to the development of the economy;
- the importance of developing an enterprise culture and addressing the learning needs of start-up entrepreneurs.

In considering the role that start-ups play in the economy, Atherton et al. also suggest that the UK's small business base is relatively weak. The main weakness, in comparison to the rest of Europe, appears to be in the actual size of the small businesses. In this respect, the UK is well below the EU average in terms of its number of small firms, ranking 13th in the 10-99 employees size category, and sixth in the 1-9 employees size category (Atherton et al., 1997, p. 2). Furthermore, they argue that the quality of the small business stock in the UK does not compare well with other European countries, with typical sales turnover figures lower than the European average for businesses employing less than 100 people. In addition, Atherton et al. (1997) report a significant increase in the number of business closures during the 1990s, with, according to Barclays Bank (1995), seemingly more closures than start-ups in each of the five years from 1991 to 1995.

In terms of policy, Atherton et al. (1997) suggest that start-ups play a significant role in providing the stock of companies from which future growth companies develop. They emphasise that start-ups are not only one of the largest creators of employment in the economy, but that job creation costs are lower for start-ups than for most existing businesses. This job creation argument is further supported by Frank and Landström (1997) who, quoting figures from the European Observatory for SMEs (1995), state that small firms have tended to show a more positive development of employment than larger ones in 13 out of 16 European countries (Frank and Landström, 1997, p. 3). A later report by the European Observatory for SMEs (1997) investigated issues of employment, working conditions and the challenges facing SMEs, and concluded that micro-enterprises with less than ten employees had the greatest growth potential. Furthermore, Daly (1991) reports that start-ups create one third of all new jobs in the UK, while Birch (1994) reports similar findings in the USA, where small firms provided the majority of all new jobs created between 1969 and 1976. Additional benefits of start-ups to the economy would appear to include their positive impact on regional prosperity, as well as the returns yielded by public investment in terms of start-up support and training. However, Atherton et al. (1997) point out that small firms experience start-up barriers that larger firms do not. This point is strongly presented by Bannock and Peacock (1989) who argue in favour of government intervention in the creation of small firms in order to compensate for the disadvantages which they experience by their small size and to offset the adverse effects of other government policies. Hence, all start-ups would appear to be vulnerable and their chances of closure are particularly high. This statement is evidenced by the fact that less than half of the new businesses created in the UK survive beyond their first five years (European Commission (EC) and Eurostat, 1994).

Like Jamieson (1984), as will be discussed in Chapter 4, Atherton et al. (1997) also emphasise the benefits of supporting start-ups in the development of a general enterprise culture, a point put forward as a key argument by Gibb and Cotton (1998) in their discussion of the individual and societal benefits of enterprise. Bridge et al. (1998) agree with this when they refer to enterprise as encouraging individuals to adopt new approaches that can lead to increased confidence and reduced social exclusion (pp. 210-211).

Arguments Against Intervention

Despite the strong case in favour of intervention, there are some arguments against it, and these are based on the notion that the small firms sector is not as important to the economy as some would believe. For example, despite the significance that has been attached to small firm activity, Frank and Landström (1997) suggest that the current expectations on small firms as creators of employment and re-organisers of the economy, whilst very strong, may well be unrealistic (p. 2). In fact Deakins (1999), referring to a UK based study, suggests that the vast majority of small firms are not the major job creators that many have believed them to be. The Fothergill and Gudgin (1979) study to which he refers, claims that firms employing less than 25 people accounted for less than one per cent of the growth in total manufacturing output during the period 1968 to 1975. This leads to the general belief that a small number of firms, in the small business sector in particular, generate a disproportionate share of employment (Storey and Johnson, 1986; Gallagher and Miller, 1991).

Others have indicated that, while there has been an increase in the business birth rate in the small firms sector, the survival rate of these firms is disappointing, with sustainability beyond the first three years posing a major difficulty (Stanworth and Gray, 1991; Deakins, 1999). Westhead and Birley (1994) use the low survival rates of small firms to argue a case for revising blanket intervention policies so that they focus more on growth businesses, a point supported by Storey and Johnson (1987).

According to Bridge et al. (1998) intervention may not even be necessary because it might not achieve a net economic benefit. If intervention is to be justified then there must be a market failure that needs to be addressed, resulting in an increase in the welfare of society as a whole (p. 209). However, some economists believe that enterprise thrives in a free enterprise economy and that governments should not interfere with market forces. It is entirely possible that enterprising people will naturally come to the fore and avail of whatever opportunities exist, without the help of intervention. Atherton et al. (1997), while making a strong case for supporting start-ups, also consider the arguments against intervention and recognise this latter point. They also accept that, since the market mechanism serves as the most efficient means of allocating scarce resources, supporting the start-up process through subsidies may distort resource allocation (p. 7).

Storey (1992) suggests that supporting new business creation displaces existing businesses. He argues that, since many start-ups are subsidised by public funds, a new business may use these funds to gain an unfair competitive advantage over another, hence causing the other business to close. In later work, Storey (1994) suggests that only a very small number of new businesses will grow to become major job creators, claiming that only a small minority of firms will grow to employ 50 or more people. Collectively, these points question the need for intervention in the process of new business creation. However, despite the debate on the rationale for intervention, the fact remains that governments and other agencies do intervene and that various types of intervention exist.

Enterprise Policy

Entrepreneurship has played a key role in economic strategy and development since the 1980s (Storey, 1994). The relationship between entrepreneurship and economic growth is quite complex, with several different factors involved (Global Entrepreneurship Monitor, 2001), and the level of entrepreneurship can vary significantly from country to country. Hence, the need for different enterprise policies that address different situations, and deal with different economic climates.

In the USA, enterprise or small business policy was re-focused during the 1930s, when large industries increased production to accommodate wartime defense contracts and smaller businesses were left unable to compete. This resulted in new government policies designed to directly encourage entrepreneurs and support small business development. However, it was not until after the 1970s, and in some cases as late as the 1990s, that enterprise and entrepreneurship started to become popular concepts among most governments in Western Europe. In areas of strong industrial decline, the need for an entrepreneurship culture that might compensate for the loss of firms, jobs and incomes, became particularly apparent.

Indeed, as Johnson et al. (2000) note, it is the work of commentators who promote the benefits of entrepreneurship, which has provided policy-makers with the rationale for providing a range of support programmes aimed at assisting the small business sector. Hence, the response of many governments was to develop a series of enterprise initiatives that would encourage individuals to set-up and run their own business. However, as the following section will show, such initiatives can take different forms, and there are several different ways in which new business creation can be encouraged and supported.

Types of Intervention

Deakins (1999) notes that there are considerable differences in the ways that intervention can occur. To begin with, he suggests that businesses, whether new or established, can be supported through either *part-funded consultancy* or through *longer-term relationships* (pp. 181-182). With part-funded consultancy, businesses can avail of general or expert advice and support at various stages of their development, the costs of which are subsidised by public funds. In the longer-term relationship type of support identified by Deakins, businesses can avail of a range of supports from mentoring and training at the start-up stage, to more in-depth diagnostic services as the business develops.

Adopting a more comprehensive perspective, Bridge et al. (1998) identify the various types of intervention in terms of the particular policies and stage of business development to which they are related. These are illustrated in Table 1.2. There is clearly a wide range of interventions that can be used to support the creation and development of new business, from inception right through to growth and eventual decline. However, as the remainder of this chapter will illustrate, despite an apparently common objective, there are several different approaches to encouraging entrepreneurship, some more successful than others. Indeed, it would appear that enterprise policy varies from country to country.

Table 1.2 Intervention Types

Stage of Business	Policy Field or Need	Intervention/Instrument
Culture	• An encouraging and supportive environment	• Community programmes, entrepreneurship education
Pre-start	• Ideas	• Spin-off ideas, technology transfer, ideas generation workshops
	• Small business know-how	• Small business skills training
	• Know-who networks	• Networking, access points
	• Counselling	• Pre-start counselling
Start-up (external)	• Customers	• Purchasing initiatives
	• Suppliers	• Sourcing initiatives & directories
	• Advice/consultancy	• Business expertise provision, training, counselling, research
	• Business plan information	• Databases/business planning
	• Premises	• Incubators, science parks
Start-up (internal)	• Finance	• Grants, loans, business angels
	• Market/admin. Expertise	• Training services
	• Financial management	• Advice/counselling, mentoring
Established	• New ideas	• Ideas generation workshops, spin-off ideas, technology transfer
	• Specialist guidance and investments	• Guidance services, including banks, accountants, solicitors
Growth	• Market opportunities/exports	• Trade missions, export advisers
	• Product development	• Market/technical information
	• Strategic approach	• Development courses
	• Management skills, finance	• Salary support, subsidies, grants
Decline	• Confidence, customers, money	• Mentors
	• Strategic review and planning	• Advice and guidance
Termination	• Legal/other advice	• Advice and counselling
Other dimensions	• Business sector	• Sectoral initiatives/training
	• Business support environment	• Information and education
All	• Info. on small business needs	• Research coordination, research databases

(Adapted from Bridge et al., 1998, pp. 241-242).

The USA Perspective

Small businesses represent more than 99 per cent of all businesses in the United States and create a significant proportion of new jobs every year. During the period 1992 to 1998, the total number of new jobs created in the USA was approximately 15 million, and 2.3 million of these (15 per cent) were generated by the small business sector (Small Business Administration, 2002). Statistics from the Global Entrepreneurship Monitor (GEM) Report (2001) indicate that approximately 11.7 per cent of the adult population in the USA is involved in the creation and growth of start-up businesses. In particular, entrepreneurial activity among women in the USA is among the highest of the GEM surveyed countries (GEM, 2001, p. 49).

Concern for the small business sector in the USA really began as a result of the pressures of the Great Depression and World War II. Although organisations such as the Smaller War Plants Corporation (SWPC); the Small Defense Plants Administration (SDPA); and the Office of Small Business (OSB) within the Department of Commerce were all involved in supporting entrepreneurship at some point, the US Small Business Administration, established in 1953, is now the official government organisation for supporting the small business sector in the USA.

The Small Business Administration (SBA) was created by Congress in the early 1950s through the Small Business Act (1953). Its primary function was to 'aid, counsel, assist and protect, insofar as is possible, the interests of small business concerns' (Small Business Administration, 2001). In addition, the SBA sought to ensure that small businesses in the USA received a fair proportion of government contracts. In 1958, the Small Business Investment Company (SBIC) Program was established through the Investment Company Act to facilitate the provision of funds for privately owned venture capital firms. The SBIC specialises in providing long-term investments to high-risk small firms. It provided more than $12.3 billion in loans to small businesses during 2000 alone, and is currently the nation's largest single financial backer of businesses in the USA. According to latest statistics (SBA, 2001), almost 20 million small businesses have been supported through SBA programmes since 1953, and the organisation is considered to be extremely cost effective in terms of economic development.

The European Perspective

There would appear to be general consensus within the EU that small and medium-sized enterprises are the key sector for generating employment opportunities and growth throughout Europe. Their role in growth, competitiveness, innovation and employment is widely recognised. The concept of an entrepreneurial Europe, which promotes the creation and development of innovative businesses, has led each of the EU member States to strengthen their SME policies. The overall aim of such policies is to create new jobs by supporting business start-ups and growth firms, as well as to preserve existing jobs by supporting established SMEs. Despite the level of employment generated by the SME sector within the EU (66 per cent of total employment in the EU comes from the SME sector – EC Report, 1995 and 2001), it is felt that the potential for SMEs to grow and create even more jobs, has not yet been fully realised. Therefore, the EC, through the Enterprise Directorate-General, has identified a number of priority policy objectives and measures for the purpose of stimulating a general entrepreneurial culture and facilitating entrepreneurs at all stages of development. The Enterprise Directorate-General, which is essentially a merger of the former DGs for SMEs, innovation and industry, aims to revitalise Europe's economy by fostering an environment that is supportive of innovation. Its policies and measures, which currently form part of the Commission's multi-annual programme for the period 1997-2000, include the following:

- The reduction of 'red tape' which hampers entrepreneurship;
- Ensuring better involvement of SMEs with State agencies in the decision making process;
- Helping to finance the SMEs which can create jobs;
- Vigorous action to promote research, innovation and training for SMEs;
- Enhancing competitiveness and internationalisation of SMEs.
  (EC Report, 1995, pp. 15-17)

Member States have also agreed on a joint employment strategy for Europe, the core or which is based on four 'pillars' or 'priorities': employability, entrepreneurship, adaptability and equal opportunities. The entrepreneurship pillar recognises that the development of new enterprises and the growth of SMEs is essential for job creation (EC Report, 2001, p. 57). EU SME initiatives include a wide range of financial instruments and programmes. The Structural Funds are the EU's main mechanism for providing financial support to SMEs. More than seven million SMEs are located in areas eligible for EU assistance (i.e. in Objectives 1, 2, 5b and 6) through the Structural Funds.

Table 1.3 shows the estimated structural fund expenditure on SMEs for the period 1994-1999.

Table 1.3 Estimated Structural Fund Expenditure on SMEs (1994-1999)

Type of Assistance   **Expenditure**

	€'000	Per cent
Financial Aid (grants)	6,820.2	31.9
Financial Engineering	570.3	2.7
Business Support Services	2,684.4	12.6
Innovation and Technology	2,499.4	11.7
Physical Infrastructure	2,126.2	10.0
SME Training Measures	3,607.3	16.9
Sectoral Measures	1,195.8	5.6
Other	1,850.4	8.7
TOTAL	**21,353.5**	**100**

(Adapted from Ernst & Young, as cited in 'Creating an Entrepreneurial Europe – the activities of the EU for SMEs', EC Report, March, 2001, Brussels, p. 79).

The EC places particular emphasis on new business creation and this is reflected in the various policies adopted by the different member States. For example, State subsidies are currently provided for start-ups in Germany, Spain, Portugal, Greece and Ireland. Various types of loan scheme and loan guarantees are offered in the UK, France, Sweden, Spain and Greece. Luxembourg and Germany offer special grant aid to employed people who wish to set up their own businesses. In fact, all EU countries have some sort of financial scheme to encourage the setting up of new businesses.

In terms of structured interventions for training and developing new entrepreneurs, there is a wide variety of initiatives in operation in the EU member States. For example, in Italy, the 'Legge 44' scheme is now well known throughout Europe as a major business start-up initiative. Approved in 1986 by the Italian parliament, the scheme is a USD $2 billion initiative developed to encourage and support young aspiring entrepreneurs aged between 18 and 29 and based in southern Italy. In an OECD Observer report (Arzeni, 1992), the scheme was estimated to have a job creation capacity of 20,000 new jobs.

In Finland, activities concerning entrepreneurship education and research have been greatly intensified since the mid-eighties. There are at least 13 universities and around eleven professors all involved in entrepreneurship education and research, as well as the development of training programmes to support aspiring entrepreneurs (Malinen and Paasio, 1997).

In the Netherlands, where the birth rate of firms is well above the EC average, the Dutch government has begun to play a particularly active role in the stimulation of the SME sector. Attention to entrepreneurship has increased dramatically in recent years and several initiatives exist to help aspiring entrepreneurs (During et al., 1997).

Spain and Sweden too have experienced a growth in entrepreneurship activities and support. Interest in both these countries is being increasingly directed toward the establishment of new firms, as well as the expansion of existing small firms (Veciana and Genesca, 1997; Johannisson and Landstrom, 1997).

The UK

The UK's enterprise policies have undergone several changes over the years. One of the most notable attempts to develop an overall enterprise strategy was represented by the Bolton Report (1971), as discussed earlier. Since then, the UK has seen the publication of the government's White Paper on 'Competitiveness and Growth' (1994, 1995), in which general intentions to upgrade arrangements for enterprise support were documented. However, Storey (1994) notes that, despite more than 100 measures being introduced during the 1979-83 period by the then Conservative government to assist small firms, no coherent policy or strategy seems to exist (p. 304). Storey (1994) has also claimed that, since most SME policies in the UK appear fragmented and ad hoc, their objectives are not easily apparent. With this in mind, he suggests that small business policy in the UK has the following broad objectives:

- increase employment;
- increase the number of start-ups;
- promote the use of consultants;
- increase competition and promote 'efficient' markets;
- promote technology diffusion;
- increase wealth.

More recently the Government has published its White Paper on 'Enterprise, Skills and Innovation – Opportunity for All in a World of Change' (DfEE, 2001), which sets out the various steps that the Government plans to take to help individuals, businesses and communities to prosper. Whilst the Paper's objectives are multiple and apparently still fragmented, the importance of creative and entrepreneurial skills and abilities are clearly recognised as crucial to the ever-changing global economy. Hence, the focus of this White Paper is on education and training.

In terms of training interventions, it is important to mention the Small Firms Enterprise Development Initiative (SFEDI). This initiative, formerly known as the Small Firms Lead Body, was established in 1990 to develop nationally recognised standards of competence for Britain's 3.5 million small businesses. It includes standards for those who provide the small firms sector with business advice, counselling, information and support. SFEDI comprises practising business owner-managers and advisers and is essentially the government appointed organisation to identify and endorse standards of best practice for small businesses and their advisors (SFEDI, 1999, p. 6).

In the UK, the main government agency for economic development is the Department of Trade and Industry (DTI), which aims to promote enterprise and innovation by encouraging business start-ups and promoting business growth. In April 2000, DTI established a special small business section – the Small Business Service (SBS), an new agency within government dedicated to the small firms sector. The SBS works closely with the Small Business Council which advises government on the needs of small firms. Invest UK, established in 1977, is the section of DTI that deals with overseas companies seeking to establish themselves in the UK. It is essentially the UK's national inward investment agency.

The Department for Education and Skills (DfES), formerly known as the Department for Education and Employment (DfEE) also has an influence with regard to enterprise policy and initiatives. Other related agencies include the Training and Enterprise Councils (TECs) and Business Links in England and Wales, and the Local Enterprise Councils in Scotland. Northern Ireland operates under the same basic structure but with Invest Northern Ireland (a combination of the organization formerly known as LEDU – the Local Enterprise Development Unit, IDB – Industrial Development Board, and the local enterprise agencies).

At the strategic level, a recent development in Ireland/Northern Ireland's enterprise support structure is the addition of a new all-Ireland trade and business development agency InterTradeIreland. Established as one of the North/South implementation bodies under the British-Irish Agreement Act (1999), InterTradeIreland was created to promote business development throughout the entire island of Ireland. InterTradeIreland's remit is concerned more with policy development and strategic initiatives rather than direct intervention, and hence, as an organisation, it does not provide support services directly to SMEs. Its strategic mission is:

> to lead the development of the island economy through distinctive knowledge-based interventions, which will produce significant returns in the areas of cross-border trade, and business development (InterTradeIreland, 2001, website – www.intertradeireland.com).

Within this broad mission, InterTradeIreland's aims include: establishing a channel for North/South trade and business development; encouraging the flow and exchange of private equity and venture capital within the two economies of Ireland, and between companies and educational establishments, and supporting business by making recommendations to increase enterprise competitiveness in a North-South context.

In summary, direct interventions for the business sector in Britain and Northern Ireland are provided through the following mechanisms:

Learning and Skills Council

The Learning and Skills Council was established in April 2001 as a result of the Government's White Paper 'Learning to Succeed' (1999). This organisation essentially replaced the Training and Education Councils (TECs) which were set up in England and Wales to support and develop local labour markets. The objective of the Learning and Skills Council is to provide all individuals, regardless of their background or education, the opportunity to learn new skills, fulfil their potential and improve the quality of their lives at home and at work The Learning and Skills Council operates through local offices throughout the country and aims to narrow skill shortages for businesses.

Business Link

The Small Business Service, essentially the Government's new small business agency, also manages a network of Business Link services on a national basis, and these provide independent and impartial business advice, as well as information and a range of services to help small firms and aspiring entrepreneurs.

Invest Northern Ireland

Up until the end of March 2002, LEDU (Local Enterprise Development Unit) and IDB (Industrial Development Board) were Northern Ireland's main economic development agencies.   While LEDU, which was originally established as part of the 1970-1975 Northern Ireland Development Plan, focused on supporting start-up and established indigenous businesses, IDB's remit was to cater for the needs of high-growth businesses and encourage overseas investment.

In April 2002, partly as a result of the New Northern Ireland Assembly, the functions previously carried out separately by LEDU, IDB, and some of the other support agencies, such as IRTU (Industrial Research and Technology Unit) and the tourist accommodation support functions of NITB (Northern Ireland Tourist Board), were incorporated into a new agency – Invest Northern Ireland – now the principal economic development agency in Northern Ireland (Invest Northern Ireland website, 2002). This organisation offers a range of supports to Northern Ireland-based companies and focuses on the promotion of capability building, encouraging innovation and new thinking in the business sector. Invest Northern Ireland, along with the local District Councils, provides funding to regional enterprise agencies currently known as LEAs (Local Enterprise Agencies). The LEAs focus on the pre-start-up, start-up and early development stage businesses in their local area. They provide a range of support services to aspiring entrepreneurs and existing small businesses, including: advice; mentoring; start your own business training; and grants for start-up and employment. The exact make-up and structure of the LEAs will undoubtedly change as Invest Northern Ireland develops to essentially become the 'umbrella' organisation for all enterprise and support agencies in the North of Ireland.

Ireland

Like the UK, Ireland's enterprise policies have undergone several changes. A major review of industrial policy in Ireland was carried out in the early 1980s by the Telesis consulting group. This group argued for better control over the instruments of industrial policy, a more selective approach to attracting foreign industry, and a shift in emphasis towards building strong indigenous companies in the export and sub-supply business sector (Telesis Report, 1982). Of particular interest to the small firms sector was the report's recommendation that internationally traded services should qualify for government support, and that weaknesses in management, marketing and technology should be addressed (Garavan et al., 1997, p. 9).

Ireland's industrial policy underwent a second major review during the latter half of 1991 with the appointment of the Culliton Policy Review Group. Their report (Culliton Report, 1992) made several recommendations concerning taxation; infrastructure; education, enterprise and technology; direct support for industry; institutional strengthening and special initiatives for the food industry. Of particular interest to enterprise policy were the Committee's recommendations regarding Ireland's development agencies. The Committee recommended that State supports to firms should be provided in an integrated and cost-effective way, and hence, all grant-giving and advisory supports should be brought together within one agency. This meant an integration of the then IDA (Industrial Development Agency), ABT (An Bord Tráchtála – the Irish Trade Board) and Eolas (the government's Science and Technology agency) into a new agency that would focus on the development of indigenous industry.

Following the publication of the Culliton Report, a special Task Force on Small Business was appointed to advise the government on how best to implement the recommendations put forward by the Culliton Committee. The report from the Task Force (1994) strengthened the case for the establishment of County Enterprise Boards that would be responsible for creating an enterprise culture at local level which would in turn generate sustainable jobs nation-wide.

Ireland's economy has witnessed unprecedented growth during the last decade, with increased inward investment and exceptional employment opportunities contributing to the so-called 'celtic tiger' phenomenon. Despite this, it is recognised that Ireland's economic climate is changing and that there is a limit to the net number of new jobs that can be created. The government's latest enterprise strategy document (Forfás, 2000) takes account of the rapid technological changes that are predicted for business and industry worldwide, and focuses on the need to create more high skilled/high knowledge-based jobs; to increase the number of these jobs in the internationally-traded sector, and to encourage more employment opportunities in less developed regions, such as rural areas and the border, midland and west regions of the country (BMW regions).

The strategy document also places a great deal of emphasis on the small firms sector, recommending that support is provided through the encouragement of high-tech start-ups; early stage investment; and developing a partnership approach between the development agencies, the financial institutions and SMEs.

The structures for the support of economic development in Ireland have been revised several times. The main enterprise development agencies currently in existence in Ireland and their methods of intervention are summarised below.

Enterprise Ireland (Ireland's State agency for enterprise development)

Established in July 1998, Enterprise Ireland comprises Forbairt (the former State agency for indigenous enterprise development), An Bord Tráchtála (the Trade Board) and the industrial training division of FÁS (Foras Áiseanna Saothair – the State's training and employment authority). Enterprise Ireland aims to work with Irish businesses to help them to: create profitable new business, build their share of international markets, harness new technologies, deepen R & D capability and build people skills and capabilities. In particular, the supports offered include development grants, equity, consulting, training and specialist assistance to existing growth businesses or new businesses employing more than 10 people in the manufacturing and internationally traded services sector.

City and County Enterprise Boards

Established in 1993/1994 to develop small or micro, indigenous businesses in each county and/or city of Ireland, in the manufacturing and internationally traded services sectors, Enterprise Boards focus on start-ups and micro firms employing less than 10 people. They provide grants for feasibility studies, capital purchases and employment of staff; start your own business training courses; business development training courses; and mentoring.

FÁS (Foras Áiseanna Saothair)

FÁS is the State training and employment authority in Ireland and provides a range of training and related supports to indigenous and foreign owned businesses, including training, grants, consultancy, and start-your own business courses. FÁS also provides support to community and social employment programmes.

IDA Ireland

The Industrial Development Authority is the State agency responsible for attracting overseas businesses to Ireland. It provides a full range of assistance, both financial and non-financial, to attract and support foreign owned multinationals to set up in Ireland.

In addition to the above, support is available for rural based businesses through the various EU funded LEADER groups, as well as from Údarás na Gaeltachta and Shannon Development. In addition to the support outlined above for new and existing businesses, Enterprise Ireland operates a Student Enterprise Award scheme for those studying enterprise at third level colleges throughout the country (Fleming, 1994). Furthermore, Enterprise Ireland funds the Young Entrepreneur's scheme, which introduces entrepreneurship into the curriculum at secondary level. The UK-originated Young Enterprise scheme, which is partly funded by the County Enterprise Boards, also operates in parts of the country. In terms of entrepreneurship research, although not directly supported by the State development agencies as yet, Jones-Evans (1987) points out that work has been conducted into the areas of enterprise development (Harrison and Leitch, 1995; Burke, 1995) and innovation (Cooney and O'Connor, 1995; Hunt, 1995). In addition, some empirical work has been conducted on entrepreneurship education and training programmes (Garavan and Ó Cinnéide, 1994; Fleming, 1994 and 1996; Hill and Ó Cinnéide, 1998; Henry and Titterington, 2001; Henry et al., 2001, 2002).

Enterprise Policy – Revisited

Although relatively late to introduce a focus on enterprise and new business creation into its economic policies, Ireland's support mechanisms for both new and existing businesses have been well developed and are currently very strong. In contrast, despite ranking lowest in the OECD index of barriers to entrepreneurship (GEM, 2001, p. 48), the UK's enterprise policy would appear to be less coherent, with a more fragmented approach to supporting new business creation. Indeed, it has been noted that enterprise policy in the UK is 'a patchwork quilt of complexity and idiosyncrasy' (Audit Commission, 1989, p. 1). Interestingly, however, support for the small business sector in the USA would seem to be more focused, with greater readiness on the part of the US Administration to take a risk. This is evidenced by a direct involvement in the financing of small firms, particularly the high risk ones, through the Small Business Administration and its Small Business Investment Company Program. On a broader level, the EC is clearly making efforts to consolidate and harmonise SME support policies as interest in the whole area of entrepreneurship continues to grow.

According to the Global Entrepreneurship Monitor (2001), governments in countries where there is more entrepreneurial activity tend to lack a long-term focus in their enterprise policies and would benefit from a more strategic approach to policy planning. In contrast, in less entrepreneurial countries, support programmes tend to lack coordination, and there is a view that governments would benefit from having their policies more closely aligned to their countries' immediate situation. While the focus in the more entrepreneurial countries is on actual government activity, it is the underlying strategy adopted for encouraging entrepreneurship that gets most attention in the less entrepreneurial countries (GEM, 2001, p. 34). Culture may well have an important role to play in enterprise policy making. For example, American culture encourages change and opportunity-seeking activity. As a result, entrepreneurship is viewed as a viable career option, and business failure is often seen as an essential part of the entrepreneurship learning experience. However, attitudes to self-employment in most countries in Western Europe remain somewhat less positive, with society continuing to be less accepting of business failure. This may change to some degree in the UK, with the introduction of the new Enterprise Bill (2002), which, if approved, will reform insolvency laws by providing those bankrupts who have failed through no fault of their own, with a second chance, hence reducing the stigma attached to bankruptcy (DTI, 2002). In addition, the Bill will ensure that companies in financial difficulty will not 'go to the wall' unnecessarily. It is clear, therefore, that culture and policy together, can be either encouraging or deterrent factors in terms of new business creation, and can significantly contribute, whether positively or negatively, toward the prevailing climate for entrepreneurship.

Summary and Conclusion

This chapter has considered the growing importance of entrepreneurship and new business creation to the economy, and in so doing, has set the context for the authors' study. The arguments both in favour of and against intervention have also been examined. While the debate surrounding these issues will no doubt continue, it would appear that there is a strong case to be made for encouraging start-ups and supporting the small firms sector. Thus, the primary motivation for the study reported in this monograph has been to contribute to the intervention debate by increasing the level of understanding with respect to structured interventions in the form of entrepreneurship education and training programmes. The chapters which make up the remainder of Part I of this monograph, continue to lay the theoretical foundation for the authors' study, the findings of which are presented in detail in Part II.

Chapter 2

Theories on the Entrepreneur –
Traditional Approaches

Introduction

In recent times, significant research has been carried out in the area of entrepreneurship and, in particular, into what characterises an entrepreneur. A plethora of research studies have attempted to establish an entrepreneurial profile and, as Caird (1991) points out, entrepreneurs are now probably one of the most researched groups of people (p. 177).

This part of the monograph aims to lay the theoretical foundation for the study presented in Part II. This chapter focuses on the various theories on the entrepreneurial personality. Beginning with some modern definitions of entrepreneurship-related terms, the chapter examines the various ways entrepreneurs have been conceptualised by economists and researchers over the years. From the literature, different approaches to studying the entrepreneur are explored and the key contributors in each area are identified. The psychological view of the entrepreneur is described and key personality traits, which, it is claimed, distinguish entrepreneurs from non-entrepreneurs, are identified. This is followed by a discussion on various measures of entrepreneurship characteristics. The chapter then examines the social, sometimes called demographic, approach to the study of entreprenenurship, and concludes with a consideration of the behavioural approach.

Defining Entrepreneurship

According to Bygrave and Hofer (1991), 'good science has to begin with good definitions' (p. 15). Definitions are particularly important in entrepreneurship because many of the terms associated with the field, such as entrepreneur, enterprise and small business are often used interchangeably. Bruyat and Julien (2000) argue that a definition is 'a construct at the service of the research questions that are of interest to a scientific community at a given time' and, as such, may be regarded as transitional. It is not surprising then, that there are many definitions of the entrepreneur and entrepreneurship in the literature. The entrepreneur has been defined as:

The owner or manager of a business enterprise who, by risk and initiative, attempts to make profits (Collins English Dictionary).

Entrepreneurs are people who have the ability to see and evaluate business opportunities; to gather the necessary resources to take advantage of them, and to initiate appropriate action to ensure success (Meredith et al., 1982, as cited in Tiernan et al., 1996, p. 280).

Scharma and Chrisman (1999) highlight Schumpeter's (1934) view that an entrepreneur is a person who carries out new combinations, which may take the form of new products, processes, markets, organisational forms, or sources of supply. Entrepreneurship then, is the process of carrying out new combinations. They point out though, that Gartner's (1989) notion of entrepreneurship as the creation of organisations, which although not offered originally as a definition, has since been taken up by others as such.

It is interesting to note that entrepreneurs themselves find definition difficult. For example, Virgin's Richard Branson has described the entrepreneur as follows:

I am often asked what it is to be an 'entrepreneur' and there is no simple answer. It is clear that successful entrepreneurs are vital for a healthy, vibrant and competitive economy. If you look around you, most of Britain's largest companies have their foundations in one or two individuals who have the determination to turn a vision into reality. A lot of people tend to forget that some of the blue chip names of the late twentieth century such as Marks and Spencers, Sainsbury's Food, Tate & Lyle were the sole traders of the late nineteenth century (cited in Morrison, 1997, p. 3).

In addition to the above, Branson highlights the exciting and rewarding aspects of life as an entrepreneur:

... the satisfaction of doing it for yourself and motivating others to work with you in bringing it about. It is about fun, innovation, creativity and the rewards are far greater than the purely financial. These were the goals with which we founded the Virgin Group and we have striven not to lose sight of them. Most of all, entrepreneurship is a state of mind. You do not have to run your own company, but you should try to look beyond the obvious and accepted in whatever you do (as cited in Morrison, 1997, p. 5).

In relation to entrepreneurship, a number of writers have focused on process and context. Low and Macmillan (1988) conceptualise entrepreneurship as the creation of new enterprise, which, of course, may be undertaken in a number of contexts. In terms reminiscent of Plato, Bygrave (1989, p. 21) describes entrepreneurship as a 'process of becoming, rather than a state of being'. Other writers, also focus on process, highlighting different aspects of it:

The process of creating something different with value by devoting the necessary time and effort, assuming the accompanying financial, psychic and social risks, and receiving the resulting rewards of monetary and personal satisfaction (Hisrich and Peters, 1998, p. 6).

The process of identifying opportunities in the marketplace, marshalling the resources to pursue these opportunities and committing the actions and resources necessary to exploit the opportunities for long-term personal gain (Sexton & Bowman-Upton, 1991).

The creation of a new economic entity centred on a novel product or service or, at the very least, one which differs significantly from products or services offered elsewhere in the market (Curran and Stanworth, 1989, p. 12).

Bruyat and Julien (2000) make the interesting observation that while entrepreneurship is to do with a process of change, emergence and creation of new value, it is also a process of change and creation for the entrepreneur.

Perhaps the most common definition of an entrepreneur is '*someone who starts his/her own business*', i.e. creates an enterprise, leading to the assumption that 'entrepreneurship' is the art of starting one's own business, and any education or training on the subject will provide one with the necessary skills and abilities to do just that. However, Drucker (1985) adopts a more specific perspective:

To be entrepreneurial, an enterprise has to have special characteristics over and above being new..., ... entrepreneurs are a minority among new businesses. [They] create something new, something different; they change or transmute values ... they see change as the norm (pp. 35-36).

For Drucker, entrepreneurship is not just about starting any new business. 'Copy-cat' type businesses, such as just another delicatessen store or another restaurant, are not strictly entrepreneurial. However, a MacDonalds type business, by virtue of its innovative approach, is entrepreneurial (Drucker, 1985, p. 35). What really defines an entrepreneur for Drucker is the fact that the entrepreneur does not simply allow change to happen and then reacts to it, rather, s/he always searches for change, responds to it and exploits it as an opportunity.

Carland et al. (1984) distinguish between entrepreneurs and small business owners. The former they perceive as capitalising on innovative combinations of resources primarily to achieve profit and growth using strategic management practices. Small business owners on the other hand, operate their businesses as extensions of their individual personalities, with the main aims of furthering their personal goals and generating family income.

Stewart et al. (1999) draw attention to the fact that entrepreneurial or venture teams are becoming more commonplace, citing Timmons (1990) who contends that such arrangements appear to improve the probability of entrepreneurial success. Nevertheless conflict can arise amongst team members if the motives for the new venture appear inconsistent or ambiguous. Bolton and Thompson (2000a, p.11) define an entrepreneur as an individual who 'habitually creates and innovates to build something of recognised value around an opportunity'. That being the case, they highlight examples of social and environmental, artistic and aesthetic, as well as business entrepreneurs.

In conclusion, there is a wide variety of definitions for the *terms entrepreneurship, entrepreneur* and *enterprise*. Furthermore, it would seem that there is no simple definition generally accepted as 'correct', since the spectrum of meanings covers everything from starting a business, to applying enterprising skills and abilities in almost any context. Indeed, Kaufmann and Dant (1999) point out that the diversity of conceptualisations used in the literature has led writers such as Low and MacMillan (1988) to suggest that entrepreneurship may be too imprecise a concept to permit tight definition. Stewart et al. (1999) regard this situation as highly unsatisfactory, on the grounds that 'definitional quandaries' surrounding the entrepreneur have hampered theory development.

In this text, an entrepreneur is defined relatively narrowly as someone who sets up and runs his/her own business, the aspiring entrepreneur being an individual who hopes to do likewise. However, in the context of exploring different approaches to the study and understanding of entrepreneurship and enterprise, it is necessary to explore a full spectrum of meanings.

Historical Overview

As intimated, the entrepreneur has been defined by economists in many different ways over the years. This section reviews the historical development of the term 'entrepreneur' in the literature, beginning with its first appearance in the eighteenth century and tracing its development up to the present day.

One of the earliest uses of the term 'entrepreneur' (from the French word – *entreprendre* – to undertake) was by the Irish economist living in France, Richard Cantillon. He first introduced the word into economic literature in his 'Essai sur la nature de commerce en général' which was published in 1755, although many claim that this piece of work was written much earlier, around 1734. Cantillon emphasised foresight and the confidence to operate under conditions of uncertainty. He also associated risk and uncertainty with the administrative decision making process of entrepreneurs. Cantillon's entrepreneur was very much of the classical type, someone who brought people, money, and materials together to create a new organisation. In addition, for Cantillon, an entrepreneur was able to identify an opportunity and then innovate to pursue it (Wickham, 1998).

The French economist, Jean-Baptiste Say, who was possibly the first professor of economics in Europe, described an entrepreneur as someone who:

> shifts economic resources out of an area of lower and into an area of higher productivity and greater yield (Say, 1803).

Say's entrepreneur was someone who combined and coordinated the various factors of production to accommodate the unexpected and overcome problems (Bridge et al. 1998). He emphasised the qualities of judgement, perseverance and the specialist problem solving skills of the entrepreneur but, as Binks and Vale (1990) point out, Say claimed that such skills had to be exhibited simultaneously if the entrepreneur was to be successful (pp. 11-12). If any of the key entrepreneurial qualities were missing, then the entrepreneurial venture would probably fail.

Knight's work is essentially an expansion of Cantillon's (1755). Knight (1940) distinguished between risk and uncertainty by emphasising that risk per se can be insured against, however, it is uncertainty that is the real problem. Therefore, as Barkham (1989) points out, the key characteristic of Knight's entrepreneur is judgement. Furthermore, his entrepreneur can exist in both large and small businesses, however, it must always be the individual him/herself who accepts all of the responsibility and the possibility of profit or loss. Knight's definition does not exclude anyone from being an entrepreneur, as everyone makes decisions.

Schumpeter (1934) saw the entrepreneur as an innovator, someone who used new business creation as a means of exploiting invention. Schumpeter argued that innovation was the key to entrepreneurship and it was this, which differentiated entrepreneurs from individuals who simply managed a business without innovating. For Schumpeter, the entrepreneur's key role was to bring innovations to the market place, but in so doing, they created new demand, destroying existing markets and creating new ones. Schumpeter described this dynamic iterative process as 'creative destruction'. He also believed that an entrepreneur was no *single* type of person but, rather, a mixture of types. Furthermore, he believed that, after the initial set-up period, entrepreneurs settle down to the task of management and thus cease to be entrepreneurs:

> Whatever the type, everyone is an entrepreneur only when he actually carries out new combinations and loses that character as soon as he has built up his business, when he settles down to running it as other people run their business (p. 78).

As Barkham (1989) points out, keenness, rigour and focus seem to be Schumpeter's key prerequisites for successful entrepreneurship, rather than specialist knowledge or excessive preparation (p. 17).

In his 1968 publication, Leibenstein distinguishes between two types of entrepreneur: the routine entrepreneur who operates in a well-established and well known environment, and the entrepreneur who is forced to operate in an unknown or uncertain environment. Like Say, Leibenstein emphasises the need for the successful entrepreneur to synchronise inputs from several different markets:

> The gap-filling and input-completing capacities are the unique characteristics of the entrepreneur (pp. 72-83).

Casson (1982) emphasises the decision-making abilities of the entrepreneur. According to him, the entrepreneur is very much an individual, as only individuals can take decisions (p. 23). However, Casson sees the entrepreneur as a specialist decision maker so, for him, not everyone can be an entrepreneur. He also believes that the entrepreneur will require a broad range of skills and abilities and will probably be a general all-rounder. Casson also distinguishes between two approaches to defining entrepreneurship: a functional approach, where the entrepreneur is defined by the functions s/he performs, and the indicative approach, where the entrepreneur is defined in practical terms which might include reference to his/her legal status and position in society (p. 23).

Hisrich and Peters (1998, p. 6) offer a simplified overview of the development of the terms *entrepreneurship* and *entrepreneur*. They begin by reminding the reader of the literal translation of these terms, which stem from the French word *entreprendre* and mean *between-taker* or *go-between*. They then trace the evolution of these up to modern times, as illustrated in Table 2.1.

Table 2.1 Historical Development of the Term *Entrepreneur*

Middle Ages	Warlike actor, person in charge of large-scale production projects
17th Century	Person bearing risks of profit or loss
1755, Cantillon	Person bearing risks who is different from the one supplying capital
1803, Say	Separated profits of entrepreneur from profits of capital
1934, Schumpeter	An innovator, developing untried technology
1961, McClelland	Entrepreneur is an energetic moderate risk taker
1971, Shapero	Entrepreneur takes initiative, organises some social and economic mechanisms and accepts risk of failure
1982, Vesper	Entrepreneur seen differently by economists, psychologists, business persons and politicians
1985, Drucker	Entrepreneur maximizes opportunities
1985, Hisrich	Entrepreneurship is the process of creating something different with value by assuming the financial, psychological and social risks, and receiving the resulting monetary/personal rewards and satisfaction
1986, Pinchot	Intrapreneur: an entrepreneur in an established organisation
1996, Kets de Vries	An entrepreneur is an individual who is instrumental in the conception and the implementation of an enterprise

Early research into entrepreneurship focused on the entrepreneur, seeking to determine personality characteristics which distinguished entrepreneurs from non-entrepreneurs and examining the influence of these on organisation formation rates (Mazzarol et al., 1999). Lee and Tsang (2001) state that both practitioners and academics appear to believe venture success is more dependent on the entrepreneur than on any other factor. Moreover, empirical studies on the characteristics of entrepreneurs have outnumbered studies of almost any other type (Churchill and Lewis, 1986). Several attempts have been made at developing a typical personality profile which identifies the key characteristics of successful entrepreneurs. Not surprisingly, qualities such as enthusiasm, commitment and attitude toward risk-taking are highly rated. In addition, authors as far back as Menger (1950) and Wiesner (1927) underline the importance of management and leadership in successful entrepreneurship. Drucker (1985) to some degree complements this viewpoint through his emphasis on decision-making and the need to be able to respond to change. In general, however, authors writing on the subject of entrepreneurship tend to adopt a psychological approach, a social (or demographic) approach, or a behavioural approach in their analysis of the entrepreneur. These three different approaches are discussed in the following sections.

The Psychological Approach

The psychological or trait approach to the study of entrepreneurship is probably the most extensively represented area in the literature. Over the years, a long list of personality characteristics possessed by entrepreneurs has been examined and discussed. These characteristics are represented in Table 2.2 below.

Table 2.2 Characteristics Identified within the Psychological Approach

Need for achievement	McClelland, 1961
Need for power	McClelland, 1961; Watkins, 1976
Need for affiliation	McClelland, 1961; Wainer and Rubin, 1969
Risk-taking propensity	Drucker, 1985; Osborne, 1995; Kets de Vries, 1996
Internal locus of control	Rotter, 1966
Confidence	Brockhaus, 1975; Gibb, 1993a
Need for autonomy and independence	Watkins, 1976; Collins et al., 1964
Innovativeness	Schumpeter, 1934, 1965; Drucker, 1985
Decision making	Scanlan, 1984
Judgement	Hornaday and Aboud, 1971
Communication abilities	Carson et al.,1995
Commitment/determination	McClelland and Winter, 1969
Leadership	Litzinger, 1965; Moss Kanter, 1983
Initiative/drive/enthusiasm	Gasse and Théoret, 1980; McClelland and Winter, 1969; Bridge et al., 1998
Tolerance of ambiguity and uncertainty	Hornaday & Bunker, 1970; Sexton & Bowman-Upton, 1985
A grip on reality	Schrage, 1965
Vision	Wickham, 1998

Despite the fact that there is still considerable scepticism over how exactly such traits can be accurately measured, there have been some significant studies in the area. A number of these are examined below.

Motivation

Motivation is the 'set of processes that arouse, direct and maintain human behaviour toward attaining some goal' (Greenberg and Baron, 2000, p. 130). Robichaud et al. (2001) state that the majority of theoretical models emphasise motivation as one of the key elements in the success of small businesses, an important aspect of this being the need for achievement, which has been associated with entrepreneurial behaviour (Lee and Tsang, 2001). Indeed, the findings of numerous studies suggest that entrepreneurs tend to have higher achievement motivation than non-entrepreneurs (Hornaday and Aboud, 1971; DeCarlo and Lyons, 1979; Begley and Boyd, 1987).

Achievement Motivation

McClelland's study (1961) highlighted the need for achievement (abbreviated in the literature as nAch) as a key trait found in successful entrepreneurs. For McClelland, the achievement motive is a precise technical term which he defines as:

> a measurable factor in groups and individuals .... measured by coding an individual's spontaneous thoughts ..... for the frequency with which he thinks about competing with a standard of excellence, or doing something better than before (McClelland, 1965, p. 8).

Using a combination of thematic apperception tests (in the Achieving Society, 1961) and specific games of skill, McClelland discovered that entrepreneurs scored high on nAch and demonstrated a strong desire to do well in competitive situations where the results of their efforts could be measured objectively. People demonstrating a high nAch are focused and committed to a task and have a burning desire to be a winner – an achiever – in everything they do in life. Achievers are people who strive to excel, avoiding very easy tasks. They prefer striving to achieve challenging but attainable targets and seek rapid feedback on their efforts. According to O'Gorman and Cunningham (1997), McClelland's need for achievement manifests itself in entrepreneurs as follows:

- a preference for decisions involving risk that is neither very high nor very low;
- a belief that one's efforts will be influential in the attainment of some goal;
- the perception that the probability of success in attaining a goal is relatively high;
- the need for feedback;
- the capacity to plan ahead;
- the desire to take personal responsibility for decisions;

- an interest in excellence for its own sake;
- an interest in concrete results from decisions.

Similarly, Schollhammer and Kuriloff (1979, pp. 14-15), in discussing the potential benefits of determining entrepreneurial potential prior to business set-up, suggest the following list of characteristics for the successful high nAch entrepreneur as a guide for self-analysis:

- innovative ability;
- tolerance of ambiguity;
- desire to achieve;
- realistic planning ability;
- goal oriented leadership;
- objectivity;
- personal responsibility;
- adaptability;
- ability as organiser and administrator.

Entrepreneurs with a high need for achievement view profits as a *measure* of success and not necessarily as a *goal* in themselves. Practical evidence of one's level of nAch could be obtained by considering one's track record or achievements in the past. In this sense, qualifications, awards and other personal achievements or demonstrations of having overcome serious difficulties and problems, could be considered proof of one's achievement motivation. Furthermore, McClelland and Winter (1971) point out that training courses designed to develop achievement motivation have improved small business performance significantly. Enterprise programmes which assist entrepreneurs at the pre-start or start-up stage have an opportunity to encourage and perhaps even measure nAch by setting target outputs against set time scales for programme participants. Such outputs can include a business plan, a marketing plan, completion of a feasibility study or securing a particular number of new customers. Any structured training that is provided could also include an assessment of the participants' newly acquired knowledge as a measure of achievement. This aspect of measuring nAch was included in a recent study (Henry and Titterington, 1997) which focused on the use of enterprise training programmes as a mechanism for testing entrepreneurial suitability in aspiring entrepreneurs. In addition to other measures of entrepreneurial flair, the study included an assessment of those participants who managed to complete the associated NVQ work within the restricted time scale of the programme and concluded that, by doing so, these participants demonstrated a high level of nAch.

Through his research, McClelland also discovered that entrepreneurs tend to take responsibility for their decisions, prefer decisions involving a moderate degree of risk, are interested in the results of decisions and dislike routine work. His research, supported later by other studies (Roberts, 1968; Wainer and Rubin, 1969), concluded that the highest performing entrepreneurs were high on nAch and low on the need for power (nPower). In fact, he further concluded that, in order to be successful, an entrepreneur should have the right balance between the need for achievement, power and affiliation (see below).

However, there have been some critics of McClelland's work. Brockhaus (1980) claimed that McClelland's empirical research did not directly connect nAch with the decision to own and manage a business. This view is, to some degree, supported by the work of Hull et al. (1980), as presented by Chell et al. (1991), who found achievement motivation to be a weak predictor of an individual's tendency to start a business. In summarising some of the key criticisms of McClelland's theory, Chell et al. add that people set up their own businesses for a variety of reasons, many of which include a mixture of 'push' and 'pull' factors which may not be associated with the need for achievement at all. In fact, according to Chell et al. (1991), a person may set up their own business simply because it offers them an attractive means of earning a living and not necessarily because such an option presents them with a challenge or goal to achieve (p. 38).

Apart from identifying achievement motivation as a strong characteristic in entrepreneurs, McClelland proposed that achievement motivation can actually be developed where it does not already exist. In his 1965 paper, McClelland challenges the thinking behind heavily funded aid programmes aimed at helping the poor in depressed areas. He believes that, before economic growth can be stimulated in underdeveloped regions, it is necessary to develop the local population's aspirations for achievement. His paper represents a powerful argument in support of the view that achievement motivation can be taught. One of McClelland's studies involved teaching the achievement motive to two different groups of individuals, one group of 16 company executives in the United States and another group of 52 small business owners in India. In each case, the training programme used was relatively short; one week in the US and ten days in India. In the case of the 16 US executives, the participants were taught about the achievement motive concept, how research had shown it to be important for entrepreneurship, and how to think, act and perceive the world like a person with a high need for achievement. The participants were then matched with other executives from the same company who had a similar type of job and salary but who had attended only the regular executive development courses run by the company. A careful study of both US groups two years later showed that those who had participated in the achievement motivation training, the experimental group, had clearly done better in the company than their matched colleagues. In the case of the 52 Indian businessmen, the achievement motivation training appeared to yield positive results after a six-month period, with a number of unusual entrepreneurial activities having been developed. Further research conducted among salaried executives in Bombay yielded results similar to the US experiment after two years.

McClelland points out that, in order to be successful, achievement motivation training must take place in a positive psychological or social climate, regardless of whether such training is conducted at a national or local level. McClelland concludes that, achievement motivation levels can be improved and, that training programmes designed for this purpose, are effective and relatively inexpensive. He also suggests that large sums of money can be wasted trying to retrain unskilled workers if, at the same time, motivation training is not undertaken.

Need for Affiliation

Apart from nAch, McClelland (1961) also identified the need for affiliation (nAff) as an important entrepreneurial characteristic. The nAff trait can be described as one's need for developed social and personal relations, the need to belong to a social grouping or an organisation. People with a high nAff tend to want to participate in tasks which allow them to interact frequently with others (Tiernan et al., 1996, p. 121). However, as McClelland also points out (1965), the need to affiliate may also be counter-productive for entrepreneurship since it may lead to 'approval seeking', a behaviour that is not normally associated with risk-taking.

Need for Power (nPow)

In addition to the nAch and nAff characteristics, McClelland (1961) identified the need for power as an important entrepreneurial trait. Abbreviated in the literature as nPow, the need for power refers to a person's need for dominance and control. People demonstrating a high nPow tend to view business ownership as a means of status provision. Watkins (1976) defines the need for power as the motivation to lead and influence group decisions and activities, and thus links it strongly to motivation. However, according to Schrage (1965, cited in Caird, 1991), some entrepreneurs may actually have a low need for power. On the other hand, in their investigation of practising entrepreneurs, Hatch and Zweig (2000) found a general desire to be in control. Moreover, their research findings led these authors to conclude that a strong desire for control is generally incompatible with the shared decision-making often implied in partnership structures (partnership disputes emerged as a major problem for the entrepreneurs in this study).

Need for Independence/Autonomy

Entrepreneurs have been characterised as people who are highly independent and, as indicated above, need to be in control. They prefer or need to do things on their own and, as a result, they actively seek situations and environments which allow them to 'do their own thing' in their own way. More importantly, they are ready to take responsibility for the results. For this reason, entrepreneurs rebel against bureaucratic structures with strict rules and regulations. They resent constraints since they regard these as counter-productive in developing innovative business ideas. Entrepreneurs, or those with enterprising tendencies, want to continually move forward, breaking down barriers and solving problems as they go, and often see more benefit in independent thought and action than in behaviour which is constrained by rules or other people. They need freedom of thought and action.

The importance of the need for autonomy as a critical indicator of entrepreneurship is supported by Shapero (1971), Scanlan (1979) and Collins et al. (1964). In his 1976 study, Watkins found that the strongest reason for starting a business was an individual's need for autonomy. Similar findings are recorded by Robichaud et al. (2001), although it is interesting to note in this study, that the need for independence and autonomy correlated negatively with sales as a financial indicator of business performance.   It is also worthy of note that those entrepreneurs who claimed to be pursuing intrinsic objectives, such as personal growth, the need for challenge and to succeed, recorded poorer sales, less profit and less funds drawn from the business than those pursuing extrinsic objectives.

Risk Taking Propensity

Risk-taking propensity is related to achievement motivation. McClelland (1961) found that risk-taking propensity depended upon an individual's achievement motives – individuals with a high need for achievement appeared to take moderate risks while those with a low need for achievement were prepared to take greater risks (McCarthy, 2000). Considerable research has been carried out in the area of the risk-taking propensity of entrepreneurs. Caird (1991) defines risk-taking as:

> the ability to deal with incomplete information and act on a risky option, that requires skill, to actualise challenging but realistic goals (p. 179).

A number of authors have disaggregated risk into different elements. For example, Dermer (1997), cited by McCarthy (2000), identifies three components of risk, namely conceptual, administrative and environmental risk. Conceptual risk is the imperfect formulation of an issue or problem, for instance, using an incorrect model, making false assumptions, choosing incorrect decision criteria, and so on. Common examples are over-estimating the size of the market or growth rates. Administrative risk concerns the fact that even a well thought out issue or plan may not be implemented appropriately, an example being poor management of cash-flow.   Environmental risk emanates from unanticipated change in the external environment in the form of changes in demand, competition and technological development primarily.   Thus Terpstra et al. (1993) have argued that risk is a product of an individual's propensity to take risks and the amount of risk attached to a particular situation.

Chell et al. (1991) however, claim that since authors have different definitions of entrepreneurs one must distinguish between risk taking and calculated risk taking: '... *from whose perspective is the decision or action considered to be risky?*' (p. 43).   Entrepreneurs, as already mentioned, are commonly considered to be opportunity seekers more than risk takers *per se* and, as O'Gorman and Cunningham (1997) point out, possibly the biggest risk an entrepreneur may have to take is deciding to leave a job in order to start a new venture. On the other hand, Simon et al. (2000) suggest that some entrepreneurs may not actually appreciate the risk involved in setting up a business, as certain cognitive biases may influence perceptions, so that individuals perceive the risk inherent in situations, differently. These cognitive biases are over confidence; the illusion of control, whereby individuals starting up businesses may not appreciate that certain factors important to the success of ventures, may be beyond their control; and the law of small numbers, which relates to some people drawing firm conclusions from small samples.

Drucker (1985) refers to the common belief that entrepreneurship is 'enormously risky' with a low level of success, and questions why this should be so. If an entrepreneur shifts resources from areas of low productivity and yield to areas of higher productivity and yield, then theoretically, s/he need only be moderately successful to have an impact, and for the returns to outweigh the risk (pp. 42-43). Given the high number of individual entrepreneurs around, Drucker questions the common acceptance of the 'high risk element' of entrepreneurship by hypothesising that entrepreneurship *per se* is nothing less than the practice of mere optimisation. He concludes that entrepreneurship is risky only because so few of the so-called entrepreneurs know what they are doing. They lack the methodology and break many of the ground rules, failing to engage in what he calls 'systematic entrepreneurship'. As indicated above, innovation is the key to entrepreneurship for Drucker, with the emphasis on doing something *different* rather than doing something *better* than what is already being done (p. 44). For this reason, Drucker preaches 'systematic innovation' and 'systematic entrepreneurship' where the entrepreneur treads cautiously, adopting an opportunity-focused rather than a risk-focused approach (Drucker, 1985). Osborne (1995) supports this view when he concludes that, contrary to popular belief, successful entrepreneurs normally select risks that avoid huge gambles. They match the level of risk with the potential reward and their personal capacity to manage uncertainty. The aspiring entrepreneur must, therefore, honestly assess his/her level of training and preparation for taking such risks. Failure to do so is often a much neglected step in the new venture creation process (p. 6). Osborne concludes that a key condition of entrepreneurial success is the capacity to assume risks by the person with the prerogative to take action – be it the owner or the manager of the business – who has the authority to place the firm's resources at risk (p. 4).

The risk-taking function draws on the entrepreneur's ability to deal with uncertainty and ambiguity, and concerns an individual's willingness to take economic and psychological risks (Kets de Vries, 1996). The entrepreneur can be considered more a creator of risk than a taker of it, since he/she is often using someone else's capital (i.e. the bank's, other investors', state agency grants, etc). Furthermore, even if the entrepreneur does not bear most of the financial risk in the business, s/he is, at the early stages in particular, exposed to a considerable amount of social and psychological risk when the risk of failure itself is high. As Bridge et al. (1998) point out, in setting up their business, entrepreneurs are breaking new ground and thus the outcomes are uncertain. Entrepreneurs must, therefore, be able to tolerate risk and be able to cope with the failure which may or may not result from their efforts. These authors however, do not suggest that entrepreneurs are high risk-takers, rather they are moderate and calculated risk-takers, taking care to assess a situation carefully before acting, and rejecting options with little probability of success. However, the reality is, as Aldrich and Martinez (2001) point out, 'only half of all potential founders succeed in creating an enterprise, and fewer than one in ten of them are able to make their organizations grow significantly'.

While admitting that risk taking is part of the entrepreneurial process, Hisrich and Peters (1995) claim that there is no real empirical evidence to prove that risk-taking propensity is, in fact, a distinguishing characteristic of entrepreneurs (p. 54). Others though, take a different view (see below).

Locus of Control

Developed by Rotter in 1966, the I-E scale measures one's perceived ability to influence events in one's life. Individuals who are deemed to have an *internal* locus of control believe that they can positively determine their own destiny by their behaviour and that fate or luck plays a relatively insignificant role. In contrast, those with an *external* locus of control believe that external forces are the primary determinants of life's outcomes. Individuals with an internal locus of control take responsibility for their successes and failures, attributing the positive results to ability and effort. In contrast, individuals with an external locus of control, relate results to the difficulty of the particular task, to the actions of others and to a combination of luck and fate.

The internal locus of control characteristic is linked with need for achievement, autonomy, independence and initiative. In relation to the external aspect, Levinson (1974) has argued that it should be split into two sub-dimensions, namely chance and powerful others. Accordingly, he developed a new scale, namely the IPC Scale. Some writers consider that while internal locus of control is useful for distinguishing entrepreneurs from the general population, it is not a valid discriminator between entrepreneurs and managers, as both managers and entrepreneurs tend to score high on this scale (O'Gorman and Cunningham, 1997). However, Chell et al. (1991) point out, that while further study in this area is needed, some researchers believe internal locus of control is a better predictor of entrepreneurship than need for achievement.

Innovativeness

Schumpeter (1934) suggested that innovation is a key factor which differentiates entrepreneurial behaviour from managerial activity. Other writers have proposed that both creativity and innovation are inherent in entrepreneurship (Timmons, 1978; Olson, 1985; Drucker, 1985). Innovativeness is a characteristic given particular emphasis by Drucker (1985):

> Innovation ..... does not have to be technical ..... creative imitation is a perfectly respectable and often very successful entrepreneurial strategy (p. 48).

For Drucker, it is important that entrepreneurs are not only innovative but that they learn to practise 'systematic innovation', which he describes as consisting of 'the purposeful and organised search for changes', and 'the systematic analysis of the opportunities such changes might offer for economic or social innovation'.

Successful entrepreneurs do not wait until the muse kisses them and gives them "a bright idea"; they go to work. ..... they do not look for the "biggie", the innovation that will "revolutionize the industry", create a "billion-dollar business", or "make one rich overnight". Those entrepreneurs who start out with the idea that they'll make it big – and in a hurry – can be guaranteed failure (p. 49).

The idea of 'purposeful innovation' leads Drucker to highlight four key requirements for a successful entrepreneurial venture: market focus, financial planning, a good management team and an appropriate role for the founding entrepreneur. Innovation implies doing things that are out of the ordinary by finding new opportunities and, in this respect, Kets de Vries (1996) identifies three key stages: the idea stage, the implementation stage and the formalisation stage. Creativity, as a prerequisite of innovation, is also an important entrepreneurial characteristic that relies on the process of innovation for a successful enterprising outcome (Bridge et al., 1998). It is interesting to note that a recent study by Stewart et al. (1999) found that achievement motivation, risk-taking propensity and a preference for innovation appear to 'represent a constellation of psychological antecedents that are associated with entrepreneurial behaviour'.

Decision Making

The decision to start a business is not an easy one. As already indicated, an entrepreneur has to operate in conditions of uncertainty, particularly during the preparation and set-up phase. According to Hisrich and Peters (1998), the entrepreneurial decision involves a movement from *something* to *something* – moving from one's present life-style to forming a new enterprise (p. 10).

Once his/her business is established, a business manager continues to make decisions under conditions of varying levels of certainty, uncertainty or risk (Mintzberg, 1973). Hence, the outcome of the decision is often unknown (Tiernan et al., 1996, p. 80). The entrepreneur operates in similar situations, particularly at the start up stage, when the success of the business venture is not yet proven. Thus, the entrepreneurial decision making characteristic is strongly linked to that of judgement and risk taking.

In their investigation of practising entrepreneurs Hatch and Zweig (2000) found that decisiveness was a common characteristic. They also found that the entrepreneurs displayed alacrity and flexibility in decision-making. Related to this was their readiness to act – the willingness to act on their own convictions.

Commitment and Determination

There has been some agreement that entrepreneurs normally display a high degree of commitment and determination in their efforts (McClelland and Winter, 1969; Brockhaus, 1980). Entrepreneurs appear to be able to maintain an accelerated work rhythm over relatively long periods of time, and persevere in their efforts (Gasse, 1990). Hatch and Zweig (2000) found that many of the entrepreneurs whom they studied, had displayed a formidable will to succeed in the face of setbacks encountered on the path towards growth.

Tolerance of Ambiguity, Stress and Uncertainty

Entrepreneurs can be viewed as people who are capable of sustaining the drive and determination to persist with a course of action when the outcomes are uncertain. They see certainty as unchallenging and actually prefer to operate in ambiguous situations. People who have a high tolerance of ambiguity, and who can cope with the stress associated with working in such an environment, are those most likely to be successful entrepreneurs (O'Gorman and Cunningham, 1997).

Grip on Reality

Schrage (1965) found that an accurate awareness of the environment, as well as an ability to see things as they really are, were more important in distinguishing the entrepreneur than achievement motivation or other personality traits. This ability to recognise people, things and situations as they truthfully are, rather than attributing to them qualities which are the products of one's own emotions or imagination, was termed 'verdical perception' by Schrage.

Confidence and Self-Efficacy

It is not surprising that many researchers mention confidence as a key characteristic of entrepreneurs. Given the wide variety of tasks the entrepreneur has to undertake, it is unlikely that people who lack confidence could become successful entrepreneurs. As Gibb argues, in certain situations entrepreneurs tend to have 'a security born of self-confidence' (Gibb, 1993b, as cited in Bridge et al., 1998, p. 47). In this respect, confidence is also strongly linked to the risk-taking characteristic of entrepreneurs since individuals who lack confidence in their own abilities will rarely take a risk. However, as indicated above, over confidence may represent a cognitive bias that can lead to individuals failing to perceive the risk inherent in certain situations.

Related to confidence is self-efficacy, which may be defined as, 'An individual's beliefs concerning his or her ability to perform specific tasks successfully' (Greenberg and Baron, 2000, p. 107). As Greenberg and Baron explain, when considered in the context of any given task, self-efficacy may not be regarded as an aspect of personality. However, people also develop generalised beliefs about their task-related capabilities that are stable over time, and thus these beliefs may be viewed as an aspect of personality.

Vision

An entrepreneur must have vision if his/her new venture is to become a reality. Wickham (1998) refers to vision as one's personal picture of the new world that the entrepreneur seeks to create. Entrepreneurial vision must exist before any planning or development can be done. Effective entrepreneurs appear able to communicate their vision of the business to others in a compelling manner, so that the motivation and commitment of those individuals are increased. In this sense, vision is strongly linked to confidence and motivation, since it is the entrepreneur's belief in his/her own ability to put the original idea into practice that enables the business to reach set-up stage and beyond.

Initiative, Drive and Enthusiasm

Entrepreneurs are clearly enthusiastic people who take initiative and drive projects forward. Successful entrepreneurs will typically be individuals who are able, and indeed prefer, to be proactive, constantly looking for and finding opportunities. This personality trait is also linked to Drucker's innovation characteristic, where the entrepreneur *acts on* rather than *reacts to* his environment (Drucker, 1985). O'Gorman and Cunningham (1997) liken the characteristics of initiative and drive to what they call 'Type-A' behaviour. Entrepreneurs can be said to exhibit 'Type A' behaviour as they are constantly struggling to achieve more and more in less and less time. They can, therefore, sometimes appear impatient, aggressive and competitive. Non-entrepreneurial people are, in contrast, typified as possessing 'Type-B' behaviour, which means that they are more easy-going and less rushed. Type A behaviour people have the ability to maintain their level of energy and interest for their product or service idea, even when progress is slow. In this respect, these characteristics are linked to commitment and determination.

Leadership

Leadership, the process whereby one individual influences others in an attempt to attain certain goals (Greenberg and Baron, 2000), has been identified by many as an important entrepreneurial trait (Litzinger, 1965; Hornaday and Aboud, 1971; Moss Kanter, 1983; Kinni, 1994). There have been three main approaches to the study of leadership, resonant with some of the approaches to the study of entrepreneurship, namely:

- The trait approach;
- The behavioural approach;
- The contingency approach.

The trait approach suggests that leaders are born and not made; that effective leaders possess a set of innate characteristics which differentiate them from ineffective or non-leaders. Greenberg and Baron (2000) identify some of the traits which have been associated with effective leaders, including: drive, honesty and integrity, leadership motivation, self-confidence, cognitive ability, creativity and flexibility. The behavioural approach acknowledges that while effective leaders may possess certain personal characteristics, what they do is important also. Leadership style is relevant in this context, an early but enduring distinction being made between a task-orientation and a people-orientation. Task-oriented leaders tend to focus on getting the job done, while people-oriented leaders are concerned with establishing good relationships with their followers or subordinates, and with being liked by them. By way of contrast, the contingency approach recognises that no single leadership style is effective in all situations. Indeed, this approach seeks to identify the conditions and factors which determine whether, and to what extent, leaders enhance the performance and satisfaction of their subordinates (Greenberg and Baron, 2000, p. 463). The importance attributed to leadership in a range of contexts, is evidenced by the fact that it is one of the most widely studied constructs in the social sciences (Bennis and Nanus, 1985).

Within a commercial setting, Kinni (1994) emphasises the fact that small businesses in particular, depend on their leaders, since in the early stages, the small business requires the support and co-operation of everyone within the organisation. Moss Kanter (1983) sees leadership as critical to successful innovation, since it takes two key elements to get a company up and running – a person in the driver's seat and a source of power (Moss Kanter, 1983).

Judgement

In their analysis of general management competencies, Carson et al. (1995) emphasise the importance of judgement skills. To support this, they list the derivatives of judgement, identifying within this core competence, the skills required for running a business:

- systematic information gathering;
- objective analysis;
- risk evaluation;
- opportunity identification;
- alternatives evaluated;
- decision-maker;
- implementation strengths;
- experience.

Communication

Carson et al. (1995), also emphasise the importance of communication abilities in small business management, and detail the derivatives of this competence as follows:

- knowledge;
- confidence;
- good listener;
- simple language;
- good use of oral media;
- experience and judgement.

Related to communication abilities are social skills. These are identified by Baron and Markman (2000) as social perception, impression management, persuasion and influence, and social adaptability. Social perception is an individual's accuracy in perceiving others, including perceptions of others' motives, traits and intentions. Impression management refers to the use of a range of techniques to elicit positive responses from others. These may include the enhancement of one's own appearance, flattery, the presentation of small gifts, and so on. Persuasion and influence represent attempts at changing the attitudes and behaviours of others, while social adaptability is the ability to adjust to a wide range of social situations and to engage with people from diverse backgrounds. Baron and Markman (2000) suggest that entrepreneurs lacking in social skills may make poor first impressions, fail to generate support for their ideas or businesses and may even inadvertently irritate people who 'hold the fate of their new ventures in their hands'. They suggest further, that training in social skills, or awareness raising of their importance, should be included in the curricula of all entrepreneurship training and education programmes.

In addition to the above, Meredith et al. (1982) suggest a total of 19 different traits which help to provide a profile of the entrepreneur. They place particular emphasis on what they call core traits which include: self-confidence, risk-taking ability, flexibility, need for achievement, and a strong desire to be independent. However, as Chell et al. (1991) point out, it is not clear how this list of traits was compiled nor is it clear whether these traits were subsequently tested by the authors (p. 46). From their investigation of practising entrepreneurs Hatch and Zweig (2000) propose that five characteristics, taken together, comprise what they term 'entrepreneurial spirit'. These characteristics are risk tolerance, desire for control, desire to succeed, perseverance and decisiveness. However, they suggest that entrepreneurial spirit is not enough to ensure success. Generating and putting a business idea into practice also involves insight and core skills to drive the business forward, as well as serendipity – an element of luck. Again, however, it is not clear whether or not this model has been tested.

Psychological Measures

It is hardly surprising, given the numerous and various characteristics which have been associated with entrepreneurs, many of which have been outlined above, that over the years a number of measures of entrepreneurial ability or flair have been developed. Many of these are described as 'objective psychological tests' and tend to focus on the personality of the individual and the measurement of various characteristics. In addition to the few already highlighted, some others are highlighted below.

McClelland (1987) reported on a psychological study carried out by McBer & Co. and funded by the U.S. Agency for International Development. The study sought to determine whether there were key competencies required for entrepreneurial success. The researchers distinguished between 'successful' and 'average' entrepreneurs in the three business sectors of manufacturing, marketing/trading and service in India, Malawi and Ecuador. They devised a method called the Behavioural Event Interview (BEI), which required the respondents to recall critical incidents in the life of the business. Through the BEI nine competencies were identified which were deemed to be more characteristic of the 'successful' than of the 'average' entrepreneur. These nine characteristics were:

- initiative;
- assertiveness;
- ability to see and act on opportunities;
- efficiency orientation;
- concern for quality work;
- systematic planning;
- monitoring;
- commitment to the work contract;
- recognition of the importance of business relationships.

Recordings of the interviews were then studied by others who made a judgement as to the types of competencies revealed by the respondents.

In 1970 Hornaday and Bunker reported a pilot study designed to systematically determine the relative importance of the several entrepreneurial characteristics which had been suggested by previous research findings. The study also sought to highlight and measure other characteristics that could potentially identify the successful entrepreneur. In the study, a structured interview was used together with three objective tests. The survey group contained 20 'successful' entrepreneurs from the Boston area who had started a business where no previous business had existed, and which had been in operation for a minimum of five years. Each business had at least 15 employees and included both manufacturing and service based firms. The interview required the entrepreneurs to rate themselves on a five-point scale against a list of 21 key characteristics. In addition, the entrepreneurs were asked to suggest other elements that they considered important. The interviews also dealt with childhood experiences, and highlighted early deprivation and the drive to overcome difficult circumstances. The findings of Hornaday's and Bunker's (1970) research can be summarised as follows:

- on the self-rating scales the areas which registered a median score of 5 (the highest score) included intelligence, creativity, energy level, need for achievement, taking initiative and self-reliance;
- those characteristics registering a median of 4, were risk taking, physical health, innovation, leadership effectiveness, desire for money, ability to relate effectively to others, accuracy in perceiving reality (verdical perception);
- the three characteristics which were rated in the middle or low area were need for power, need for affiliation and tolerance of uncertainty – characteristics which the researchers thought would have been rated higher.

In addition, the analysis of the entrepreneurs' childhood experiences showed that over half of the entrepreneurs in the survey mentioned deprivation in early years and their determination to overcome its effects. There were also some references by the entrepreneurs to fathers who had provided insufficient emotional and/or financial support. Interestingly, only two of the 20 entrepreneurs surveyed made mention of a positive paternal influence as encouraging their choice of an entrepreneurial career. With regard to the results from the use of the Edwards Personal Preference Scale, the entrepreneurs also scored high on achievement and autonomy. Hornaday and Bunker concluded that there was a need for further research involving a larger survey group and including control groups. In a follow-up study (Hornaday and Aboud, 1971) it was suggested that achievement, support, independence and leadership were key characteristics which differentiated successful entrepreneurs from others.

Cromie and Johns (1983) argue that entrepreneurship is a personality characteristic and that entrepreneurs display greater achievement values, persistence and self-confidence than other groups in society. They also suggest that entrepreneurs have stronger economic values and possess an internal rather than an external locus of control. In suggesting that personality characteristics are indeed important in determining the entrepreneurial profile, Cromie and Johns offer an objective assessment method to help agencies select suitable clients for support. Their study analyzes the personal characteristics of 42 entrepreneurs and 41 middle/senior managers. A one-hour interview formed the basis of the research methodology. The questionnaire administered comprised several scales that measured entrepreneurial characteristics, as well as background questions on age and education.

While the entrepreneurs in their survey scored slightly higher on achievement motivation and internal locus of control, the managers surveyed scored higher on independence of family and planning. Cromie and Johns conclude that there are more similarities than differences between established entrepreneurs and managers. The authors also studied a small sample (23) of aspiring entrepreneurs and claim their results suggest that new, aspiring entrepreneurs possess unique personal characteristics but that, after some years, the entrepreneurial qualities may diminish and established entrepreneurs begin to resemble career executives (p. 323). These findings support Schumpeter's (1934) view of the entrepreneur as someone who eventually 'settles down' to running his/her own business, as discussed above. This recidivism may not apply to serial entrepreneurs such as Richard Branson however, who in a 30-year period has been instrumental in the start-up of many new businesses within the Virgin Group. Bolton and Thompson (2000a, p. 92) quote Branson as stating that, 'the challenge of learning and trying to do something better than in the past, is irresistible'. It is interesting to note too, that Branson encourages intrapreneurial activity and internal corporate venturing on the part of his employees, and is prepared to offer developmental capital when appropriate.

In a recent (2001) paper Robichaud et al. present a new instrument to measure entrepreneurial motivation. It measures four motivational factors namely: autonomy and independence (make my own decisions, maintain personal freedom, self-employment, be my own boss, and personal security); extrinsic motivators (increase sales and profits, acquire a comfortable living, increase personal income and maximise business growth); security and well-being of the family (build a business for retirement); and intrinsic motivators (meet the challenge, personal growth, gain public recognition, prove I can succeed). The authors claim that their instrument possesses the desired metrical qualities of construct validity, content validity, predictive validity and internal consistency reliability. Nevertheless, they acknowledge the limitations of their work – for example, the need to study the differential validity of the instrument by applying it to different groups of entrepreneurs such as male/female, new/established and so on.

Kurder's 'Occupational Interest Survey' (OIS) (1968), measures occupational interests and allows researchers, through its application, to effectively discriminate between occupational groups. It is intended for use with students to help them choose a field of study or select a suitable career. It can also be used with adults contemplating a change in occupation. The author cautions users not to consider OIS scores as measures of ability. The approach adopted by the OIS is firstly to sample the subject preferences among a number of easily understood activities in areas that have been found to be related to occupational choice, and then to compare these preferences with those of people in each of a wide range of occupations – people who have met certain standards for satisfaction with their chosen field. The rationale behind the OIS is that people in a given occupation have characteristic preferences that distinguish them from people in other occupations. Kurder concludes that people who enter occupations which match their interests are more likely to be satisfied workers than those who do not. 'Measured' interests, it is claimed, are more accurate/more realistic than 'expressed' interests. Preferences for occupations, particularly in young adults, are often unrealistic (Nunnally, 1959) as young people are usually quite unaware of the specific activities entailed in different occupations. Kurder strongly suggests that the OIS should not be used in isolation, but with other tests/surveys.

Durham University's General Enterprising Tendency (GET) scale, developed by Caird and Johnson in 1987-88, is applied to the aspiring rather than to the well-established entrepreneur. Based on a review of the literature regarding existing measures of entrepreneurial attributes, Caird (1991) identified five key entrepreneurial characteristics:

- calculated risk-taking;
- creative tendency;
- high need for achievement;
- high need for autonomy;
- internal locus of control.

These characteristics were deemed to be indicative of general enterprising tendency (Caird, 1991, p. 179). The GET scale incorporates these five characteristics into a structured pencil and paper self-assessment test comprising 54 items which test respondents' attitudes, preferences and habitual behaviours. Half of the 54 items are assessed positively and the other half negatively. One point is given for correct items and the maximum achievable score is 54. The application of the GET scale as a viable measure of enterprising tendency is tested in Caird's (1991) study of six different occupational groups in which she compared the enterprising tendency of business owner managers (73), teachers of enterprise (101), nurses (33), clerical trainees (10), civil servants (20) and lecturers and trainers (25). Her study revealed that business owner-managers have higher average scores than every other occupational group for all measures of enterprising tendency tested by the GET scale. Her analysis also showed that the mean differences between the groups were significant (Caird, 1991, pp. 177-186). Caird also suggests that there is a need to determine whether entrepreneurs actually possess a unique psychological profile and whether psychological testing has any real value in entrepreneurial studies.

Cromie and O'Donaghue (1992) review Caird's work and report on the usefulness of the General Enterprising Tendency scale as a measure for distinguishing between the entrepreneurial attributes of three different groups of individuals. The authors take Caird's study, in which she applied the GET scale to a group of 73 entrepreneurs, and compare it to the results of their own study where they applied the GET to two different groups – 194 managers and 661 undergraduates (across a range of faculties). Cromie and O'Donaghue's paper concludes that there is good evidence to suggest that the GET scale is valid and suggests that further applications should be considered, particularly to test the discriminant and predictive validity of the instrument.

From the above, it would appear that researchers adopting a psychological perspective to the study of entrepreneurship, tend to focus on the assessment of specific entrepreneurial traits. Kets de Vries (1996), however, feels that there is a lack of consistency among the analytical instruments used, which leads to overall disagreement about the emerging entrepreneurial profile. Modern researchers, again in an attempt to produce a more accurate picture of the entrepreneur, tend to use a combination of measures and scales when testing for entrepreneurial flair. Most often, statistical background data will be combined with objective and subjective tests administered by means of paper based questionnaires and semi structured interviews.

The Social or Demographic Approach

As McCarthy (2000) indicates, the shortcomings of the psychological or trait approach to the study of entrepreneurship are well documented. Concerns tend to focus on lack of specification in relation to the entrepreneurial personality, conceptual and methodological problems surrounding the measurement of traits, the reductionist nature of the approach and a stereotypical portrayal of entrepreneurs. Some writers expose a failure to acknowledge the significance of other factors, such as social learning (Chell, 1985) and context, process and outcomes (Aldrich and Martinez, 2001). Thus alternative approaches have been adopted. Researchers investigating entrepreneurship from a social or demographic approach, tend to focus on the effects of an individual's background and include some analysis of his/her family history, the education and occupations of the parents, the entrepreneur's childhood experiences, birth order, religion and culture, age at start-up (if the business is already set-up), and his/her education and work experience. This approach is represented in the literature by Kets de Vries (1977), Collins and Moore (1970), Davids (1963), Gould (1969), Howell (1972), and Garavan and Ó Cinnéide (1994), among others.

From a sociological perspective, a factor such as societal upheaval is considered to have considerable impact on the making of new entrepreneurs. Societal disruptions which affect family life may influence the choice of non-traditional career paths (Hagen, 1962). If the family of the entrepreneur does not seem to 'fit in' to society or is seen to be different, then their children may feel the need to create a new niche for themselves (Kets de Vries, 1996). Some studies indicate that entrepreneurs are more likely to come from ethnic, religious or minority groups (Weber, 1958; Hirschmeyer, 1964).

Family History and Childhood Experiences

Some authors (Collins et al., 1977) pay close attention to the entrepreneur's family background. It is suggested that the fathers of several entrepreneurs were self-employed and that this familiarity with enterprise facilitates their children's creation of their own businesses (Kets de Vries, 1977; Roberts, 1991). In addition, factors such as an absent father, an overbearing or controlling mother, as well as major upsets such as illness, separation or a death in the family, are often cited as influencing the entrepreneurial decision.

Dyer and Handler (1994), in suggesting that the career of the entrepreneur should be studied from an individual's entry into the business world right up to his/her exit from it, explore how the family can influence an entrepreneur's career. Based on the literature, several empirical studies conducted by themselves and others, and their own experiences, Dyer and Handler (1994, p. 71) identify four 'career nexuses' that reflect the different points in time where family and entrepreneurial dynamics intersect, as follows:

The Early Experiences in the Entrepreneur's Family of Origin

McClelland (1965) claims that parents providing a supportive yet challenging environment in the home can develop children with high nAch. Roberts and Wainer's (1968) and Ronstadt's (1984) emphasis on entrepreneurial parents, and Dalton and Holdaway's (1989) study of entrepreneurs who had significant family responsibilities at a young age, are all quoted in support of the point that the entrepreneur's early family experiences can impact on his/her success or failure in later life.

Family Involvement in the Entrepreneur's Start-up Activities

In stressing the importance of the relationship of the family to the entrepreneur's business, Dyer and Handler (1994) mention such factors as the family's willingness to support the business venture, both financially and emotionally, the ability of the entrepreneur to 'use' family members in the business to reduce start-up costs, and the ability to manage the obligations of both the business and the family.

Employment of Family Members in the Entrepreneurial Firm

Dyer and Handler (1994) note that little empirical work has been conducted to investigate the connection between family involvement and business performance but suggest that conflicts are likely to arise where close family members become key figures in the business and the entrepreneur must be aware of and able to manage these conflicts.

The Involvement of Family Members in the Ownership and Management Succession

Here the authors cite Sonnenfeld (1988) regarding founders' resistance to planning for succession. They also refer to Levinson (1971) and Barnes and Hershon's (1976) view of the difficulties an entrepreneur faces when contemplating the transfer of ownership.

Dyer and Handler strongly suggest that the role of the family may be a much more important determinant of business success than other factors, and conclude that it is only by studying the entrepreneurial career over a period of time, that the true influence of the family is recognised. They emphasise the lack of systematic studies in the area, suggesting that there is a need to develop a more comprehensive theory of how child-rearing practices and the family dynamic can encourage or discourage entrepreneurial behaviour.

In his 1996 paper, Anatomy of the Entrepreneur, Kets de Vries presents a very detailed clinical case study of an entrepreneur whom he studied over a four-year period. By presenting a rare look at the inner world of an entrepreneur, Kets de Vries gives the reader an insight into the complexity of the human condition and its effects on decision making in organisations. His study highlights the entrepreneur's need for control, sense of distrust, desire for applause and use of primitive defence mechanisms. The author also reveals that entrepreneurship is not necessarily a rational process, rather, it is one which involves the retrospective rationalising of decisions already made.

Kets de Vries emphasises the inter-disciplinary approach to the study of entrepreneurship, with contributions to the subject being made from disciplines such as economics, sociology, anthropology, psychology and organisational theory. He suggests, however, that there is a shortage of entrepreneurship material in the psychoanalytical literature. His paper (1996) concludes that economists writing on the subject of entrepreneurship, tend to talk about the need for a receptive economic climate, referring to favourable factors such as the availability of risk capital, an accommodating bank system and the benefits of incubator organisations. He quotes Schumpeter (1934), Knight (1940), and Baumol (1968) as examples of such economists (p. 856). Other studies by Kets de Vries (1970), as well as Collins et al. (1964) and Collins and Moore (1970), reveal, perhaps surprisingly, that the behaviour of many entrepreneurs is based not on confidence and high self-esteem, but rather on a sense of inferiority. Some entrepreneurs counteract their feelings of low esteem and helplessness through excessive control and a high degree of activity. Hence, many entrepreneurs are seen to be 'allergic' to authority and strive to be in control (Kets de Vries, 1977).

Parents' Education and Occupations

Some studies suggest that entrepreneurs are more likely to come from families where the parents were business owners. It is thought that the owner-manager or self-employed family environment may not only serve to encourage and develop entrepreneurial tendencies, but can also foster certain skills in the individual that will help him/her to operate in the business world. Individuals tend to look upon their parents as role models and, as the owner-manager/own-boss mentality is developed, the option of self-employment is seen as a viable career option. Blair (1997) supports this view in his study of 49 top public company owners in the UK in which he found that over 75 per cent of the entrepreneurs surveyed had fathers who owned their own businesses.

O'Gorman and Cunningham (1997) point out that this pattern of following in one's parents' footsteps seems to hold true regardless of whether the parents have been successful, and they quote the US figure of 50 per cent of company founders having self-employed fathers (p. 13). While accepting that successful new ventures are as much due to an 'abundance of luck and timing' as they are to a 'driving entrepreneurial personality' (p. 3), Garavan and Ó Cinnéide (1994) suggest that, to be a successful entrepreneur, it is desirable to come from:

> two learned, successful entrepreneurial parents [and] to have work experience [and] to have an adequate education (p. 3).

They feel that this scenario will not only significantly enhance the probability of success, but also lend support to the belief that entrepreneurs are often made and not born.

Birth Order

There has been some research to suggest that children who are the first born in a family are more likely to become successful entrepreneurs than those who are not. This could be due to the fact that the eldest in the family is given more attention and encouragement initially, and often takes on more responsibility at an earlier age, than their siblings, thus developing early self-confidence. In a study of 272 Irish entrepreneurs conducted by Hisrich and Ó Cinnéide (1985) it was found that the biggest proportion (32 per cent) were first born. Moreover, a study by Hisrich and Brush (1994) of 408 female entrepreneurs, revealed that 50 per cent of them were first born. However, Hisrich and Peters (1995) suggest that the relationship between the first born element and entrepreneurship has, to date, only been weakly demonstrated, and that further research is needed to determine whether it really does have an effect on an individual's ability to become an entrepreneur (p. 55).

Religion and Culture

Some researchers have found that entrepreneurs often come from ethnic, religious or other type of minority group (Hagen, 1962; Kets de Vries, 1970; Roberts and Wainer, 1996). Exposure to discrimination may restrict minority groups in their choice of employment and social status, and thus they are sometimes forced into self-employment when no employment option is open to them. Furthermore, according to Kets de Vries (1977), the process of social deterioration and the experience of religious oppression, can give rise to creative, innovative entrepreneurial activity. A recent exploratory study by Mueller and Thomas (2001) found support for the proposition that some cultures are more conducive to entrepreneurship than others. Individualistic cultures, for example, seem to foster an internal locus of control. These authors have concluded tentatively, that a 'supportive national culture will, ceteris paribus, increase the entrepreneurial potential of a country'. The corollary is presented by Lee and Tsang (2001) who describe how a 1985 government report on Entrepreneurship Development in Singapore, revealed that there was a low tolerance of failure in that society. Indeed, the report outlined a prevalent view that failure in the job or in business would mean castigation and ruin – a mindset not conducive to risk-taking. Since then, of course, the government of Singapore has tried hard to promote a spirit of entrepreneurship in the city-state. Lee and Tsang (2001) also make an important point in relation to this discussion. They assert that other studies of the entrepreneurial characteristics associated with venture performance have been based on Western countries, in particular the United States. Lee and Tsang assert that entrepreneurship is a culturally embedded phenomenon and that cross-cultural or cross-national generalisations, unaccompanied by empirical support, lack substance.

Age

There have been a number of attempts to establish a link between the entrepreneur's age and the performance of the particular venture in which he/she is involved. While one might justifiably hypothesise that a more mature entrepreneur will have significantly more experience and thus may be more likely to succeed, it has also been suggested that younger entrepreneurs are possibly more likely to take more risks in an attempt to grow their business. Almost all of the entrepreneurs analysed in the survey by Blair (1997), mentioned above, started their entrepreneurial careers when they were quite young, with most of them becoming millionaires by the time they had reached 30 years of age. However, as

O'Gorman and Cunningham (1997) point out, if age is a measure of experience and possibly wealth accumulation it could also be seen as a form of milestone which can trigger an individual towards self-employment (p. 14). In contrast, from the findings of their own research into established entrepreneurs, Hatch and Zweig (2000) observed, that people can become entrepreneurs at almost any age.

Oldfield (1999), reporting in the Sunday Times Business section, refers to a Lloyds TSB survey which showed that a quarter of all new firms were started by individuals over the age of 45. Based on a survey of 250,000 of their small business bank accounts, the Lloyds survey revealed that this 'third age' entrepreneurial phenomenon is particularly strong among women, with 26 per cent of 1998's female fledging entrepreneurs in the 45-59 age range. These findings appear to be supported by similar research conducted by Barclays bank, which found that the businesses run by individuals over the age of 50 not only lasted longer but outperformed those led by younger people. However, more recently, there have been a number of examples of very young individuals successfully setting up their own businesses. Brennan and Waterhouse (1999) report the growing trend for young executive high-flyers to quit the stressful lifestyle of the City in favour of an opportunity to set up their own internet businesses. The ability to work from home in a more relaxed, family environment, has the added appeal of a better quality of life with unlimited future earning potential – despite lower financial rewards initially. It would appear that, in addition to the 'third age' entrepreneurial phenomenon mentioned above, the younger 'dot.com' (internet-based) entrepreneurship revolution is also sweeping through Britain (Brennan and Waterhouse, 1999, p. 14).

Education and Work Experience

Studies have shown that, in the past, entrepreneurs received very little formal education (Collins et al., 1964; Stanworth and Curran, 1971). However, more recent studies have indicated that entrepreneurs now tend to be better educated, with up to 23 per cent of those surveyed in O'Farrell's study (1986), a quarter of those in Hisrich's study (1988), and 68 per cent of those in Henry's study (1998) holding primary university degrees or higher. Furthermore, many enterprise training programmes are now geared specifically towards graduates. As Caird (1989) and others (Murray and O'Donnell, 1982) have pointed out, the uneducated entrepreneur may well be a dying breed. This assertion is qualified however, by Lee and Tsang (2001) who observe that the evidence presented in the literature concerning the effect of education on venture performance, is inconclusive. Indeed, the findings of their own study of venture growth in Singapore, suggest that education has a small negative effect on venture growth, though this effect is mediated by venture size – positive for larger firms and negative for smaller ones. Taking a somewhat different perspective, Bolton and Thompson (2000b) argue that the efficacious effect of education is undermined by the influence of a risk-averse culture. While education may teach analysis and sound judgment, these writers claim that it can devalue flair and instinct, resulting in a diminution of entrepreneurial spirit.

Work experience has been seen by some researchers as an important factor in entrepreneurial success, particularly if the experience is in the specific industry sector of the proposed business venture. Mukhtar et al. (1998) and Oakey et al. (1998) have argued that the propensity to be interested in working in SMEs is strongly linked to previous work experience. Lee and Tsang (2001) state that most studies reported in the literature suggest a positive relationship between the entrepreneur's prior experience and venture performance. Indeed, their own research found that achievement motivation, the personality trait which had greatest influence on venture growth, had a smaller impact than previous experience. Of all the factors in the study (including internal locus of control, number of partners, networking activities, extraversion and education) an entrepreneur's industrial and managerial experience had the greatest effect on the growth variable.

Important studies investigating the background of Irish entrepreneurs include the work of O'Farrell (1986) and Hisrich (1988). Their findings, as presented in O'Gorman and Cunningham (1997), are summarised in Table 2.3.

Table 2.3 O'Farrell and Hisrich Studies

Characteristic Variables	O'Farrell Study	Hisrich Study
Age at time of establishment	32 years	40 years
Married	84%	Most were married with 2 children
University degree holders	22%	25%, mostly in Business and Engineering
Had a self-employed parent	46%	Not surveyed
Previous management experience	50%+	Not surveyed
International work experience	42%	Not surveyed
Established businesses as partnerships	50%+	Not surveyed
Held at least two full-time jobs prior to start-up	73%	50% had previous experience in the actual area of the business

(Adapted from O'Gorman and Cunningham, 1997, p. 8).

As can be seen from the table, the studies had some common findings with regard to the entrepreneurs' educational background, their previous work/management experience, age and marital status.

The social/demographic approach is supported particularly in the psychodynamic model of Kets de Vries (1977) where the entrepreneur is a person whose family background and other deprivations have been formative in shaping a somewhat deviant personality. While Kets de Vries quotes high achievement motivation, the need for autonomy, power and independence as the most common qualities attributed to successful entrepreneurship in the literature, he feels that a confusing and inconsistent picture of the entrepreneur has emerged. For him, the entrepreneur is a complex individual whose character is often enveloped in a strong element of mythology in popular journals and commercial magazines. However, Kets de Vries stresses that closer analysis of the entrepreneur often reveals an individual who has suffered hardship, has had an unhappy family upbringing and who feels displaced or even a 'misfit' in his own environment. His concept of the social mis-fit, the reject or marginal human being, is presented in his 1977 paper, aptly entitled 'The Entrepreneurial Personality: a person at the crossroads'. Thus, as already stated, the entrepreneur is for Kets de Vries a loner, a reject or a marginal individual (p. 35). He/she is inconsistent and confused about what they want, often acting irrationally, and is frequently impulsive. The entrepreneur is a 'reactive' individual who uses his/her rebellious nature to facilitate adaptation to changing situations. Tension and anxiety exist within such an individual as any potential success is viewed only as a prelude to failure.

> Rejection, dissatisfaction and a sense of failure follow the entrepreneur like an inseparable shadow (Kets de Vries, 1977, p. 51).

He/she is, however, someone who demonstrates remarkable resilience in the face of set-backs, with a strong ability to start all over again when faced with absolute failure. For Kets de Vries, the entrepreneur can be defined as an individual who is instrumental in the conception and implementation of an enterprise. He defines the entrepreneurial process as one where the entrepreneur fulfils the functions of innovation, management, coordinating and risk taking, and likens the entrepreneur to Schumpeter's 'creative destructor' (p. 37). Social, economic and psychodynamic forces all combine in influencing the entrepreneur and contribute to the complex and sometimes conflicting definition that has emerged over the years. Of particular importance is the entrepreneurial work environment which, for the entrepreneur, symbolises his/her capacity to compensate for past hardships by creating an environment where s/he is in control and not dependent on the whims of undependable authority figures. The various psychodynamic forces influencing Kets de Vries' entrepreneur are illustrated in Figure 2.1.

Kets de Vries warns that this complete psychological immersion of the entrepreneur, a contributory factor to initial success, can lead to serious problems during the growth phase of the enterprise. The entrepreneur will tend to run his/her business in a very autocratic way in which all the decision making centres around him/herself. They will, by their very nature, refuse to delegate and make no distinction between day-to-day decision-making and more long term strategic planning. The organisational structure is undefined and totally unsuited to development and growth:

It basically resembles a spider's web with the entrepreneur in the center, who is constantly changing loyalties and keeping his subordinates in a state of confusion and dependence. The organisation has usually a poorly defined or poorly used control and information system (no sharing of information); there is an absence of standard procedures and rules and a lack of formalisation. Instead, we notice the use of subjective, personal criteria for the purpose of measurement and control (Kets de Vries, 1977, p. 53).

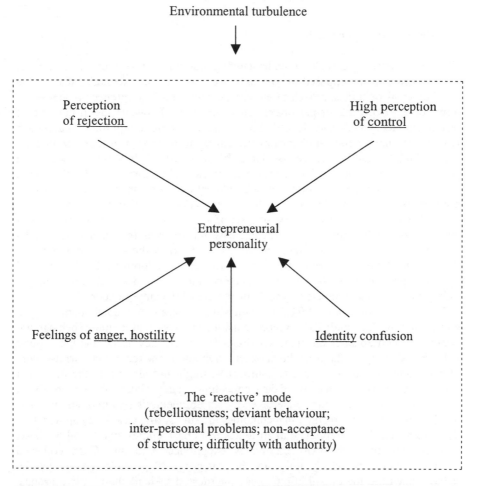

(Adapted from Kets de Vries 1977, p. 52).

Figure 2.1 Psychodynamic Forces Influencing the Entrepreneurial Personality

Unfortunately, the characteristics which help the entrepreneur to guide his/her new firm through the development period into the growth stage may be the very same characteristics which eventually lead to his/her own self-elimination. S/he is then:

> a person at the crossroads, an enigma, on the one hand highly creative and imaginative but, on the other hand, highly rigid, unwilling to change, incapable of confronting the issue of succession (Kets de Vries, 1977, pp. 56-57).

The Behavioural Approach

The behavioural approach to understanding entrepreneurship deals with *what entrepreneurs do* as opposed to *who they are*. As has been demonstrated, in the psychological or trait approach to entrepreneurship, the entrepreneur is viewed in terms of a set of traits or personality characteristics. However, as in the case of leadership theory and as evidenced above, a major problem with the trait approach is that very many personal characteristics appear to have significance. Moreover, the research to date has not yet satisfactorily identified sub-sets of these which are predictive of entrepreneurial activity or success. In contrast, the behavioural approach focuses on the entrepreneur's interaction with the environment which both shapes, and is shaped by, the entrepreneur (McCarthy, 2000). The entrepreneur is seen in the context of a set of activities involved in the creation of an organisation (Gartner, 1989). In this case the focus is on understanding how attitudes, behaviours, management skills and know-how, all combine in determining entrepreneurial success. Researchers adopting the behavioural approach tend to do so because they perceive the trait and social approaches as failing to provide a complete and accurate picture of the entrepreneur.

Lau and Chan (1994), in criticising the trait and social/demographic approaches to the study of entrepreneurship, suggest that a more behavioural approach could enhance our understanding. However, they argue that the popular behavioural study methods of direct observation and diary recordings, whilst more effective than the trait and social approaches, might not always be the most cost effective or consistent means of data collection. They claim that a more direct examination of the activities undertaken by entrepreneurs is required, and propose an alternative incident method that combines the survey and case study approaches. They identified 15 entrepreneurial attributes from past studies and, based on these, and drawing on their own consultancy experience, Lau and Chan collected company incidents which fell into the category of possible entrepreneurial behaviour within the organisation. They then tested their method on two groups: twelve middle to senior managers in the process of setting up their own business, and 35 executive MBA students in managerial positions. They concluded that executive MBA students are, in general, less entrepreneurial than managers in the process of setting up their own business, and claim that their incident method is effective in distinguishing more entrepreneurial managers from less entrepreneurial ones.

Drucker (1985) mainly supports the behavioural approach by strongly rejecting the psychological approach to entrepreneurship, and the claim that entrepreneurs are exclusive individuals with pre-determined characteristics. According to Drucker, entrepreneurship is a behavioural pattern rather than a personality trait and something that people can be taught so that they can, indeed, learn how to behave entrepreneurially.   As explained above, Drucker draws a clear distinction between just another business venture and what constitutes true entrepreneurship (i.e. a delicatessen store as opposed to a McDonalds). He also emphasises the importance of practising entrepreneurship in existing businesses and not just in new ventures. His work explains the essential practices and strategies for successful entrepreneurial management, using international case studies to illustrate key points.

Drucker's entrepreneurs take risks and make decisions.   Anyone, therefore, who is involved in making decisions can learn to be an entrepreneur. For Drucker, a distinct feature of an individual or an organisation and its foundation, lies in concept and theory rather than in intuition. Regardless of the field an individual is operating in, change is normally inevitable and it is in the perception and handling of change that the entrepreneur distinguishes him/herself:

> Entrepreneurs see change as the norm and as healthy. Usually they do not bring about the change themselves.   But – and this defines entrepreneurship – the entrepreneur always searches for change, responds to it, and exploits it as an opportunity (Drucker, 1985, p. 42).

Schultz (in Barkham, 1989), to some degree, supports the behavioural view by believing that the entrepreneur's prime role is being able to deal with disequilibrium, and thus he views a very wide range of people as potential entrepreneurs. In fact, Schultz believes that anyone who controls resources, either their own or those of someone else, is, in fact, an entrepreneur.

Gartner (1989) also argues strongly against the psychological or trait approach to studying entrepreneurs. For Gartner, an entrepreneur is part of a complex process of new venture creation; someone who performs a series of actions that result in the creation of an organisation. However, like Schumpeter (1934), Gartner believes that:

> Entrepreneurship ends when the creation stage of the organisation ends (p. 62).

Gartner's entrepreneur creates an organisation whereas the non-entrepreneur does not.   His 1989 paper criticises the trait approach to entrepreneurship, claiming that the behavioural approach is more effective and could be more useful to future researchers. 'Who is an entrepreneur?' really is the wrong question, as far as Gartner is concerned, since it forces one to focus on the traits and personality of the individual and does not lead to a true definition of the entrepreneur nor indeed to a better understanding of what entrepreneurship is all about. To emphasise his viewpoint, Gartner uses the example of a baseball team, and illustrates what would happen if a profile of the typical, successful baseball player were developed based solely on a set of traits – height, weight, age, and so on, and failed to consider the key activities involved in baseball playing, namely pitching, running and throwing. Just as abilities in these activities are obvious prerequisites for successful baseball, so too are abilities in the area of innovation, management and securing finance critical for successful entrepreneurship.

Gartner sees the entrepreneur at the very centre of the process of new venture creation and, in this sense, he views the personality characteristics of the entrepreneur as ancillary to his/her behaviour. Entrepreneurship is all about the creation of an organisation, with the entrepreneur performing a series of actions which ultimately result in the set-up of a new business. If this definition is accepted, then one must look at the process by which new organisations are created. To do this, Gartner suggests that one should follow Mintzberg's lead in his analysis of managerial behaviours (Mintzberg, 1973) and that one should ask the same questions about the *entrepreneur* as Mintzberg asks about the *manager*, i.e. What kinds of activities does the manager [entrepreneur] perform? What are the distinguishing characteristics of managerial [entrepreneurial] work? What roles does the manager [entrepreneur] perform in handling information, in making decisions, in dealing with people? (Mintzberg, 1973, cited in Gartner, 1989, p. 63). Gartner recommends that researchers should observe entrepreneurs in the process of creating organisations, and describe in detail the specific roles they undertake and the activities involved. Aldrich and Martinez (2001), echoing Low and MacMillan (1988) go further, arguing for an evolutionary approach to the study of entrepreneurial activities, whereby a concern for entrepreneurial outcomes and the processes and contexts which make them possible, are united in a single framework using concepts of variation, adaptation, selection and retention (Aldrich, 1999).

Timmons (1985) suggests a comprehensive approach to understanding entrepreneurship drawing on both the trait and behavioural ones. He adopts the view that many entrepreneurial traits, skills and behaviours may be developed and acquired, so that the individual's probability of entrepreneurial success can be improved. These Timmons identifies as follows:

- Total commitment, determination and perseverance.
- Drive to achieve and grow.
- Orientation to goals and opportunities.
- Taking initiative and personal responsibility.
- Persistence in problem-solving.
- Verdical awareness and a sense of humour.
- Seeking and using feedback.
- Internal locus of control.
- Tolerance of ambiguity, stress and uncertainty.
- Calculated risk taking and risk sharing.
- Low need for status and power.
- Integrity and reliability.

- Decisiveness, urgency and patience.
- Dealing with failure.
- Team builder and hero maker.

Those characteristics, which according to Timmons (1985), while desirable, are not as acquirable as those listed above, include:

- High energy, health and emotional stability.
- Creativity and innovativeness.
- High intelligence.
- Vision.

For Timmons, the key to entrepreneurship is understanding opportunity, coupled with an achievement orientation, i.e. the ability to recognise an appropriate opportunity, identify the goals involved and pursue a successful outcome. Different situations present different challenges and problems, and an entrepreneur will assess the probable outcome of a given situation in terms of what s/he is likely to achieve. Thus, external factors appear to be highly influential in determining entrepreneurial success. The process of entrepreneurship presented in Timmons et al.'s model, involves a combination of what the individual brings to the particular situation and the specific demands of that situation. Accordingly, Timmons et al. (1977) compare the personal attributes and role/job demands of the successful and the unsuccessful entrepreneur. These are illustrated in Table 2.4.

Table 2.4 Characteristics and Role Demands of Successful and Unsuccessful Entrepreneurs

	Successful Entrepreneur	**Unsuccessful 'Entrepreneur'**
Personal attributes/ characteristics	<ul><li>Personal drive</li><li>Strong character</li><li>Competitive/independent</li><li>Takes educated risks</li><li>Realistic goals</li><li>Ethics</li></ul>	<ul><li>Self-centred</li><li>Unwilling to listen</li><li>Takes big or small risks</li><li>Unclear goals</li><li>Money more important than building a business</li></ul>
Role/job demands	<ul><li>Own values/standards</li><li>Hard work and sacrifice</li><li>Business comes first</li><li>Knows the business</li><li>Team builder</li><li>Long hours in early years</li><li>Innovation and creativity</li></ul>	<ul><li>Same as the successful entrepreneur but doesn't meet many of the demands</li></ul>

(Adapted from Timmons et al., 1977, p. 56)

Beaver and Jennings (1996) emphasise the need for entrepreneurs to have good managerial skills when they suggest that the root cause of small business failure is poor managerial competence. Through the use of case study examples, they examine the difference between prescribed and assumed models of entrepreneurial behaviour provided by management theorists and the actual behaviour of small business owner-managers. They conclude that management in a small business is strongly influenced by the personality, experience and competence of the entrepreneur and, supporting Greiner (1972), identify the capability to adapt to changing circumstances as a key requirement for sustainable entrepreneurial success. They also view the small firm management process as an abstract rather than a readily visible process, where a number of core skills must be utilised if a successful business is to be established and operated (p. 186). These skills include entrepreneurial skills, strategic skills, management skills and ownership skills, with an emphasis on the core competence level of the entrepreneur. Such emphasis would appear to be justified since, as Cromie (1994) points out, if individuals who are less than competent in the core business skills embark on an entrepreneurial venture they should not be too surprised if they fail:

> Lack of ability in technical and managerial areas can have serious consequences for the future performance of ventures, and Storey (1989) confirms that this is so. Inadequately equipped entrepreneurs are an unfortunate reality and in these circumstances, the failure of small firms is quite common (Cromie, 1994, p. 66).

Bhide (1994) views the entrepreneur in terms of the strategies s/he pursues. He suggests that the text book based analytical approach to planning a new venture does not actually suit most start-ups, since entrepreneurs typically lack the time and money to conduct such comprehensive market and product research. Referring to a series of interviews with the founders of 100 companies on the 1989 'Inc. 500 list' of the fastest growing private U.S. companies, and subsequent research conducted by his own MBA students, Bhide claims that most entrepreneurs spend little time researching and analysing. Bhide goes on to quote a 1990 National Federation of Independent Business study of nearly 3,000 start up companies as further evidence that not only do entrepreneurs spend little time planning, reflecting and analysing, but those who do, are no more likely to survive their first three years than people who seize opportunities without planning (p.150).

Whilst entrepreneurs do not take risks blindly, Bhide suggests that they use:

> a quick, cheap approach that represents a middle ground between planning paralysis and no planning at all. They don't expect perfection – even the most astute entrepreneurs have their share of false starts. Compared to typical corporate practice, however, the entrepreneurial approach is more economical and timely (Bhide, 1994, p. 150).

Bhide also claims that there is no ideal entrepreneurial profile, however, he suggests that there are three critical elements in successful entrepreneurial behaviour which are demonstrated in the entrepreneur's approach to start-up:

- screening opportunities quickly to weed out unpromising ventures;
- analysing ideas parsimoniously, focusing on a few important issues;
- integrating action and analysis, not waiting for all the answers but being ready to change course if necessary (Bhide, 1994, p. 150).

Apart from behaving in the above manner, successful entrepreneurs, according to Bhide, also demonstrate a high level of creativity together with a superior capacity for execution. Like Drucker (1985), Bhide sees the ability to seize short-lived opportunities and execute them brilliantly, as being far more important for entrepreneurial success than the ability to develop long-term competitive strategy.

Contrary to Bhide's suggestion that the aspiring entrepreneur need only adopt a 'quick, cheap approach' to planning the new venture, Osborne (1995) claims that the essence of entrepreneurial success derives from developing a strategy that innovatively links a business's products or services to its environment. For Osborne, a successful start-up strategy emerges from a specific process that includes such arduous tasks as:

- studying the environment to identify unmet marketplace needs;
- developing a product or service to respond to needs and marketplace trends;
- creating a marketing and financial plan to animate the selected product/service concept;
- sorting out the suitable level of personal and business risk that corresponds to the entrepreneur's capacity and potential marketplace rewards;
- marshalling the requisite resources to launch the business (Osborne, 1995, p. 5).

To some degree, Bhide, in a later paper (1996) which focuses on the key areas an entrepreneur must address prior to setting up a new venture, changes his opinion in line with that of Osborne. He suggests that aspiring entrepreneurs must clarify their goals, determine their strategy and then execute it. Having started the business, the tasks of planning and analysing, which were perceived as superfluous by Bhide in his earlier work, must eventually be undertaken by the entrepreneur as s/he sets about finding the right growth rate for the business and determining an appropriate organisational structure.

> Entrepreneurs, with their powerful bias for action, often avoid thinking about the big issues of goals, strategies and capabilities. They must, sooner or later, consciously structure such inquiry into their companies and their lives. Lasting success requires entrepreneurs to keep asking tough questions about where they want to go and whether the track they are on will take them there (Bhide, 1996, p. 130).

Bruyat and Julien (2000) identify four entrepreneurial strategies namely, entrepreneurial reproduction, entrepreneurial imitation, entrepreneurial valorization and entrepreneurial venture, each of which involves different behaviours and modes of operation, and results in different outcomes. According to Bruyat and Julien (2000) *entrepreneurial reproduction* requires little new value creation, usually no innovation and very few changes for the individual. In this case the entrepreneur may become self-employed through the performance of activity in which they have already acquired expertise – a hairdresser opening their own salon perhaps. *Entrepreneurial imitation* may involve insignificant new value creation, but require the entrepreneur to acquire new knowledge and develop new networks. The creation process is longer and more risky than with entrepreneurial reproduction, not least because the entrepreneur must learn a new occupation while attempting to ensure that the business survives. An illustrative example given is that of a senior organisational executive taking the life-changing decision to open a restaurant. Bruyat and Julien describe *entrepreneurial valorization* in terms of an engineer who has experience of developing innovative projects in a large organisation. The individual then goes on to develop a new project for themselves in an area which s/he knows well and with good prospects for growth. The engineer is one of only a small group of people who really understand the technology and has a unique network of customers and suppliers who appreciate his/her expertise. Thus, in this instance there is innovation and creation of significant new value through the valorization of the entrepreneur's knowledge, expertise and contacts. By way of contrast, as Bruyat and Julien point out, examples of *entrepreneurial venture*, such as Microsoft and Apple, are rare, but when they are successful, they lead to significant changes in the environment through the creation of new value, innovation and sometimes a new economic sector. This involves considerable transformation for the creator; however, the outcomes of the process are highly uncertain.

Summary and Conclusion

This chapter has reviewed the main traditional theories on the entrepreneur, and these have included psychological/trait, social/demographic and behavioural approaches. The above review suggests that there are a number of different ways in which the entrepreneur can be studied. However, defining the successful entrepreneur appears to be a near impossible task, and any attempt could be compared to Kilby's 'hunt for the heffalump', the fictional creature which is often sighted but never caught (Kilby, 1971).

The available evidence suggests that the innate psychological dimension of entrepreneurship is a strong one (McClelland, 1961; Rotter, 1966; Schrage, 1965; Hornaday and Bunker, 1970; Meredith et al., 1982; Caird, 1991). Indeed, entrepreneurship itself, in terms of a skill or competence, remains very much an enigma. This point is emphasised further in the next chapter, where elements other than the entrepreneurial persona are taken into account, and the process of entrepreneurship is expanded to take account of factors such as product, market and team variables.

Chapter 3

Theories on the Entrepreneur – Alternative Approaches

Introduction

As discussed in the previous chapter, the literature reveals three main approaches to the study of entrepreneurs, namely, the psychological, social and behavioural perspectives. However, many modern researchers take the view that a combination of all three of these approaches is more likely to yield greater insights.

This chapter will consider some of the more integrated and modern approaches to studying the entrepreneur, including those that take account of other variables outside of the entrepreneurial personality, such as the type of business, the product, the market and the expertise available within the firm. In this context, this chapter continues to lay the theoretical foundation for the study presented in Part II.

Entrepreneurial Potential and Intent

The concept of entrepreneurial potential in terms of actual intent has been addressed by several authors (Shapero, 1982; Ajzen and Fishbein, 1980; Ajzen, 1991; Krueger, 1995; Kruegel and Brazeal, 1994; Autio et al., 1997; Bridge et al., 1998). Such an approach studies the entrepreneurial process not by examining traits, but by focusing on entrepreneurial intent which, it is claimed, may be a more accurate predictor of entrepreneurial behaviour and potential success (Bird, 1988; Boyd and Vozikis, 1994; Cox, 1996). Some of the models which aim to integrate the various approaches to analysing the entrepreneur are discussed below.

Shapero's model assumes that inertia guides human behaviour until something interrupts or displaces that inertia. The interruption or displacement may be *positive* (i.e. an inheritance, a commercial opportunity or strong entrepreneurial influences in the workplace); or *negative* (i.e. discouraging influences in the workplace, job frustration or job loss); and the choice of behaviours resulting from it will depend on how credible, desirable and feasible the alternative behaviours appear to the individual. In addition, there needs to be some propensity to act since, if there is not, the individual may not take any action. Shapero sees propensity to act as a stable personality characteristic and links it strongly to locus of control.

Ajzen's theory of planned behaviour (Ajzen and Fishbein, 1980; Ajzen, 1991) suggests that there are three independent attitudes that predict intentions: attitude toward the behaviour, which concerns the individual's perception of the likely personal outcomes of the proposed behaviour or act; social norms, which concern the perceived influences or social pressures on the decision-maker to perform the behaviour; and perceived behavioural control, which involves the individual's perceptions of the feasibility of the proposed behaviour, i.e. whether or not the individual feels s/he has the ability to execute the proposed behaviour or act. Perceived behavioural control reflects the individual's past experiences as well as perceived future obstacles. The stronger the attitude, social norms and perceived behavioural control of the individual, the stronger the intention to perform the behaviour will be.

In 1995, Krueger developed a model of entrepreneurial potential based on an individual's intentions and perceptions. For Krueger, it was important that, in order to be an entrepreneur, a person could perceive the outcome of his/her efforts and truly believe that s/he had the ability to succeed. Kruegel and Brazeal (1994) believe that before there can be entrepreneurship there must be the potential for entrepreneurship, and propose a model based on Shapero's model of the entrepreneurial event (1982) and Ajzen's theory of planned behaviour (1980, 1991), which they see as overlapping. Their model is based on a combination of three critical elements:

- *Perceived venture desirability* – this concerns how attractive the individual finds the proposed business venture together with how s/he views the likely personal impact of the outcomes of embarking on an entrepreneurial career. This aspect would include the individual's preference for a particular type and size of venture.
- *Perceived venture feasibility* – this concerns the extent to which the individual believes that s/he is capable of setting-up the business and might involve her/him questioning her/his entrepreneurial abilities.
- *Propensity to act* – this concerns the individual's ability and readiness to take action, without which nothing will happen.

Kruegel and Brazeal conclude that entrepreneurship is not something mystical and that entrepreneurs are made and not born. Their creation and success, however, depend very much on support and perceptions; the support they receive from others and on how they perceive the entrepreneurial process themselves.

> [Entrepreneurship is not] confined to some anointed group of people. They [entrepreneurs] are made through a perception-driven inactive process that begins with forging a potential for entrepreneurship. As educators, as consultants, as policy advisers we can assist this process through helping empower potential entrepreneurs who will be better able to seize opportunities when the environment presents them (Kruegel and Brazeal, 1994, p. 103).

Autio et al. (1997) build on Ajzen's theory of planned behaviour to analyse factors influencing entrepreneurial intent among groups of technology and science students in four different countries. Their model is based on that of Davidsson (1995) and includes Ajzen's concept of attitude toward the behaviour and Shapero's concept of perceived desirability. The model they propose analyses entrepreneurial intent in the context of career choice, and includes variables relating to the prevailing supportive environment (in this case the university), the image of entrepreneurship and the perceived related rewards.

The study by Autio and his colleagues involved a survey of nearly 2000 university students in Helsinki, Linköping, Colorado and Thailand, and collected data on:

- personal background variables (i.e. gender, marital status, age, work experience);
- perceived image of entrepreneurship;
- perceived benefits or 'pay-off';
- entrepreneurial conviction (Davidsson, Shapero and Ajzen combination);
- perceived support of the university environment ;
- entrepreneurial intent (likelihood of starting a business in the near future).

Based on their empirical study, Autio et al. conclude that entrepreneurial conviction among university students is influenced by the image of entrepreneurship as a career alternative, and by the perceived level of support from the university environment. They suggest that entrepreneurship training programmes, such as university spin-off schemes, could be used to influence students' entrepreneurial conviction by fostering an encouraging attitude toward the creation of campus-based SMEs. They quote the establishment of a clear IPR (Intellectual Property Rights) policy, the use of successful role models in teaching and the fostering of a positive image of entrepreneurship as a career alternative, as practical examples of how such an encouraging attitude might be developed. Whilst their study assumes, as do others, that intentions predict entrepreneurial behaviour, they recognise that there is a lack of research on the extent to which such intent is carried through.

Another interesting use of Ajzen's Theory of Planned Behaviour to predict intentions is that of Orser et al. (1996). In their empirical study of 112 SME owners in Canada, they build on Azjen's theory and apply it to the small business setting in an attempt to predict growth. Orser et al. developed a model of determinants of owner intentions which reflects positive and negative owner evaluations of firm growth. Their study concludes that growth is a consequence of a conscious decision process on the part of the venture promoters rather than a result of environmental factors.

The Attributes and Resources model (Bridge et al., 1998) is based on the attributes and resources an individual may possess at any one point in time. Such attributes include self-confidence, diligence, interpersonal skills and innovative behaviour. Resources include finance, experience, network of contacts and a track record. It is the interaction between these factors that produces the best result when a business opportunity arises. The attributes and resources model, as presented by Bridge et al., is illustrated in Figure 3.1.

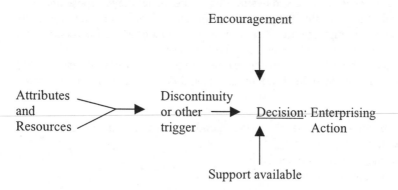

(Adapted from Bridge et al., 1998, p. 57).

Figure 3.1 Attributes and Resources Model

      In relation to organisation formation, Bird (1988) acknowledges that both personal characteristics and environmental factors define entrepreneurial intentionality. In her model, individuals are disposed towards entrepreneurial intention by a combination of both personal and contextual factors. Moreover, entrepreneurial intention directs strategic thinking and decision-making, and serves as a filter for viewing relationships, resources and exchanges (Mazzarol et al., 1999).

Chell's Approach

Chell's (1985) contribution to the study of entrepreneurship has focused on questioning the sufficiency of the psychological and social approaches in helping to understand the entrepreneur. She discusses the many criticisms of the psychological techniques used to measure personality traits, and concludes that there is little agreement in the literature on the actual profile of the entrepreneur. Chell calls for more radical ways of conceiving entrepreneurial traits, and suggests that models should be designed to measure the entrepreneurial behaviours exhibited in the development of business contacts.

      Chell suggests that, to date, research on the entrepreneurial character has centred on the following three key conceptual models:

- The psychodynamic model of Kets de Vries (1977) which, as discussed above, depicts the entrepreneur as a person whose family background and other deprivations have contributed to the development of a deviant personality, resulting in an individual who has difficulty 'fitting in' and who becomes a non-conformist, a rebel or mis-fit.

- The social development model of Gibb and Ritchie (1981) which argues against the view that entrepreneurs are born and not made, suggesting that a series of social influences shape a person as s/he goes through life.

- The personality/trait model, which adopts the view that there is a clear set of characteristics differentiating entrepreneurs from non-entrepreneurs with achievement motivation (McClelland, 1961), being the most important of these traits.

Chell (1985) takes the view that these models are inadequate, and that a more comprehensive one is required which encapsulates appropriate person variables and takes account of the variation in behaviour due to differences in persons and situations. She suggests that a more adequate model might be one which would include Mischel's (1973) social learning person variables, combined with Harré's (1979) situational-act model.

Mischel (1973) suggests the following set of cognitive social learning variables that result from each individual's life experiences and determine how new experiences affect him/her:

- competencies: the various skills and abilities of the individual;
- encoding strategies and personal constructs: the different ways individuals represent, symbolise and think about environmental stimuli;
- expectancies: a person's expectations of what might happen will determine how s/he performs in a given situation;
- subjective values: individuals will choose different courses of action because the outcomes have different values for them;
- self-regulatory systems and plans: the different goals and standards which an individual tries to achieve.

Chell (1985) illustrates how Mischel's variables can be applied to entrepreneurial behaviour by asking the following questions:

- What skills and abilities does the entrepreneur need?
- How does the entrepreneur perceive his/her environment?
- What are the entrepreneur's expectations for the performance of the business?
- What outcomes does the entrepreneur value?
- What are the entrepreneur's goals and objectives?

Harré (1979) suggests that it is the meaning of a specific situation to an individual that is of utmost importance. He suggests that individuals learn how to manage situations by learning the rules that govern them. Situations, therefore, require the individual to act out appropriate roles and engage in various activities. These activities have two main functions. Firstly, they have a practical function: to manage the situation and fulfil the individual's needs. Secondly, they have an expressive function: to convey impressions to others.

Chell suggests that Harré's model can easily be applied to entrepreneurship, as businesses create situations that the entrepreneur has to deal with. Such situations, according to Harré, are governed by rules and require an appropriate role to be acted out. As Chell points out, the entrepreneur, in reacting to a specific situation, brings his/her own set of person variables to bear on that situation. As s/he may not have the necessary experience or skills to deal with every situation encountered, it is often necessary to play a particular role, for example, that of manager, sales executive, general 'dogs-body', and so on (p. 50).

Identity Structures and Entrepreneurial Typologies

In an attempt to examine whether identity theory can add to our understanding of entrepreneurship, McNabb (1996) reports on her study of over 200 small business owners in Northern Ireland in which she used the Identity Structure Analysis (ISA) method to measure aspects of the small business owners' identities. Recognising that entrepreneurship is contingent on individual, social and situational variables, (p. 303), the study investigates group allegiance, similarities and differences among entrepreneurs. The instrument used in McNabb's study (ISA) was first developed by Weinreich (1980) and provides a means of investigating people's value systems and their identifications with others in the context of social, family and historical contexts. It is based on the belief that people tend to construct and re-construct their values and beliefs according to their experiences. The results of McNabb's study revealed that there was clear group allegiance in the identification patterns of small business owners. The entrepreneurs in McNabb's study were more inclined to perceive themselves as having characteristics in common with successful entrepreneurs than with non-entrepreneurial types (p. 315).

In terms of entrepreneurial type, Gartner et al. (1989) recognise the importance of typology in classifying and comparing types of entrepreneur, and defined typology development as follows:

> Taxonomy development is a method for identifying the most salient characteristics for differentiating among entrepreneurs as well as describing how each entrepreneurial type behaves. Every taxonomy of entrepreneurs begins with the same fundamental premise: all entrepreneurs are not the same (Gartner et al., 1989, p. 183, cited in Robichaud et al., 2001).

Typological studies tend to associate various types of entrepreneur with different objectives. Smith (1967), for example, categorised entrepreneurs into two types: the craftsman entrepreneur and the opportunistic entrepreneur. For Smith, the craftsman type is a person with narrow education and training, low in social awareness with a lack of competence in dealing with the social environment. This type of entrepreneur will, according to Smith, normally build a rigid firm, that is, one which is fixed in terms of its product range, markets and production methods. The opportunistic type of entrepreneur, on the other hand, probably has a breadth of education and training, a high social awareness and is confident in dealing with the social environment. This entrepreneur will tend to create a more adaptive firm and one that will be open to change in the future.

In many ways, opportunistic entrepreneurs may be considered as those who are interested in growing and maximising their returns from the business venture, while craftsmen entrepreneurs may be considered as those simply interested in earning a living from selling their specialist skills without being overly concerned with profits. Wickham (1998) points out that the *opportunistic* and *craftsman* entrepreneur terms were later developed and replaced with the more definite *growth-oriented* and *independence-oriented* terms. The former type describes an entrepreneur who pursues opportunities to maximise the potential of their ventures, while the latter merely prefers the option of working for him/herself (p. 16). This view is further developed by Gallagher and Robson (1996) who distinguish between entrepreneurs who are 'goodwill builders', i.e. those who are interested in the improvement of quality, reduction of costs, and the development of better technology; and entrepreneurs who are 'empire builders', i.e. those who are more aggressive and who are interested in competitive strategies and increasing their business through acquisition (p. 22). Other typologies include that of Filley and Aldag (1978), which classifies entrepreneurs into three categories, namely, those who have the goal of comfort-survival, those with the goal of personal accomplishment, and those whose goal is adaptation to the market (Robichaud et al., 2001). Braden (1977) employs two categories, the caretaker and the administrator, the former focusing on activities which s/he enjoys and the latter focusing primarily on financial objectives. As can be seen, the common feature of typological studies is that they associate the various types of entrepreneur with different goals and objectives (Robichaud et al., 2001).

In their Indian study of 30 small new ventures, Ramachandran et al. (1996), attempted to determine whether the same entrepreneurial characteristics which are suited to start-up can also be relevant to growth stages. They identified six main types of entrepreneurs at the new venture stage, as illustrated in Table 3.1.

The firms studied by Ramachandran et al., which were either in the process of setting-up or had just passed through the start-up stage, were all being run by the founding entrepreneur as 'one man shows' with little formal structure to support them. Ramachandran et al. conclude that the range of critical success factors for each stage of new business development includes a variety of entrepreneurial and managerial factors, and that their relative importance varies from stage to stage.

Table 3.1 Types of Entrepreneur at the New Venture Creation Stage

Path-breaking high achievers	Mostly graduates; innovative; highly flexible, developing modern, often technology based products or services.
Pioneering early birds	Develop products which are too early for the market; have work experience in an area related to the target market.
Comfortable growth stage entrants	Start their business when the industry is in a rapid growth phase; demonstrate phenomenal growth.
Pushed-around losers	Start a business primarily to make money; lack clarity of mission and of the product/service; may incur losses.
Risk-averse rich business people	Come from business oriented families; enter mature markets; select tried and tested products with minimal risk; start their own business as an additional source of income.
Last resort survival seekers	Start their own business after years working for others; avoid risk; enter mature markets where they have gained previous experience; limited financial resources; are more managers than entrepreneurs.

(Adapted from Ramachandran et al., 1996, pp. 399-401).

Gibb and Ritchie (1981) suggest that the trait approach to entrepreneurship, which assumes that entrepreneurs are born and not made, ignores environmental influences. Their alternative social development model suggests that entrepreneurship can be understood in terms of the types of situation encountered and the social groups to which people relate. Gibb and Ritchie assume that individuals are shaped by their transactions with specific social contexts and reference groups, and hence they change as they go through life. They place considerable importance on the stage in life at which an individual decides to set up a business and the particular event that influences this decision. Just as an individual's circumstances change as they go through life, so too does their behaviour. Accordingly, Gibb and Ritchie (1981) propose four types of entrepreneur:

- Improvisors: those who set up a business at an early stage in their life or career.
- Revisionists: those who set up a business in the middle of their life or career.
- Superceders: those who set up a business in the second half of their life, possibly in a new career.
- Reverters: those who set up a business in the later part of their life.

Other writers such as Aldrich and Martinez (2001) and Mazzarol et al., (1999) also highlight the importance of context. 'As intellectually stimulating as it may be to find out what motivates entrepreneurs and how they differ from ordinary mortals, the more critical question is how these individuals manage to create and sustain successful organizations, despite severe obstacles', Aldrich and Martinez (2001, p. 42). These writers argue that understanding entrepreneurial success requires consideration of the context in which entrepreneurs develop their efforts. Mazzarol et al. (1999) point out that a new firm requires some external resources and information to emerge. They cite Specht's (1993) classification of five main types of environmental factors that affect organisation formation, namely social, economic, political, infrastructure development and market emergence factors. Thus Mazzarol et al. (1999) argue that in addition to personal characteristics, environmental influences also play a central role in the start-up process (p. 51).

Carson et al. (1995) also support the integrated approach to the study of entrepreneurs, suggesting that a combination of psychological, social and behavioural elements have a direct impact upon how the term entrepreneur or enterprise is ultimately defined.

Product-Market Characteristics

In addition to supporting both the trait and behavioural approaches to the study of entrepreneurship (1985), Timmons et al. (1987) identified five categories of factors that affect new venture success:

- product-market characteristics;
- competitive dynamics;
- business economics;
- business performance;
- management.

In light of the above, with regard to the screening and selection of potential investment opportunities, Timmons et al. recommended that investors should:

- try to understand the economics of the product and the business;
- ensure that a prime market for the product has been identified;
- ensure that the management team possesses general management skills as well as an ability to cope with uncertainty.

In a similar vein, Hay et al. (1993) claim that entrepreneurial success is due more to product-market characteristics than to anything else. Based on their analysis of 37,000 new U.S. businesses and a number of UK based case studies, they suggest that the key to success lies not so much in the barriers to entry for a new venture, but rather in the barriers to survival (p. 32). Their study suggests three sets of significant factors: customer buying patterns, competitors' marketing and channel strategies, and production requirements. Under these headings, their study identifies a total of ten different indicators:

Customer Buying Patterns (3 Indicators):

- the frequency of purchase;
- the significance of the purchase, (i.e. whether or not the particular product represents a major purchase for the consumer);
- customer fragmentation (i.e. whether the customer base consists predominantly of end-users, retailers or wholesalers).

Competitors' Marketing and Channel Strategies (3 Indicators):

- pull marketing – the firm's expenditure on advertising calculated as a percentage of total sales revenue;
- push marketing – the cost of the firm's direct marketing as a percentage of total sales activities, excluding advertising;
- channel dependence – the percentage of the firm's products that have to pass through an intermediary before reaching the end-user.

Production Requirements (4 Indicators):

- labour versus capital intensity – expressed as the ratio of total employees to the total book value of plant and equipment in the particular industry sector;
- employee skill requirements– expressed as the number of high-skilled jobs as a percentage of total employees involved in producing the product;
- service requirements – the percentage of product lines requiring a moderate to high degree of sales or technical service;
- made-to-order supply – the percentage of product lines which were made to order based on customer specifications.

Hay et al. (1993) also suggest that the above indicators can help an entrepreneur to choose the best market segment in which to start and hence increase his/her chances of survival. They conclude quite simply that entrepreneurs are more likely to succeed in some markets than in others and, hence, analysing the product-market characteristics prior to set-up in order to choose the right 'battle field', is critical (p. 31).

The Business Platform and Growth Orientation

Building on the importance of product-market characteristics, Klofsten (1998) suggests that there are eight key factors affecting entrepreneurial outcomes and that these can be measured at the start-up and early stages of a firm's development.

These eight elements, which Klofsten terms 'cornerstones' include: the business idea, the product, the market, the organisational structure of the firm, the core group expertise within the firm, the promoter or prime-mover (i.e. the entrepreneur him/herself), customer relations and the firm's relationships with other businesses. All eight cornerstones must be in place, albeit to varying degrees, if a new firm is to survive and grow, and together, they make up the business platform. Table 3.2 shows the different levels at which the cornerstones can exist, and how these may be measured.

Recognising that it may not be possible for a firm to reach the highest level in all eight cornerstones, Klofsten suggests that there is a minimum level that must be attained in each, if a firm is to survive. These minimum levels are indicated in the extreme right hand column of the table. According to Klofsten, four of the eight cornerstones must be developed to a high level very quickly if the firm is to survive, namely the product, the market, customer relations and the prime mover. However, Klofsten sees the 'prime mover' cornerstone (i.e. the entrepreneur him/herself) as the most fundamental, since it must already be in existence at a high level when the firm is at the set-up stage.

It is interesting to note that, in his business platform, Klofsten makes a distinction between the business 'idea' and the 'product'. The idea involves the formulation and clarification of the concept behind the firm, as well as the development of the firm's activities and strategic direction. The product, on the other hand, refers to the development of actual finished products or services that are accepted by customers in the marketplace. In order to survive, a firm must reach at least the intermediate level on the business platform for the business 'idea' and the high level for the 'product'.

Table 3.2 Klofsten's Eight Cornerstones of the Business Platform

Cornerstone	Low Level (L)	Intermediate Level (I)	High Level (H)	Target Level
Idea	Idea is vague; business concept not yet articulated.	Clear, articulate understanding of products + know-how.	Business concept in initial version.	I
Product	No finished product exists.	Prototype is tested on pilot customers.	Finished product available.	H
Market	Market not clearly defined.	Early mapping of customer categories.	Market basics are defined; one or more profitable niches.	H
Organisation Structure/ Development	No organisational structure; no key functions.	Reduced overlapping of functional roles.	Organisation structure that enables problem solving.	I
Core Group Expertise	Necessary business and technical expertise is lacking.	Necessary business/ technical expertise available.	High level of balanced business and technical expertise.	I
Prime Mover	No driving force; founder treating the idea as a hobby.	Small scale commitment.	At least one committed individual striving to create a business.	H
Customer Relations	Underdeveloped customer relations; no sales procedure.	Adequate customer relations; pilot selling and evaluation.	Market acceptance; opportunities for on-going sales.	H
Other Firm Relations	No network for complementary resources.	Financial relations established for capital supply.	Network to supply capital; management credibility.	I

(Adapted from Klofsten, 1998, pp. 27-28).

In terms of growth orientation, Storey (1994) found that the entrepreneurs establishing growth businesses are more likely to be well motivated, well educated middle-aged individuals, with a significant amount of previous management experience. Such firms are also likely to be team based as opposed to individual based ventures. A number of other studies (Birley and Westhead, 1994; Kinsella et al., 1994) have supported the view that new businesses set up by teams will not only have a better than average chance of survival, but they will also have a greater ability to grow. These findings are unsurprising, since a team will almost certainly possess a wider range of traits, knowledge, expertise and experience than one individual. Furthermore, a team is better placed to ensure that the necessary 'cornerstones of the business platform' are in place, thereby raising the probability of survival and growth.

The Technology Based Entrepreneur

There appears to be some indication that the profile or make-up of the classical entrepreneur is different to that of the more high-tech or growth-oriented entrepreneur. Just as Gallagher and Robson (1996, p. 22) distinguish between entrepreneurs who are 'good will builders' and those who are 'empire builders', Ramachandran et al. (1996) differentiate between the entrepreneurial characteristics suited to start-up and those relevant to growth stages. The technology-based entrepreneur is normally a technical expert who requires general business management as opposed to product development skills to set up his/her business. Moreover, some studies (Schrage, 1965; Cooper, 1971) have found that technical entrepreneurs rarely possess the management expertise comparable to their technical skills. Thus, the high-tech entrepreneur must possess a combination of management and technical skills, as well as having the ability to build an entrepreneurial team with a repertoire of marketing, sales, technical and general skills (Flynn and Hynes, 1999). However, due to the long lead time normally associated with high-technology businesses, Deakins (1999, p. 56) suggests that the technology-based entrepreneur may begin to set up his/her business while still completing R & D or securing a patent. This 'non-technical' start-up period can provide an important preparation phase for the entrepreneur, laying the foundation for the development of more advanced strategies concerned with the risk involved in such businesses. It also provides the entrepreneur with a practice ground where s/he can make mistakes and develop contacts.

Intrapreneurship

Despite the range of definitions available, Sharma and Chrisman (1999) point out that the term entrepreneurship has become more hypothetical and abstract over time, being used to describe the activities of any individual or group creating new combinations, either on their own or in existing organisations. To illustrate, they refer to Collins and Moore, who in 1970 differentiated between 'independent' and 'administrative' entrepreneurs, the former creating new organisations from scratch, and the latter forming new organisations within, or adjunct to, existing business structures. They also cite Lumpkin and Dess (1996) who more recently have stated that launching a new venture can be done either by a start-up firm or by an existing one. Hatch and Zweig (2000) make the point that a number of individuals have become intrapreneurs as a means of gaining greater control over corporate decision-making, before launching their own businesses.

It would appear that the term *intrapreneur* was first introduced during the 1970s when it was used to describe those individuals operating as entrepreneurs within existing organisations (Macrae, 1976). Pinchot (1986) refers to an intrapreneur as someone who works within the confines of an established organisation but whose work parallels that of an entrepreneur. He later develops the term further to incorporate entrepreneurial behaviour within large organisations (Pinchot, 1986, cited in Carter and Jones-Evans, 2000, p. 244). However, as Carter and Jones-Evans point out, intrapreneurship is not just about developing a small business within a large organisation, as there are significant differences between creating a new independent venture and establishing a corporate venture through intrapreneurship (pp. 244-245).

Elsewhere in the literature, reference is made to the importance of recognising what the established non-entrepreneurial organisation has to offer its stakeholders (Wickham, 2001; Hisrich and Peters, 1998). For example, Coulson-Thomas (1999) warns against employees being too quick to 'burn their boat', i.e. to leave their place of employment:

> The value of what people have to offer is often employer, sector or context specific. It may not be recognised elsewhere. Many of those who resign from companies subsequently rue the day they cut themselves adrift from a corporate cocoon. They wish, with the benefit of hindsight, that they had established some form of continuing relationship (pp. 127-128).

Coulson-Thomas suggests that aspiring entrepreneurs in established organisations should make serious efforts to involve their employer as a business partner in their plans for a new venture. There may be considerable scope for co-operation in the form of complementary or part-time work that would generate both income and security for the aspiring intrapreneur, and this may well prove invaluable during the start-up phase. This would seem to be hugely beneficial even if the intrapreneur's new venture eventually becomes completely separate from his former employers' business (p. 128).

Unfortunately, formal, bureaucratic structures do little to generate a creative environment, and this is very much the case with intrapreneurship. An enterprising attitude can only be developed within an encouraging, open and flexibly structured organisation. The commitment from senior management is also critical and some sort of system needs to be put in place to accommodate enterprising activity and behaviour. It has been suggested that an ideal structure for encouraging entrepreneurship, innovation and creativity, should include some of the eight attributes identified by Peters and Waterman (cited in Guest, 1992) as common to 'excellent' companies:

- A bias for action: getting on with something rather than over-analysing it.
- Close to the customer: concern for and interest in customers.
- Autonomy and entrepreneurship: company is broken down into small units.
- Productivity through people: employees are seen as important resources and their contribution is recognised and appreciated.
- Hands-on, value-driven: senior management promote a strong corporate culture and keep in touch with core activities/get feedback.
- Stick to the knitting: staying close to the business best known to the company.
- Simple form. lean staff: a simple organisation structure with few senior staff.
- Simultaneous loose-tight properties: considerable freedom for innovation with errors tolerated but with strict focus on company values at the same time (adapted from Guest, 1992).

The importance of the 'simultaneous loose-tight properties' would appear to be an important element in encouraging creativity within organisations. An organisation needs to have some sort of control – a 'tight' structure, while at the same time allowing staff enough scope and freedom – a 'loose' structure – to try out new ideas and be more enterprising in their behaviour.

In a similar vein, Bridge et al. (1998) identify a number of key barriers to intrapreneurship, and these include:

- resistance to change;
- organisational structure;
- communication systems;
- creating slack in the organisation;
- championing and empowering;
- lack of an appropriate reward system.

Intrapreneurship starts with good people who in turn attract more good people. Therefore, staff recruitment and retention strategies must be strong on incentives, motivation and staff development opportunities. Attention must be paid to job design, career path planning and human resource strategy if good enterprising people are to be recruited, developed and retained in an organisation.

The need for good human resource practices to encourage entrepreneurial behaviour is also emphasised by Jones et al. (1995). Based on their study of managers from firms in seven industries, they found that the greatest differences between entrepreneurial and non-entrepreneurial firms lay in the practices and policies they adopted with regard to performance appraisal, compensation and training. Their study calls for more participative HR practices which can be adapted to develop the particular level of entrepreneurial philosophy required within a firm. Finally, they suggest that entrepreneurial activity has three key dimensions:

- innovation – which requires an emphasis on developing new and unique products, services and processes;
- risk-taking – involving a willingness to pursue opportunities which have a chance of costly failure;
- proactive behaviour – which is concerned with implementation and doing whatever is necessary to bring a concept to fruition (Jones et al., 1995, p. 86).

Even in today's business environment, nearly 30 years after the term intrapreneurship appeared in the literature, management in large established organisations still tend to focus too much upon the achievement of corporate objectives and less upon the personal interests and goals of their staff. This often results in employees feeling exploited or used. Hence, there has been a renewed call for personal and corporate interests to be reconciled through encouraging and supporting enterprise (Coulson-Thomas, 2001).

The Dot.com Entrepreneur

In recent years, the development of the Internet and its extensive range of applications have opened up new and exciting opportunities for start-up and developing SMEs, especially micro businesses. In the late 1990s, young executive high-flyers began to leave the stressful lifestyle of the 'City' in favour of an opportunity to set up their own internet businesses. Such ventures adapted well to early flotation on the stock market and appealed strongly to investors, making millionaires out of their founding entrepreneurs. For a while, it appeared that the 'dot.com' revolution was truly in vogue. However, this revolution was relatively short-lived and many businesses in this particular sector failed. A number of explanations have been offered as to why so many dot.com businesses, once heralded as exciting investment opportunities, were caught in the 'crash'. For example, the trend for the founding entrepreneur to quickly abandon his/her business after floatation and reap the financial rewards of the stock market was a key issue for researchers, and it has been suggested that investors and shareholders had unrealistic expectations for these businesses from the outset.

While the dot.com hype appears to have settled somewhat, the question of what exactly is a dot.com still tends to cause some confusion. It would appear, and logically so, that the term *dot.com* originated from the generic part of the Internet address used by most websites. Definitions of a dot.com company range from the broadest perspective of 'any website intended for business use' (searchwebmanagement.com, 2001), to 'an organisation that offers its services or products exclusively on the Internet' (TechEncyclopedia, 2002), the emphasis in the latter definition being on *exclusively*. The literature also reveals a couple of relatively new terms closely associated with the dot.com sector – 'bricks and mortar' and 'clicks and mortar' companies. 'Bricks and mortar' appears to refer to those businesses that have *physical* rather than *on-line* presences, while the latter term can be applied to a business that sells its products and services on the web as well as from its physical location (searchEBusiness.com, 2001). As part of the dot.com trend, those businesses that existed before the arrival of internet technology are now becoming 'clicks and mortar' firms, using the internet as an additional rather than a sole trading channel. While companies like Ebay or Amazon are generally considered to be dot.com companies in the strictest sense, i.e. they were set up as internet based businesses from the outset, other firms such as Barnes and Nobel would fall under the 'clicks and mortar' category. In addition, firms involved in web-based software or support, for example, would not typically qualify as dot.coms.

The literature also reveals another interesting new term closely associated with dot.coms – the New Economy. In many ways, the so-called New Economy has been defined by the very success of the dot.com sector, however, Florida (2000) believes that the most important thing about the New Economy is the way in which it has become a catalyst for a set of powerful societal changes (p. 1). In this context, Florida emphasises the importance of people: 'What's really new is that we are shifting from a *company-driven* economy to a *people-driven* economy, which means that talented people have much greater choice in where they work and live' (Florida, cited in Crane, 2001).

Atkinson (cited in Mahoney, 2001) offers a more academic definition for the New Economy:

> This is a structural change in the economy that happens once about every 50 years. Last time – in the 1940s and 50s – the New Economy was the change from small manufacturers to a mass-production corporate consumer economy. Information technology is the driver – it has nothing to do with whether or not some dot-coms go out of business.

Leavy (cited in Mahoney, 2001) concurs with the information technology association, referring to the New Economy as the Internet Age, the third major age in Society's growth following Agriculture and Industry. However, some believe that the role which information technology could play in such an economy has been exaggerated (Cassidy, 2002). One must not forget that the New Economy also consists of dynamic global markets, where risk and innovation are key players (Mahoney, 2001). This view is also reflected to some degree in Paul and Joyner's (2000) definition of the New Economy as a 'youth movement – possibly the greatest youth movement since the 60s'.

During the late 1990s, many aspiring entrepreneurs were lured into starting their own internet-based business by expectations of independent working and instant wealth. Speculators believed the hype and dot.com shares boomed. The dot.com sector was set to revolutionise traditional business models and blow away the 'Old Economy' (Economist.com, 2002). Cassidy (2002) tracks this phenomenal rise in economic and financial terms in his controversial book 'Dot.Con'. The stock market rose at an unprecedented rate, causing economic growth to accelerate well beyond the rate predicted by many New Economy proponents. The Nasdaq had risen by 85.6 per cent since the start of 1999, and the Dow Jones was up 25.22 per cent for the year by end 1999. On January 14th, 2000 the Dow Jones peaked at 11,908.50, closing at the end of the day's trading at 11,723 (Cassidy, 2002).

January 2000 saw the beginning of the fall of the dot.com revolution, with a slump in technology shares, particularly the on-line retailers, causing the IPO market to virtually snap shut (Economist.com, 2002). During the second half of January, the Dow Jones fell by almost 1,000 points to below the 11,000 level. From then on, it was 'sell, sell, sell', with investors not only shifting their funds out of technology stocks, but out of traditional 'old economy' businesses as well. By the close of business on Friday April 14th, the day that came to be known as 'Black Friday', both the Dow Jones and the Nasdaq had witnessed their biggest points' drop, down 617.58 and 355.49 respectively (Cassidy, 2002). The dot.com bubble had truly burst (Yoffie and Kwak, 2001).

In terms of what went wrong, there are really several factors that can be attributed to the fall of the dot.com sector. According to Walden (cited in Van Slambrouck, 2000) it was quite simple: 'the cart got way ahead of the horse' (p. 3). In other words, the consumer marketplace was just not ready for the plethora of on-line services on offer. Indeed, many dot.coms appear to have failed because they viewed the Internet as a revolutionary business model, rather than simply a tool that can help a business to grow and develop (Cassidy, 2002).

Cramer (1999) highlights the Net's negative impact on stock commissions and the underwriting process. He views it as having empowered a new class of buyer – the Net buyer – who cared little about management or financials, and equated buying stock in a dot.com to simply voting for their favourite website (Cramer, 1999). Cramer also believes that the fall of the dot.coms can be attributed to people's belief in what he describes as 'the 10 biggest Internet myths'. These range from the belief that 'it is cheap to do business on the web' and 'anyone can start a dot.com', through to 'don't worry, profitability is just around the corner', and 'you don't need a second revenue stream' (Cramer, 1999).

Another factor that contributed to the fall of the dot.coms was that the difficulties involved in up- (or down) scaling knowledge-based companies were seriously underestimated. After all, people, not machinery, are the key resource in a dot.com company (Scaife, 2001), and you cannot acquire (or dispose of) a staff member as easily as a piece of equipment.

In many cases, it appears that dot.comers forgot about the need to maintain the principles of competitive strategy and economic value (Yoffie and Kwak, 2001). From the dot.comers' point of view, popular funding models of the 1990s encouraged exit strategies for investors, entrepreneurs and employers alike, almost predicting that stock options would eventually become so valuable that no one would have to work anymore (Scaife, 2001). So, who was going to be left to run the company?

Plenty of advice has been offered to established and aspiring dot.comers. O'Neill (2001) suggest that a good Internet business plan had to take into account the 3 Cs: content, community and commerce. Yoffie and Kwak (2001) offer more specific advice for successful dot.com businesses and suggest that the aspiring dotcomer should:

- position his/her business alongside competitors rather than against them;
- use partnerships to befriend competitors;
- compete only in areas where his/her business has an edge;
- challenge competitors to destroy their own assets thus making it difficult for even the larger businesses to fight back.

The human capital aspect of the dot.com sector has also been highlighted as a critical success factor (Florida, 2001). After all, entrepreneurship – new business creation – does not take place in a vacuum but amidst *real* people working in a *real* world (Florida, 2001, p. 1). Ostermann (2001) supports this view and, while recognising the significant positive changes that the dot.com era has brought, suggests that the New Economy is beginning to look suspiciously like the old one. In describing the business skills necessary for success in the New Economy, he highlights the need to return to the traditional skills of strategy, operations and communication – 'old skills in a new order' (Ostermann, 2001, p. 30).

Elsewhere in the literature, commentators warn of the need for internet companies to be 'scaleable companies that can adapt and change' (Scaife, 2001); to see the Net as 'a means by which to conduct business rather than a business in itself' (O'Neill, 2001); not to expect to 'get rich quick' (McGovern, 2001); and have 'modest ambitions' (Griffith, 2001):

> Successful dot.coms, therefore, are not out to revolutionise how Americans shop; they are simply looking to increase sales' (Griffith, 2001).

General Advice from Successful, Established Entrepreneurs

According to Lussier (1995), regardless of what type of new business venture an entrepreneur is attempting to establish, there are several factors which can contribute to its success or failure. Therefore, aspiring entrepreneurs would do well to listen to the advice of successful established business owners. Based on a review of 20 studies from the literature, Lussier (1995, p. 10-11) identifies the following critical factors that can lead to entrepreneurial success or failure:

- adequate capital;
- good record keeping/financial control;
- industry experience;
- management experience;
- good planning;
- use of professional advisors;
- adequate level of education;
- quality employees;
- product/service timing;
- economic timing;
- age of the founding entrepreneur;

- business partners;
- parents;
- minority (background);
- marketing.

Lussier also notes that there are discrepancies between the studies represented in the literature, and concludes there is no generally accepted set of reasons why businesses fail or succeed. He goes on to compare the above list of factors with advice compiled from his own study of 160 US based business owners across a wide variety of industry sectors. These are summarised in Table 3.3.

On comparing the findings of his own study with the key determinants of entrepreneurial success identified in the literature, Lussier concludes that there are additional factors which may contribute to success or failure. He suggests that these merit further research and could eventually be added to those listed in the general body of entrepreneurial literature. The main additional factors identified by Lussier are those italicised in Table 3.3, and include the preparedness to work long hours, researching the market prior to start up and watching overhead costs.

Table 3.3 Summary of Advice from Successful Business Owners to Aspiring Entrepreneurs

	Summary of Advice Given	Per cent
1	Start a business in which you have industry knowledge	44%
2	*Be willing to work long hours and be persistent*	19%
3	Get help from as many professional sources as possible	15%
4	*Research your market and ensure there is sufficient demand*	14%
5	Keep good records, especially of cash flow	13%
6	Ensure you have adequate start-up capital	12%
7	Develop a business plan	9%
8	Set goals for sales, profits and market share	8%
9	Hire good employees	7%
10	*Watch overheads and fixed costs*	6%

(Adapted from Lussier, 1995, pp. 10-13).

Nulty (1995) in his interview with a highly successful Texas businessman, found that one of the keys to his success was having 'good people' working in the business. Logue, the business man interviewed, had founded or acquired 28 companies by the time he was forty-seven, and attributed his success to a combination of having good staff, 'sticking to the knitting' and what he called the *third tenet of management*:

> watch the business like a hawk and don't wait until the end of the year to go over the figures (Nulty, 1995, p. 182).

Blair (1997) examined the characteristics of 49 top public company owners in the UK. His survey focused on successful UK quoted companies that were still being run by the individuals who founded them. Apart from finding the common denominators of an entrepreneurial parent, a poor academic record, and the young age at which these individuals started their business, Blair could find no common personality traits. The characteristics of the individuals surveyed ranged from 'bullies' to 'those genuinely concerned for the wellbeing of their staff' (p. 47). He did, however, find that the individuals in his survey showed exceptional skill in selling themselves to customers and bankers.

Blair underlines the difference between setting up and running a small private company and managing a large public company, suggesting that only a few of the newly floated company bosses continue to run the business they originally started. He introduces a new term into entrepreneurship literature, that of the *ownerdriver* (p. 45) whom he defines as an individual who sets up and enthusiastically directs and drives forward his/her own business. Hatch and Zweig (2000) report similar findings, describing the entrepreneurs in their study as exhibiting a relentless pursuit of success and constantly thinking of how to expand their businesses. In addition, Blair found that many of the successful businesses in his survey were one-product companies, or at least, started out that way.

Summary and Conclusion

Building on the previous chapter, this chapter has considered the more integrated approaches to studying the entrepreneur, presenting alternative perspectives to the trait, social and behavioural views. The chapter has also included a discussion on the *high-tech* or *growth-oriented* entrepreneur, and in this respect, some studies appeared to indicate that team rather than individual based ventures may have greater capacity for growth. A discussion on intrapreneurship – entrepreneurship within existing businesses – was also included.

Having reviewed a range of approaches to studying the entrepreneur, one is still left with the fundamental question: can entrepreneurship be taught? If one believes that entrepreneurship relates to a collection of mostly innate psychological characteristics, or that it depends on one's social background, as discussed in Chapter Two, then the conclusion is that entrepreneurship is difficult to teach, implying that entrepreneurs are *born*, or possibly inadvertently shaped, and not *made* in the intentional sense. However, it was noted that some researchers, like McClelland and Timmons, believe that certain innate characteristics such as achievement motivation and locus of control, are acquirable. Furthermore, if one accepts Drucker's (1985) view that entrepreneurship is a set of behavioural patterns, as explained in Chapter 2 and that several other factors in addition to the entrepreneurial persona are at play, as discussed in this chapter, then it may be possible, and indeed necessary, to teach people how to be entrepreneurs.

Thus the potential for, and benefits of, entrepreneurial development through the introduction of enabling factors such as structured training interventions cannot be ignored (Stanworth and Curran, 1971; Shapero, 1982;

Garavan and Ó Cinnéide, 1994; Atherton et al., 1997; Gibb and Cotton, 1998). The issue of structured training interventions clearly merits further attention, and hence, is explored in more detail in the next two chapters, where the literature on entrepreneurship education and training programmes, as well as evidence of their effectiveness, is reviewed.

Chapter 4

Entrepreneurship Education and Training Programmes

Introduction

In the previous chapters the issue of who or what is an entrepreneur was discussed, leading to the question of whether entrepreneurs are born or made. This in turn leads commentators to ask whether or not entrepreneurship can be taught, and in this respect, there is still considerable uncertainty. For instance, Feit (2000a, p. 1) has noted that, 'there is an on-going debate in the entrepreneurship academy about whether we can actually teach students to be entrepreneurs'. He further observes that the resolution of this debate is inextricably linked to our theoretical assumptions about the field, because these will determine how and what is taught. This is problematic, however, for the field, as it is currently constituted, does not have one overarching theory. 'Despite the creation of more theory in entrepreneurship, entrepreneurship scholars have noticed the difficulty of integrating entrepreneurship theory-development efforts into any coherent scheme' Gartner (2001, p. 28).

This chapter begins by highlighting the lack of theoretical rigour in the area of entrepreneurship and discusses the extent to which entrepreneurship can be taught. The focus then shifts to entrepreneurship education and training programmes, considering the ways in which such programmes have been categorised, as well as their objectives, structure and content. Attention is also given to the various difficulties associated with programme design and delivery.

Entrepreneurship – a Lack of Theoretical Rigour?

Fiet (2000a, p. 12) suggests that, 'all theories in the social sciences, including those that examine entrepreneurs, are in some ways inaccurate, contradictory or incomplete'. However, while this might be the current position, he notes that those who believe entrepreneurship can be taught, assume that those engaged in research in the area will eventually develop a more general theory of the field.

As has been highlighted in preceding chapters, the sustained interest in entrepreneurship is more than just a fad. Indeed, as Venkatraman (1996, cited by Fict, 2000b, p. 102) has commented, this interest accurately reflects an 'emerging economic environment created by the confluence of changes in the corporate world, new technology and emerging world markets'. However, despite the attention currently being paid to entrepreneurship, Brazeal and Herbert (1999) believe that the study of the concept is still in its infancy and, in consequence, those working in the field continue to be engaged in conceptual and methodological debates. In particular, there are two areas of concern regarding research conducted in the field. On the one hand, research has tended to run ahead of theoretical developments, and on the other, there has been a bias towards research which has been conducted in an *ad hoc* way without theoretical underpinnings being developed.

It is in this context that Low (2001) has described entrepreneurship as being in its adolescence, and while much research activity has occurred over the past decade, only a modest level of academic legitimacy has been achieved. The fundamental problems, which the field has to address, stem from the number of issues to be explored, as well as the diverse range of disciplines from which these issues might be examined. The result of this is that each discipline views entrepreneurship from its own perspective without taking cognisance of approaches in other disciplines. As Herron et al. (1991) have observed, 'many "uni" – rather than one or more "multi" – disciplinary views of our field currently exist'. Indeed, Ucbasaran and Westhead (2001, p. 58) have noted that there is, 'growing concern that entrepreneurship as a discipline is fragmented among specialists who make little use of each other's work'. Thus, while a large body of knowledge has been generated, some commentators are concerned that this has not necessarily been cumulative. For example, Greenfield and Strickon (1986) state that when there is no consensus on, at least, the main research object of the field, researchers tend to speak after one another rather than to one another. Indeed, the question posed by Sexton (1988) regarding whether the field of entrepreneurship at that time was growing (i.e. developing) or just getting bigger, is still applicable today. As Bruyat and Julien (2000, p. 166) have observed, 'even though the field of entrepreneurship is to a large extent, formed... the problem of defining the word "entrepreneur" and establishing the boundaries of the field have still not been solved'. This is despite the fact that those working within the field have, as Low (2001) notes, spent a disproportionate and unproductive amount of time engaged in trying to define entrepreneurship. However, he also asserts that, while the fundamental question of what is meant by entrepreneurship remains the same, at least the discourse surrounding it has improved in quality.

It is appropriate to consider the link between research and teaching within the field of entrepreneurship, as there would appear to be a correlation between the theoretical rigour of research conducted and the theoretical rigour of courses designed. If theoretically rigorous research is not conducted, then the content of entrepreneurship courses may suffer. In particular, 'we weaken our teaching effectiveness when we try to teach the answers to questions that have not been addressed in the literature from a theoretical stream of research' (Fiet, 2000a, p. 4). In addition, there is a danger that unresolved debates concerning the definition of both the entrepreneur and entrepreneurship can lead to confusion when assessing the state of entrepreneurship education as it currently exists.

Can Entrepreneurship be Taught?

Despite the fact that the debate surrounding whether or not entrepreneurship can be taught continues, there has been much interest in entrepreneurship education over the last couple of decades (Sexton et al., 1997). For instance, in the early 1990s Gibb (1993b, p. 11) observed that there had been considerable activity throughout the world 'in what can be broadly termed the field of enterprise and entrepreneurship education in schools and colleges'. Not surprisingly, given the fact that this type of activity occurs on a global basis, great diversity in the type of courses that have been developed, their target audiences, and the way in which they are delivered, can be found. It is, therefore, difficult to make comparisons within the field due to the variability that exists, not only in programme objectives, but also in the meanings of the words employed to describe the courses.

For example, within the UK, Gibb (1993b) states that a number of different types of programme aimed at developing the concept of 'enterprise', and sponsored by both the public and private sectors, were developed in the 1980s. After a decrease in activity in the early 1990s, the idea of developing 'enterprise' amongst students, at both secondary and tertiary levels, has been rejuvenated (Gibb, 2000). However, the emphasis has shifted from 'enterprise' to 'entrepreneurship'. As Gibb (1993b) pointed out almost a decade ago, much of what was promoted within the entrepreneurship education and training arena in the UK, was termed 'enterprise' and focused upon the development of personal enterprising skills and attributes. Further, at university level, under the Enterprise in Higher Education Initiative, potential confusion existed between the development of 'interpersonal' and 'enterprising' skills. While the former can be synonymous with the latter, Gibb suggests that general skills, on their own, are probably not sufficient for developing entrepreneurial behaviour. He believes that confusion still exists, and recently warned that it is particularly important 'to clarify notions of the relationship between enterprise, entrepreneurship, business skills and personal transferable skills in developing an approach to entrepreneurship education' (Gibb, 2000, p. 16). This is despite the fact that in earlier work Gibb (1987a) clearly distinguished between entrepreneurship, enterprising behaviour and small business management. He did this by defining the entrepreneur in terms of attributes, and the small business owner or manager in terms of tasks. In subsequent work, Gibb and Nelson (1996, p. 98) also differentiated between these three categories. They defined entrepreneurship as the functional management skills and abilities required to start, manage and develop a small business, while small business management was concerned with the personal capability of the individual or individuals at the helm of the business. Enterprising behaviour referred to the development of learning skills to enable learning to be personalised, applied to the workplace and continued beyond the education or training programme, with the participant firmly in control of the process.

Despite repeated calls for more clarity in the definition of these terms, confusion still appears to exist. For instance, one of the conclusions of the recently conducted survey by Gorman et al. (1997) of the entrepreneurship education literature, was the need for clarity in definition. In particular, the need to differentiate between entrepreneurship, enterprise and small business management education, taking care to distinguish each of these from traditional approaches to management education, was highlighted. This confusion is surprising, for as Laukkanen (2000, p. 27) has noted, 'the field itself customarily differentiates entrepreneurship and small business ownership: the former stressing new business and wealth creation, the latter being more occupied with management and business function know-how in small firm contexts'.

Within the US, where there has been interest and activity in the teaching of entrepreneurship for almost forty years (Sexton et al., 1997), the term 'entrepreneurship education' has been employed (Gibb, 1993b). Entrepreneurship education in the US is not just conducted within the domain of the universities, where its presence is pervasive, but as Sexton et al. (1997) point out, there has been a contemporaneous increase in the number of seminars on entrepreneurship offered by private consultants and trade associations. Indeed, interest in the area of entrepreneurship education, by both practitioners and academics, appears to be undiminished. Although not extensively represented in the literature, the subject of entrepreneurship education and training is continuing to receive increased attention, and research in the area is growing. Gibb (2000) states that there has been a substantial growth not only in the academic literature, but also in the grey literature, which includes press and professional journal articles, as well as consultancy reports. However, despite the increase in academic knowledge he argues that, within the UK, there has also been a growth in ignorance. This has manifested itself in the emergence of, what he terms, mythical concepts that are currently influencing policy. In addition, at a less macro level, Gorman et al. (1997) report that there has been an increase in the amount of empirical research conducted, especially in the areas of educational process and structure. Not surprisingly, they also report that the findings from the studies which they assessed, indicated that entrepreneurship can be taught, or if not taught, at least developed by entrepreneurship education. This supports the findings of Vesper's (1982) US based study of university professors, which demonstrated an overwhelming consensus that entrepreneurship can be taught. Supporting this view, Kantor (1988) claims that, based on his study of 408 entrepreneurship students in Ontario, most generally believed that the majority of entrepreneurial traits and abilities can be taught, with abilities perceived as being more teachable than traits. This concurs with the findings of the study conducted by Clark et al. (1984), which indicated that teaching entrepreneurship skills aided the creation and success of new businesses.

Jack and Anderson (1998) have suggested that teaching entrepreneurship is a bit of an enigma since the actual entrepreneurial process involves both art and science. The 'science' part, which involves the business and management functional skills, appears to be teachable using a conventional pedagogical approach. However, the 'art' part, which relates to the creative and innovative attributes of entrepreneurship, does not appear to be teachable in the same way.

Instead this aspect is inductive, which contrasts with the rational deduction of resource management. Saee (1996) also compares the teaching of entrepreneurship to an art form and suggests that some individuals are naturally talented, whilst others must work hard to achieve similar ends. He suggests that a curriculum cannot create an entrepreneur, rather it can only demonstrate the process involved in being successful. The individual will always be responsible for their own success.

This perspective concurs with that held by Shepherd and Douglas (1996) who support the need to teach both the art and the science elements. Indeed, 'since the spirit of entrepreneurship may not be endemic in every person, or may require awakening and enhancing, business education should teach not only the various business disciplines but also the essence of entrepreneurship' (Shepherd and Douglas, 1996, p. 1). However, for them the gap between what is art and what is science is much wider. They depict science as something that is selective, analytical, sequential and fixed while they describe art as generative, provocative, jumping and without constraint. While they do not suggest that the essence or art of entrepreneurship is completely unteachable, they propose that this area has been largely neglected by those involved in delivering entrepreneurship and business courses.

However, it is in developing this *essence* that schools and universities have a key role to play, since they are ideally placed to influence entrepreneurial attributes from an early age (Mahlberg, 1996). In examining the contribution of business schools to the development of entrepreneurship, Shepherd and Douglas (1996) point out that many entrepreneurship educators are teaching *logical* thinking when they should, in fact, be teaching *entrepreneurial* thinking, and argue that logical thinking can lead to incorrect and unworkable answers. They call for a shift in emphasis from teaching to learning, suggesting that an individual can really only learn when he or she performs the particular skill in an environment as close to real life as possible. The challenge for entrepreneurship teachers and trainers, therefore, is to find innovative learning methods that coincide with the requirements of potential entrepreneurs. Unfortunately, having criticised a range of teaching methods, including those thought to be more modern and possibly more innovative, Shepherd and Douglas fail to answer the fundamental question of *how*?

Miller (1987) also separates the teachable from the non-teachable aspects of entrepreneurship. He believes that not all aspects of entrepreneurship can be taught, and that educators cannot create entrepreneurs any more than they can produce foolproof, step-by-step recipes for entrepreneurial success. However, Miller (1987) believes that educators can provide an understanding of the rigorous analytical techniques required to set-up a new business and an appreciation of the limitation of those techniques. He also claims that many of the entrepreneurial characteristics, like self-confidence, persistence and high energy levels, cannot be wholly acquired in the classroom. Boussouara and Deakins (1998), in examining the development of high technology small firms, suggest that entrepreneurs learn, not through structured teaching, but through experience and trial and error. Whilst they believe that intervention at the critical stages of business development has an important role to play, they view a firm's performance and development as dependent on critical incident decision making. Their study of 23 technology based entrepreneurs who had started out in non-technical ventures demonstrated that this type of start-up can in fact act as a 'nursery' for these individuals in the development of their technology based businesses. Indeed this preparation and nursery stage is an important part of the entrepreneurial creative process.

Categorising Entrepreneurship Education and Training

The idea that the learning needs of entrepreneurs will vary at different stages of development has been acknowledged for some time. For example, one of the categories adopted by Gorman et al. (1997) when conducting their survey of entrepreneurship education literature, was that of the target market of each course or programme. Indeed, their 'underlying assumption for using audience segmentation was that educational objectives, subject matter and pedagogical approach might be expected to vary depending on the nature of the target audience' (Gorman et al., 1997, p. 56). In this survey the authors have differentiated between education and training targeted at the pre-startup which appears to involve the aspiring entrepreneur, and the post-startup phase consisting of the established entrepreneur or small business owner. However others, including McMullan and Long, 1987; Monroy, 1995; O'Gorman and Cunningham, 1997; Bridge et al., 1998; van der Sijde et al., 1997, have more specifically identified that the training needs of an individual will vary according to a particular stage of development such as awareness, pre-startup, startup, growth and maturity. Drawing attention to the fact that the stage of development of an individual, or his/her business, can have an impact upon the nature of entrepreneurial education that might be received, provides an opportunity for educators and trainers to improve the entrepreneurial learning process as much as possible. Indeed, Gorman et al. (1997, p. 65) call for a 'more in-depth assessment of the matching process between what are perceived to be entrepreneurial characteristics and the attempt of educational institutions to enhance them'.

Jamieson (1984) has suggested a three-category framework by which to organize entrepreneurship education. He distinguishes between education *about* enterprise, education *for* enterprise and education *in* enterprise, and in so doing recognises the roles different types of education have to play. The first category, education *about* enterprise, deals mostly with awareness creation, and has the specific objective of educating students on the various aspects of setting up and running a business mostly from a theoretical perspective. Indeed, enterprise modules within business and other courses at undergraduate or postgraduate level which seek 'to foster skills, attitudes and values appropriate to starting, owning, managing or working in a successful business enterprise' would be included in this category (Jamieson, 1984, p. 9).

The second category, education *for* enterprise, deals more with the preparation of aspiring entrepreneurs for a career in self-employment with the specific objective of encouraging participants to set-up and run their own business. Participants are taught the practical skills required for small business set-up and management, and the courses are often geared towards the preparation of a business plan. Business start-up schemes and start your own business programmes, would be examples of this type of entrepreneurship training. Jamieson (1984) sees this as the narrowest definition as it refers to educating people to start-up their own small business, with an emphasis on start-up and small.

The third category, education *in* enterprise, deals mainly with management training for established entrepreneurs and focuses on ensuring the growth and future development of the business. Management development and growth training programmes, as well as specific product development and marketing courses, might fit into this category. In addition, such training provides skills, knowledge and attitudes for people to go out and create their own futures and solve their own problems (Jamieson, 1984, p. 19). Although this definition refers strongly to the world of business, it is by no means restricted to it. Hence, education *in* enterprise can refer to courses aimed at helping individuals or groups to adopt an enterprising approach, irrespective of the type of organisation for which they work.

In a similar vein, Watts (1984) distinguishes between education concerned with the implementation of enterprise, and straightforward awareness raising. The former category involves helping people to create their own work practice, whether in the form of self-employment, of setting up a small business or setting up a co-operative. Examples of this type of training include help with developing the business idea, guidance on researching and writing the business plan, and training in business methods to enable implementation. The latter category identified by Watts (1984), involves stimulating individuals to consider the possibility of self-employment, not immediately, but as an option at some point in the future.

In categorizing entrepreneurship education and training, Garavan and Ó Cinnéide (1994) adopt a broader view, differentiating between, on the one hand, entrepreneurship education, and on the other, education and training for small business owners. In the former category they describe entrepreneurial education which is aimed at providing an opportunity to learn about the conditions favouring new business creation, as well as the various theories concerning the type of characteristics required for successful entrepreneurship. However, the authors place more emphasis on education and training for small business owners and have classified the type of training that these individuals might receive into three categories, which relate specifically to stage of development. The first of these is termed small business awareness education and normally appears in secondary school syllabi. As with Jamieson's (1984) education about enterprise, the aim of this type of training is to increase the number of people who are sufficiently knowledgeable about small business to consider it, at some stage in the future, as a career option. The second category describes education and training for small business ownership. The aim of such provision is to provide practical help to those seeking to make the transition from traditional employment to self-employment. As such, this type of training would include instruction on raising finance, marketing problems and legal issues. The third type of education and training identified is that of continuing small business education. This is a more specialist type of education designed to enable people to enhance and update their skills.

Even though commentators acknowledge that the learning needs of an entrepreneur vary at different stages of development, there is actually very little uniformity in the programmes and courses offered at each stage. For instance, Gorman et al. (1997) in their survey of the entrepreneurship education literature, which comprised mainly post-secondary courses, identified diversity within teaching strategies, learning styles and curricula design. While one would expect a degree of diversity in courses and programmes developed, taking into consideration the diversity of backgrounds from which teachers and facilitators might be drawn, Fiet (2000a) suggests that such differentiation is actually indicative of the lack of theoretical rigour within the field of entrepreneurship. This he feels has resulted in little consensus on fundamental questions, which in turn is reflected in differing views on developing entrepreneurship courses. Indeed, the content of syllabi of courses developed by entrepreneurship scholars differs to such an extent that it is difficult to determine if they even have a common purpose. Although specifically referring to the development of entrepreneurship courses within American universities, this apparent lack of rigour and the associated problems in definition are not necessarily confined to the design of courses at this level. Indeed, Laukkanen (2000) has observed there is still insufficient knowledge of what can or should be accomplished by entrepreneurial education under different situations. This is despite the considerable effort that has been expended in this area. He continues, however, by noting that 'in terms of teachable contents and didactics, the situation is better, assuming narrow, individualistic views of entrepreneurial education' (Laukkanen, 2000, p. 26).

Objectives of Entrepreneurship Programmes and Courses

The above, however, has resulted in problems when attempting to classify entrepreneurship education and training activities, due to the level of differentiation and disaggregation of concepts and objectives (Gibb, 1993a; Vento, 1998). Hills (1988), for example, in his survey of 15 leading entrepreneurship educators in the USA, identified that there were two important objectives of entrepreneurship education programmes. These were to increase the awareness and understanding of the process involved in initiating and managing a new business, as well as to increase students' awareness of small business ownership as a serious career option. Cox (1996) believes that a primary objective of training interventions targeted at the awareness stage of entrepreneurial development is the promotion of self-efficacy with regard to new venture creation. Instruction at this stage, therefore, should seek to provide *mastery experiences* or opportunities to *act entrepreneurially*, as well as exposure to several real-life entrepreneurs. An advocator that the objectives of entrepreneurship should differ with the particular stage at which the intervention is targeted, he suggests that the main focus of training intervention at the start-up stage should be to heighten students' resolve to become entrepreneurs. Accordingly instructional emphasis should be on the development of a viable business plan which should be supported by individualised assistance in the form of financing, networking or counselling.

Garavan and Ó Cinnéide (1994) provide a European-wide evaluation of six enterprise programmes across five European countries consisting of Ireland, France, Italy, Spain and England. They compared the design features, comprising objectives, content, duration learning styles and outcomes of each, as well as the target population. In their review they discovered that there were seven commonly cited aims of entrepreneurship programmes. While broadly similar to those described by Hills (1988) in that the development of new start-ups as well as the acquisition of various skills and abilities believed to be necessary in such courses were highlighted, the objectives identified were more specific. These included the need to identify and stimulate entrepreneurial drive, talent and skills, undo the risk-averse bias of many analytical techniques, develop empathy and support for all unique aspects of entrepreneurship and to devise attitudes towards change. In addition, emphasis was placed on the acquisition of knowledge germane to entrepreneurship as well as the development of skills to analyse business situations. In terms of content, the focus of the programmes reviewed by them varied from idea generation and business planning to the identification of products, market research and business formation. They concluded that entrepreneurship itself is not usually what is taught; rather, it is small business management skills that are provided.

Instead of considering the objectives of entrepreneurship programmes from the viewpoint of facilitators and teachers, Hisrich and Peters (1998) examined these from the participants' perspective. While awareness raising was not listed, those features that participants believed should be included in potential courses were more practically oriented and geared at improving one's chances of success. Some of the key learning aims of entrepreneurship students included developing an understanding of the strengths and weaknesses of different types of enterprises, as well as the opportunity to assess one's own entrepreneurial skills. In addition, knowing the essentials of marketing, finance, operations planning, organisation planning and venture launch planning, together with obtaining resources, were also considered essential. Consideration of the views of participants was a feature of the development of a small business training programme by Le Roux and Nieuwenhuizen (1996). To ascertain those elements deemed to be most important by prospective students, they surveyed 220 aspiring and developing entrepreneurs. They discovered that the main areas of interest were similar to those cited by Hisrich and Peters (1998) and included marketing, entrepreneurship, business planning, management and financial management.

Content and Duration of Entrepreneurship Programmes and Courses

In terms of the skills required by entrepreneurs, Carney and Turner (1987) are quite specific.   Based on work carried out on the CITY project (Community Improvement through Youth Programme) in Adelaide, South Australia, they identify a set of twelve core enterprising skills that are essential for successful entrepreneurship. They include the ability to assess and appreciate one's strengths and weaknesses as well as evaluate one's performance, to communicate with other people, to negotiate, to deal with people in power and authority, to resolve conflict and to cope with stress and tension. In addition making decisions, planning one's time and energy, seeking information and advice, carrying through agreed responsibilities and solving problems were highlighted.   These skills are not necessarily confined to entrepreneurship education but, as the authors acknowledge can be transferred into also adult life, enabling young people to be active participants in their community, exercising their political rights and taking control over their employment situation.

Hisrich and Peters (1998, p. 20) categorize the various skills required by entrepreneurs as follows:

- Technical skills: includes written and oral communication, technical management and organising skills.
- Business management skills: includes planning, decision making, marketing and accounting skills.
- Personal entrepreneurial skills: includes inner control, innovation, risk taking and innovation.

In addition, Hisrich and Peters (1998) stress that the development of particular skills, namely inner control, risk taking, innovativeness, being change oriented, persistence and visionary leadership, differentiates an entrepreneur from a manager.

Interestingly, Timmons et al. (1987) suggest that that there is a limit to what can be taught in entrepreneurship training programmes, and that the only way to learn is through one's own personal experience. With this in mind, they see the quality of the resulting business plan as a key measure of effective experiential learning.   However, Gibb (1997) questions the emphasis placed by many entrepreneurship programmes on producing a business plan, despite the fact that business plan development would appear to be a common element in most entrepreneurship programmes (Hills, 1988). He suggests that excessive focus on the business plan as an output may inhibit entrepreneurial response to subsequent changes in the environment. Gibb (1997) recommends that trainers should realise a business plan is only one way of exploring a new venture, and that it is often of more use to the bank manager or grant-aiding body than to the entrepreneur him/herself. Wan (1989), to some degree supports this view, claiming that the business plan is only one of the criteria which venture capitalists use to evaluate new proposals. A business plan does not reflect the abilities of the individual entrepreneur, which have a strong impact on the ultimate funding decision.

Financial management and marketing have also been highlighted as critical areas where entrepreneurs require help in the various surveys reported on by Dunsby (1996). However, Atherton and Hannon (1996) suggest broader requirements for entrepreneurs seeking success. Based on a survey of 70 owner-managers in north-east England and south-west Australia, they examined entrepreneurs' perceptions of success. They found that the key entrepreneurial competencies required to develop a business include the ability to manage events and conditions in the external environment, and envisioning a future for the business. In addition, the importance of the need to develop or enhance one's personal capabilities (as opposed to abilities) in order to manage the environment and develop direction and purpose for the business, was stressed. Based on their work, they suggested that teachers in business schools should consider building curricula around such key success factors, rather than merely providing instruction on the functional areas of expertise. This is similar to Laukkanen's (2000, p. 26) view that university-level entrepreneurial education is 'concerned with learning and facilitating *for* entrepreneurship (what to do and how to make it happen by being personally involved) and less with studying *about* it (in a detached manner, as a social phenomenon among others)'.

Despite the increase in the amount of research conducted into the area of entrepreneurship training and education, Jennings and Hawley (1996) suggest that many entrepreneurship training initiatives do not actually address the real needs of entrepreneurs. They feel that there is often a significant gap between the perceptions of the training providers and those of the entrepreneurs in terms of training needs, for, what sometimes appear as key problem areas to the trainer, may have little importance for the entrepreneur. This may be because many providers have limited managerial or vocational experience of small firms and fail to understand the practical problems facing entrepreneurs.

If one begins to examine what is actually taught in an entrepreneurship programme, it becomes clear that some programmes tend to be more task oriented rather than behaviour oriented, focusing on specific skills for small business management such as finance and marketing, as opposed to creativity, innovation and problem solving abilities (Deakins, 1996). Many structured training interventions do little to alter the approach of the entrepreneur to solving business problems. Entrepreneurs who become task-oriented are more likely to fail (McCabe, 1998). With this in mind, Garavan and Ó Cinnéide (1994) question what can actually be taught in entrepreneurship programmes that is specific to entrepreneurship itself. They support Vesper's view (1982) that most entrepreneurship programmes do not even promote entrepreneurship in that they are not 'resource effective' and their results are poor in comparison to the throughput of participants.

For example, Garavan and Ó Cinnéide (1994) have commented upon the wide variety in the duration and content of entrepreneurship training programmes, as well as the variety of learning methods used. The programmes they reviewed seemed to range from one day to one year and, in general, were very short, perhaps too short, when one considers what needs to be included and also when they are compared with other career development courses. Hills et al. (1996), reporting on entrepreneurship training developments in Puerto Rico, suggest that there are three emerging models for entrepreneurship education and training programmes. First, introductory courses which focus on the development of a business plan; second, courses for established businesses on which the focus is growth; and, third, management related courses which emphasise innovation, teambuilding and entrepreneurial characteristics.

Van Voorhis et al. (1996) incorporated a 30-week entrepreneurship training schedule into 'B-17 Educational Plan', a Swedish pilot programme for teaching entrepreneurship to the unemployed. The course, involving a cross-functional team approach with 20 team members and one 'president' per business proposal, has been designed so as to progressively develop and/or enhance the core enterprise skills required for setting up a new business.

Strong emphasis has been placed within the course on sales training. As Van Voorhis et al. (1996) point out, in their experience, selling skills are not only crucial to the successful start-up of a new business venture, but these skills are highly valued by government agencies and funding bodies whose ultimate goal is to create more exports. Hence, the 'B-17 Educational Plan' uses sales capability as a discriminating factor as participants progress through the programme. Since the 'B-17 Plan' is still in its infancy, no empirical data has yet been gathered to test the long-term effectiveness of the programme.

Approaches to teaching Entrepreneurship Programmes and Courses

It is clear from the literature that the learning methods employed in entrepreneurship education and training programmes vary considerably from lectures, presentations and handouts to video and case study based learning with group discussion and role-plays. In addition, both traditional and non-traditional approaches to learning were featured. Some commentators such as Davies and Gibb (1991) are critical of the adoption of traditional education methods, which focus mainly on theory and a didactic approach, suggesting that they are inappropriate in the teaching of entrepreneurship. Young (1997) supports this view when he questions the relevance and value of a theoretical approach to a subject which deals almost exclusively with activity, suggesting that the experience and practical skills used by entrepreneurs are possibly not something that can be acquired through conventional teaching methods. However, Shepherd and Douglas (1996) criticise the use of the less traditional case study, role play, simulation and problem solving teaching methods, arguing that, in the confines of the classroom where guidelines are provided and outcomes are known, such mechanisms are actually promoting logical rather than creative or entrepreneurial thinking. In an attempt to assess alternative approaches to teaching entrepreneurship, McMullan and Boberg (1991) compared the case method of teaching with the project method by conducting a survey amongst current MBA students and alumni at the University of Calgary. They discovered that the students felt the case method was effective in developing analytical skills and the ability to synthesise information. However, courses based on the project method were perceived to develop and enhance knowledge and understanding of the subject area, as well as the ability to evaluate, and were felt to be more effective in teaching entrepreneurship.

In exploring the relationship between education and entrepreneurship, Gibb (1987b) has contrasted the classroom learning situation with the real world learning environment of the entrepreneur. He suggests that the learning emphasis in many educational establishments and business schools is very much on the past, with a focus on the understanding, feedback and analysis of large amounts of information. In reality, the entrepreneur is focused on the present, with little time for critical analysis. He/she spends most of the time dealing with problems and learns through his/her own experiences and through doing. The classroom situation involves a high level of dependence on authority and on what Gibb terms 'expert validation', whereas in the real world the entrepreneur must rely on the validity of his/her own knowledge and personal values. The main differences between the classroom and the real world entrepreneurial learning situation are outlined in Table 4.1.

Table 4.1 Learning Processes

University/Business School – Classroom	Entrepreneurial – Real World
Critical judgement after analysis of large amount of information	'Gut feel' decision making with limited information
Understanding and recalling the information itself	Understanding the values of those who transmit and filter information
Assuming goals away	Recognising the widely varied goals of others
Seeking verification of the truth by study of information	Making decisions on the basis of judgement of trust and competence of people
Understanding basic principles of society in the metaphysical sense	Seeking to apply and adjust in practice to basic principles of society
Seeking the correct answer with time to do it	Developing the most appropriate solution under pressure
Learning in the classroom	Learning while and through doing
Gleaning information from experts and authoritative sources	Gleaning information personally from any and everywhere and weighing it up
Evaluation through written assessments	Evaluation by judgement of people and events through direct feedback
Success in learning measured by knowledge-based examination passed	Success in learning by solving problems and learning from failure

(Adapted from Gibb, 1987b, p. 18).

In view of the differences illustrated in Table 4.1, therefore, Gibb suggests a more flexible, in terms of location and time, as well as a more active experience-based, learning approach to teaching entrepreneurship. For example, such an approach should encourage students, among other things, to find and explore the wider concepts relating to a problem, to learn by overcoming failure and to develop more independence from external sources of information and expert advice and to think for themselves.

However, in terms of entrepreneurship education and training, Gibb (1987b) suggests that very little is known about the knowledge transfer process between trainers and entrepreneurs or owner-managers, and it is not entirely clear how participants in entrepreneurship programmes prefer to learn. Recently, the emphasis on learning methods within entrepreneurship education has been to encourage an active approach, though not necessarily at the expense of theory. For example, Fiet (2000a), who advocates that those involved in teaching entrepreneurship should increase the theoretical content of their courses if they wish to develop in students the cognitive skills necessary to make better entrepreneurial decisions, believes that this can be achieved via theory-based activities (Fiet 2000b). However, other commentators argue that the adoption of a more practically focused and active-based approach to entrepreneurship teaching is more valid. For instance, this point is highlighted by Hills (1988), whose survey of leading educators showed that students attributed more importance to practical work on business plan development and entrepreneurial guest speakers, than to lectures and readings. This point was supported by the results of his later evaluation of entrepreneurship courses at the University of Puerto Rico.

Timmons and Stevenson (1985) suggest that entrepreneurship is an ongoing lifelong learning experience and, as such, the best way to learn is to combine experience with formal educational activities. Based on their study of 100 established entrepreneurs attending a management programme at Harvard Business School, they claim that analytical thinking, accounting, finance, marketing, management information systems and manufacturing are among those aspects of entrepreneurship that can be taught. However, other more critical skills such as judgement, handling people, patience and responsibility cannot be taught directly and can only be learned in the real world.

Connor et al. (1996) suggest that, for learning to be effective, experiential methods that go beyond case studies and role plays must be incorporated into curricula. Stumpf et al. (1991) suggest the use of behavioural simulations in the teaching of entrepreneurship, claiming that these have more benefits over traditional teaching methods, while Wright (1996) supports the use of case incidents or mini-case studies in the delivery of business education. Kirby and Mullen (1990) suggest the use of work-based placements as an effective method of teaching entrepreneurship. They feel that this gives the students more of an insight into the holistic approach to managing a small business and begins to develop in them competencies and skills relevant to enterprise. For entrepreneurial development programmes to be effective, learning must be based in real work situations so that managers can better implement what they have learnt. Based on the belief that aspiring entrepreneurs require more flexibility in their learning, Sexton and Bowman-Upton (1991) call for the need to experiment more with entrepreneurship teaching, even to the point where an unstructured approach is adopted. In a similar vein, Connor et al. (1996) refer to Kolb's learning cycle (1984) in which practising business managers are involved in experiencing, reflecting, conceptualising and experimentation. They see this process as critical in helping business managers to apply what they have learnt in the real organisational or business setting.

Profile of Participants on Entrepreneurship Programmes and Courses

It is clear from the literature, as well as from the variety of programmes on offer, that different types of entrepreneurship programmes attract different types of participants. As Jack and Anderson (1998) point out, the audience for entrepreneurship education is a wide one. In fact, not all individuals who take a course in entrepreneurship wish to be entrepreneurs. Some may wish to explore entrepreneurship on an intellectual level while others may recognise the need for entrepreneurship in society, and attend a programme so as to better understand this discipline (Block and Stumpf, 1992, Jack and Anderson, 1998). Hills et al. (1996) support this point, suggesting that although some entrepreneurship students may seek to start a business, others may wish merely to satisfy their curiosity, consider possible career alternatives or work in a supporting role to existing entrepreneurs.

Douglass (1976) suggests that, although traditionally entrepreneurs tended to have a relatively low level of formal education, this is no longer the case. Hence, as the studies by O'Farrell and Hisrich indicate, (cited by O'Gorman and Cunningham (1997)), participants on entrepreneurship training programmes are now better educated. There is also evidence to support the fact that individuals participating in entrepreneurship training programmes now tend to have more work experience. This is important since many researchers, including Gasse (1990), emphasise the benefits that such experience can bring to the entrepreneur. Collins et al. (1964) indicate that it is often the sense of stagnation, lack of power and deterioration of job satisfaction that can lead an individual to considering an entrepreneurial career, thus, entrepreneurship programme participants may be driven by frustration and a desire to be more independent.

Kailer (1990), in his study of Austrian firms, discovered that attitudes towards training were affected by several elements. These included the innovativeness of the firm, the clarity of vision articulated for the firm, the length of planning horizon, the profile and qualifications of employees, the age of the employer and his own past experience with education. Watkins (1983) suggests that many entrepreneurs have a low regard for business education and training because they themselves received little or no formal education and, as a result, many owner-managers are unwilling to commit the time or resources to it. This perspective concurs with one of the findings from Gorman et al.'s (1997) survey, which indicated that a large percentage of small business owners possessed a negative attitude towards formal education and training. Curran (2000) concurs by observing that a recurrent theme in the findings from both independent and sponsored evaluations is the low level of take-up. He advances that there are three reasons to explain why small business owners decline help. Firstly, is the belief by the small business owner that support providers do not understand their particular business. In referring to Lightfoot (1998), Curran suggests that this does not refer to a lack of knowledge of a business by a business adviser because such knowledge can always be acquired, but instead refers to a reluctance to accept external advice. This is because accepting such assistance can be perceived, by the small business owner, as a threat to his/her personal autonomy. Secondly, small business owners are sceptical about the benefits of the advice given to small firms with respect to, for example, business planning and financial management because the content of courses in these areas is often derived from large firm practice. As Curran (2000) observes small businesses are not just scaled down versions of larger businesses, and good practice in one context may not necessarily be applied to the other. Thirdly, the standardised approach to developing training courses, which makes them easier to administer and monitor, ignores the fact that small firms are heterogeneous and will thus have different needs. As a result, business owners, both aspiring and actual, may not immediately see the benefits for them of attending programmes. The issue of uptake does not arise to any serious degree when dealing with aspiring entrepreneurs since many of the pre-start-up support schemes are inextricably linked to grant incentives and access to financial aid is often dependent upon successful completion of the training element. Furthermore, most aspiring entrepreneurs nowadays are better educated than in previous years (Caird, 1989) and thus, tend to place a higher value on training.

Curran (2000) observes that, despite there being strong consensus from policy makers on the continued need for policies targeted at promoting the small firm and its role in the economy, the fact that too few firms avail of the support offered would suggest otherwise. There is a clear need, therefore, to assess the effectiveness of small business policy at both the macro and micro levels to evaluate the impact of the training courses and programmes which have been developed for this sector. Although there has been a growth in the number and type of entrepreneurship programmes and courses, it would appear that little empirical research has been directed towards evaluating the content and pedagogy of these programmes, and also their effectiveness. Further, Caird (1989) has observed that much of the information on enterprise training tends to be descriptive rather than evaluative, and that this creates problems for the evaluation of all small business education.

Determining and Measuring Effectiveness

Many researchers including Curran and Stanworth, (1989), Gibb (1987b), Block and Stumpf (1992), Cox (1996) and Young (1997) have identified the need for evaluating entrepreneurship education and training programmes. To date, Hill and

Ó Cinnéide (1998) have noted that only a few studies have investigated the effects of entrepreneurship education. In addition, such studies have tended to focus on a particular programme and its immediate outcomes. Despite this, McMullan et al. (2001) have argued that it is necessary to assess the effectiveness of entrepreneurship courses on a number of grounds. First, there is an expectation that the net benefits of entrepreneurship programmes should outweigh their costs and risks. Second, training programmes and courses can be expensive in terms of money for sponsors and in time for participants. Third, in addition to the more obvious costs highlighted by these authors there are hidden costs which should also be taken into consideration when assessing a programme's effectiveness. For example, extra costs might be borne by guest speakers, mentors and unpaid consultants associated with programme delivery. Fourth, participants may take additional risks if they decide to implement advice from entrepreneurship programmes. Thus, they suggest that central to such evaluations are an assessment of the cost effectiveness of a particular programme as well as its opportunity costs.

However, conducting such evaluations can be problematic. In considering the substantial research that has been undertaken into the cost-benefit analysis of training, Gibb (1997) doubts whether a definitive answer could ever be found to the question of effectiveness in terms of pay back. Furthermore, Wyckham (1989) has noted that there has been difficulty in identifying appropriate output measures of programmes as well as determining causality. Despite this, however, Storey (2000) and McMullan et al. (2001) suggest that the best means by which to evaluate training courses is to directly relate programme outcomes to objectives. Indeed McMullan et al. (2001, p. 38) advance that the objectives of entrepreneurial courses should be 'primarily economic' and as such 'appropriate measures would include businesses started or saved, revenue generation and growth, job creation and retention, financing obtained and profitability'. Clark et al. (1984) have noted that few surveys actually evaluate the impact a particular programme has had on new venture creation following its completion. Instead most entrepreneurship programme evaluations measure such variables as instructor's knowledge, preparation and presentation style, as well as the degree of difficulty and level of interest of the programme itself. There is, therefore, no emphasis on the financial implications of a training course.

Stake (1980) has proposed a more *responsive* approach to the evaluation of education and training programmes in general and suggests that the purpose of evaluation should be to produce information that can guide decisions concerning modifications to a programme. His approach is less reliant on formal communication and places more emphasis on natural communication. His method is based on what people do naturally to evaluate things: they observe and react. Thus, various individuals conduct observations, regarding the value of the programme to the participants. However, Stake (1980) warns against what he calls 'meta-evaluation' where the evaluator exercises a type of quality control over the evaluation process, choosing to emphasise the areas where the programme has been most successful rather than the unsuccessful aspects. This may be prompted by an unwritten requirement of programme funders to produce a favourable report.

With particular respect to the evaluation of small business policy Curran (2000) has observed two approaches. The first comprises evaluations sponsored by the government funding body responsible for delivering the policy and conducted by private-sector, profit-oriented bodies. He suggests that most of the evaluation conducted in the UK is of this nature. In general the findings of such surveys do not enter the public domain. The second type of evaluation is that which is conducted by independent (usually academic) researchers on a not-for-profit basis. A body other than that responsible for funding or delivering the initiative will sponsor these assessments. The results of such evaluations usually enter the public domain with the aim of promoting constructive discussion. One important distinction to note between the two approaches is that the first type of evaluation is likely to be more favourable to the policy or programme than the second, which due to its independent nature should be more detached. On this basis therefore, Curran (2000, p. 39) argues that 'small business initiatives receive more favourable recognition for promoting small business, employment and economic performance than they merit'. If this is the case, then there is a very real danger that policies, which perhaps are not as effective as they might be, are perpetuated. Although making his observation with respect to the evaluation of small business policies, the general principles advanced are nevertheless applicable when considering evaluation of entrepreneurship courses and programmes. There is a danger that, if the evaluation of such courses is not conducted in an independent and non-biased fashion, any limitations inherent within a programme are not addressed.

Wyckham (1989) has argued that most entrepreneurship education programmes are measured in three ways. Interestingly none of the approaches he presents attempt to address the financial consequences of developing such courses. First, the knowledge and skills of students are assessed through examination. Second, courses and teachers are evaluated through student evaluation surveys. Third, after the course has been completed data on the employment and income status of the graduate participants can be obtained and evaluated. Further, he has noted that no universally accepted criterion which can be used to evaluate the effectiveness of an entrepreneurship programme has yet been identified. However, while McMullan at al (2001) suggest that designing a methodology to evaluate programmes and courses is comparatively easy, it is more difficult to ensure that the approach adopted is actually valid. Indeed, Westhead et al. (2001, p. 167) caution that 'precise and careful methodologies are required to evaluate training programmes'. They have observed that initially researchers attempting to assess the outcomes of training programmes asked participants for their views. Indeed this approach is not uncommon and as McMullan et al. (2001) indicate, it is likely that most evaluations of entrepreneurial programmes will continue to employ this particular methodology. However, they do advise that this type of subjective judgement should be confined to determining the satisfaction of participants, and cannot be used as a proxy for measuring the performance outcomes of a programme. Thus, when attempting to assess the impact or effectiveness of a course they suggest that objective measures be employed instead.

Westhead et al. (2001) have highlighted the limitations of adopting a purely subjective approach to evaluation. First, there is the issue of whether the participants on a particular course are representative of the target population as a whole. Second, respondents to a survey can be tempted to give answers that they feel the evaluator wants, instead of providing an honest response. Third, the impact of a programme can only be judged by comparing it with what would have happened had the respondent not participated on the course. Fourth, failure to take into account the personal characteristics of individuals might lead to an exaggeration of the effectiveness of a programme. Fifth, researchers should appreciate that participants actually self-select themselves onto programmes, which can, when evaluating courses, lead to inaccurate assessments being produced. Sixth, the subsequent behaviour of respondents is actually more important than reporting their opinions.

One means by which to measure the behaviour of participants on completion of a training course is to employ a model such as that advanced by Jack and Anderson (1998). They have developed a five step framework for assessing the effectiveness of entrepreneurship education and training programmes, which is based on an earlier version developed by Block and Stumpf (1992). The model, which is illustrated in Figure 4.1, is comprehensive, and emphasises the measurement and impact of different elements of training courses over time from the outset of a programme and even after its completion. Such a model is useful for it raises awareness of the importance of tracking the development of participants on a course over time. Indeed, a number of authors have noted the lack of longitudinal studies conducted within the area of entrepreneurship and training and a clear need to evaluate entrepreneurship education and training programmes over time has been identified (Wyckham, 1989; Fleming, 1996; Clark et al., 1984; Westhead and Storey, 1996; Barrow and Brown, 1996).

Garavan and Ó Cinnéide (1994, p. 5) have suggested that 'longitudinal research designs, using control groups to compare participants with individuals who did not have entrepreneurial educational experience, are needed to examine the lasting effects of entrepreneurship education and training interventions'. Storey (2000) also advocates such an approach but suggests that the most appropriate way to assess the effectiveness of entrepreneurial support programmes is to include a control sample of matched firms which are identical on the basis of age, sector, ownership and geography. Ideally such matching should take place immediately before a programme commences so as the two groups can be monitored over time.

　　　　10 years+
- Contribution to society and economy
- Firm performance
- Career satisfaction
- Personal self-actualisation and psychological success

　　　　3-10 years post course/programme
- Survival and reputation of new firms and start-ups
- Change in reputation and innovation level of established firms

　　　　0-5 years post course/programme
- Number and type of start-ups
- Foothold acquisitions
- Entrepreneurial positions obtained
- Entrepreneurial positions sought

　　　　Pre and post course/programme measures
- Intentions to act
- Knowledge gained
- Self-perception of learning and capability

　　　　Current and on-going measures
- Student enrolment
- Number/type of course
- Interest in entrepreneurship
- Awareness of field

(Adapted from Jack and Anderson, 1998, p.10).

Figure 4.1 Jack and Anderson's Evaluation Framework

　　　　Even if such a methodological approach is adopted, researchers should be aware of inferential problems, so even though the matching characteristics of the two groups are kept constant, there may be other ways in which they differ. With specific reference to participation in courses and programmes, Storey (2000) suggests that motivation and selection might be differentiating factors. For example, those firms or individuals seeking assistance or attending courses might be more dynamic and growth-oriented and, therefore, more open to new ideas. By definition individuals who voluntarily participate on courses have self-selected themselves.

　　　　Another source of bias can occur when participants are selected onto a scheme. In a competitive situation, selectors will have to choose between various applicants and will choose those who appear to be the 'best' applicants. This could potentially have ramifications when comparing against a control group, for as

Storey (2000) notes, the performance of the selected group will be superior to that of the matched group since the better cases have been selected.

Awareness of the limitations of adopting a purely subjective approach can be overcome when designing the methodological approach to be employed in a programme evaluation. For example with respect to the first limitation, Westhead et al. (2001), in their assessment of the impact of the 1994 Shell Technology Enterprise Programme (STEP), ensured that the highest possible response rate to the questionnaire administered, was obtained. This meant they could be reasonably sure that they had obtained as representative as view of the respondent population as possible. In order to minimise the impact of the second limitation the researchers explored objective outcomes of the programme by using a series of structured questionnaires, which were separated in real time over a 36-month period. Control groups were employed as a means of addressing the remaining constraints. Students who had participated in the 1994 STEP initiative were 'matched', in terms of age, gender, degree course and location of home address, with a control group of students who had not participated on the course. This enabled the research team to identify the contribution of the programme.

Assessing the effectiveness of programmes and courses is a complex issue due to the number of variables that have to be taken into consideration. It is important however, that analyses conducted are as sophisticated as possible in order to provide rigorously derived information from which accurate conclusions might be drawn. This is applicable not only at the policy level, but also at a more micro level when assessing if a course or programme has met its objectives or not.

Conclusion

The area of entrepreneurship education and training is continuing to receive increased attention and research in the area is growing. While there has been much debate in the literature as to whether entrepreneurship can be taught, most commentators believe that at least some elements associated with the subject can be developed and enhanced via education and training. However, despite the growth in entrepreneurship education and training programmes and courses at all levels, little uniformity can be found. In part, this stems from the fact that there is still much debate about the theoretical assumptions underpinning the field of entrepreneurship. In addition the many different disciplinary perspectives from which the subject can be studied has resulted in great diversity in the curricula of programmes and courses that have been developed. Some commentators have also noted that great confusion with respect to definition of the concept and its associated ideas of enterprise and small business ownership still exists, and this has impacted upon course design, content and structure. One area in which little research has been conducted is that of assessing the impact of educational and training initiatives. This is perhaps surprising, given the fact that the development and running of courses and programmes is potentially expensive in terms of time and money, both to participants and sponsors. Researchers have observed that one of the most efficient means by which to evaluate programmes is to assess the extent to which the programmes objectives have been met. It is vital, therefore, that entrepreneurship educators and trainers have a complete understanding of what they wish to achieve from a course or programme from the outset, as this will have ramifications for its accurate assessment.

PART II

A STUDY OF EFFECTIVENESS

Chapter 5

Methodology

Introduction

This part of the monograph presents the findings from the authors' study which aimed to investigate the effectiveness of entrepreneurship training programmes in supporting and developing aspiring entrepreneurs. This is still an under-represented area in the literature, with most commentators to date tending to focus on the difficulties associated with evaluation (Adams and Wilson, 1995; Gibb and Nelson, 1996; Gorman et al., 1997) rather than conducting much needed evaluative studies over time (Caird, 1989; Garavan and O'Cinnéide, 1994; Curran and Storey, 2002). Furthermore, since a great deal of taxpayers' money continues to be spent in this area (Gavron et al., 1998; Curran, 2000), the need for on-going evaluation that leads to a 'virtuous policy circle' (Curran and Storey, 2002, p. 169) has never been more important.

This chapter presents the main research questions that this study sought to address, and describes the research methodology used, explaining how and why the particular cases and groups were selected. The findings from the research are presented in the chapters that follow.

Research Questions

As stated at the outset in Chapter 1, while this study is essentially an investigation into the nature and effectiveness of entrepreneurship education and training in general, its principal aim is to make a valuable contribution to the area of entrepreneurship training programmes. With this in mind, the study sought to address the following research questions:

- Why are agencies, universities, and/or other support organisations providing and/or funding entrepreneurship training programmes? Do the reasons differ from programme to programme and/or from country to country?

- What exactly are entrepreneurship programmes attempting to achieve and at what cost? Do the objectives, content and cost differ with each provider/programme, and, are there particular differences between programmes operating in Ireland and those in other parts of Western Europe?

- What type of individual participates in entrepreneurship training programmes? Do aspiring or very early stage entrepreneurs actually possess (or believe they possess) the key characteristics, which, in the literature, are deemed critical for entrepreneurial success?

- What do entrepreneurship training programmes actually achieve, and are there measurable benefits for the participants? Do the participants' perceptions of these benefits change over time?

- Is it possible to develop a framework for improving the effectiveness of entrepreneurship training programmes, and, if so, what would such a framework comprise?

As stated at the outset, for the purposes of this study, aspiring entrepreneurs are defined as *individuals who are considering starting their own business and who may be at various stages of the preparation process.*

Considerations for Research Design

There is no doubt that evaluating the effectiveness of enterprise programmes can be extremely difficult due to the intrinsic procedural and methodological problems involved (Bennett, 1997; Storey, 2000). In addition, other issues, such as the susceptibility to what Stigler (1971) calls 'regulatory capture', i.e. where failures are downplayed due to pressures from sponsors to produce favourable results; the overwhelming power of the very notions of entrepreneurship (Curran and Storey, 2002), and the lack of specific performance measures, only serve to further complicate the evaluation process.

In terms of actual measures of effectiveness, it would appear that there is no universally accepted set of criteria for programme evaluation (Wyckham, 1989). Evaluative methods used to date have included the use of a responsive approach (Stake, 1980); the assessment of knowledge and skills through examinations, participant surveys and collecting data on income and employment (Wyckham, 1989), and a combination of mechanisms to track participant development over time (Jack and Anderson, 1998). It has also been suggested that many evaluations of entrepreneurship programmes have tended to rely on surveys of clients where participants are simply asked for their views (Nahavandi and Chesteen, 1988; Pelham, 1985). However, simply reporting participants' opinions is only partly of interest to any study of effectiveness, since the real objective must be to consider the subsequent behaviour of participants upon completion of the programme.

McMullan et al. (2001) suggest that there are three standard methods of evaluating the effectiveness of entrepreneurship programmes:

- subjective assessments of client satisfaction;
- clients' attributions of the impact of assistance on their subsequent performance;
- objective measures, such as the growth in jobs created, sales, etc.

However, as discussed in the previous chapter, there are a number of limitations with these types of approaches. Furthermore, there also seems to be a range of intrinsic difficulties associated with conducting effectiveness studies, and these include missing data, problems in sampling, inadequate or absent control groups, as well as the need to make manipulations and assumptions in analysing the data (p. 38). McMullan et al. (2001) imply that programme evaluations which rely exclusively upon participants' satisfaction or subjective judgements of programme effectiveness, can lead to erroneous conclusions (p. 37). With this in mind, it has been suggested that measures of attribution, when used in conjunction with objective measures, may well have some value in supporting effectiveness claims (McMullan et al., 2001).

In designing the research programme for this study, consideration was also given to the use of quantitative and qualitative approaches. Quantitative research typically concerns the collection of facts, and involves conventional survey methods that use scientific techniques to produce quantified and normally generalisable conclusions (Bell, 1991). However, a key problem with quantitative studies based on large, statistically representative samples is that they tend to offer statements about populations rather then individuals or individual cases.

Qualitative research, on the other hand, is more concerned with understanding individuals' perceptions and attitudes, and seeks insight rather than statistical analysis (Bell, 1991). Its techniques normally address aspects of research that cannot be effectively addressed by quantitative approaches (Eisenhardt, 1989; Walsham, 1995). Interestingly, such techniques are sometimes seen as inferior because they typically involve a *softer* approach as well as a smaller data set than quantitative methods, thus suggesting that the research does not meet the statistical criteria required for establishing validity. However, qualitative research methods are based upon human action and social phenomena, thus allowing the researcher to monitor and assess changing perceptions of what is actually happening '*out there*' (Curran and Storey, 2002).

Research Method

In view of the range of difficulties associated with effectiveness studies, and the drawbacks of the various evaluation measures, the programme of research adopted for this study includes both quantitative and qualitative approaches developed within a multi-method framework. While it has been argued that some multi-method studies focus purely on statistical analysis (Diesling, 1971), the need to integrate such analysis with qualitative data has also been emphasised (Smithson,

1991). Furthermore, in terms of evaluating entrepreneurship programmes, it has been suggested that measuring only quantitative (i.e. economic) results of a programme will fail to provide a full picture of its true value (Johnson and Sack, 1996). Thus, this study considers a combination of objective, subjective and attribution assessments, and includes:

- Case studies ($n = 8$) which integrate both quantitative and qualitative data derived from an analysis of documentary evidence (programme literature and evaluation reports) and in-depth interviews.
- A paper-based questionnaire, designed to profile aspiring entrepreneurs, and administered to various entrepreneurship programme participants ($n = 102$).
- A series of paper based questionnaires (5 questionnaires) – designed to gather both quantitative and qualitative data and administered on a longitudinal basis over a three year period to a specific group of aspiring entrepreneurs ($n = 35$).
- An established pen and paper type of entrepreneurial assessment test – the General Enterprising Tendency (GET) – administered to three groups of aspiring entrepreneurs – a treatment group, a control group and a comparator group ($n = 38$), two groups of programme participants, and a group of non-participants.

While single cases can prove to be appropriate if the researcher is investigating a previously unresearched subject area, there is some debate as to whether single case designs adequately address the concerns of validity, reliability and generalisabilty (Yin, 1994). In order to achieve an important construct, a researcher needs to see different instances of a case, at different times and with different people (Glaser and Strauss, 1967). Multiple case research also offers a deeper understanding of processes while facilitating theory building and theory testing (Yin, 1981). For these reasons, a multiple case design was chosen for this study. The case study approach was also chosen because it offers comprehensiveness of perspective that provides insights not normally gained with other methods (Pettigrew and Whipp, 1991; Gable, 1994; Babbie, 1995). For the purposes of this study, *typical cases* (Hammersley, 1985) were used, with data derived from at least two sources, i.e. documents, archival records and interviews (Yin, 1994). The documentary evidence included promotional literature, policy documents plus various associated reports and academic papers. The archival records included organisational records, lists of names, programme plans, budgets, and survey data in the form of previously collected data and evaluation reports (Yin, 1994, p. 83).

Further justification of the choice of research method can also be found by considering the methodologies used in other studies in this field, elements of which have been included in this particular study (O'Farrell, 1986; Hisrich, 1988; Garavan and Ó Cinnéide, 1994; Adams and Wilson, 1995; Fleming, 1996). In addition, it is worth noting that Jack and Anderson's (1998) adaptation of Block and Stumpf's (1992) evaluative framework for entrepreneurship programmes strongly recommends pre and post programme evaluation measures which include the number and type of start-ups, knowledge gained and the participants' self-perception of learning and capability. Such frameworks have had a direct influence on the design of the research programme adopted for this study.

Preliminary Research

Prior to commencing the actual research, a preliminary study was conducted with a small group of aspiring entrepreneurs who had just completed an entrepreneurship training programme. At the same time, a study was conducted with a small group of established entrepreneurs who had not apparently participated in any type of entrepreneurship training programme and whose business had been operating for a period of between one and eight years (see Henry and Titterington, 1996). This preliminary research proved to be important, as it helped to inform the main research programme by uncovering additional questions that could be explored in a more comprehensive study, and illustrated the sorts of useful insights to be gained by using a control group. In addition, the preliminary research emphasised the difficulties of accessing a sufficient number of non-exposed/non-supported entrepreneurs (i.e. those who had not participated in entrepreneurship training programmes) to make up a representative control group. This latter point was due to the fact that most entrepreneurs were required to participate in some sort of entrepreneurship training programme in order to qualify for State grant aid. This implied that a slightly different type of control group would be required.

Selection of Cases

The study presented in this monograph was conducted by the authors over a three-year period. It begins with the analysis and comparison of eight entrepreneurship programmes operating in five different European countries. This analysis helps to lay the foundation for the studies that followed, by providing an overview of the type of entrepreneurship training programme available, as well as the structure, content and objectives of each. The programmes analysed in this study include: four programmes from Ireland, one of which operated on a cross-border basis and covered both the north and south of the country; a programme from Sweden; one from Spain; one from Finland, and one from the Netherlands. These particular programmes were selected for three reasons. Firstly, they represented *typical* cases, and met one of the main objectives of the research design. Secondly, they were all managed by universities or third level colleges through their industrial liaison office or incubation centre, and hence, despite their diversity, had this one element in common. Moreover, these providers were dealing primarily, though not exclusively, with aspiring entrepreneurs. Thirdly, these initiatives were selected because they were directly accessible to one of the authors through her European contacts. The case study approach allowed for a thorough analysis and comparison of the structure, content and cost of each of the eight programmes. Any gaps in the original data were covered in the structured interviews with the providers and funders.

The In-depth Interviews

In-depth interviews were conducted with the providers and funders of the programmes mentioned above. The in-depth interview method was chosen as it represents one of the most important sources of information, and, as a research method, has a major advantage over questionnaires, particularly in terms of adaptability (Bell, 1991). Since in-depth interviews are used primarily for exploratory research and can uncover more complete answers to questions that might otherwise only be answered superficially by quantitative survey methods (Domegan and Fleming, 1999), the authors felt it was the most appropriate method for this type of study. This approach helped to facilitate the interviewees in fully expressing their opinions towards the provision and funding of entrepreneurship training programmes (Kinnear and Taylor, 1996). The interviews were designed primarily to determine the main reasons why organisations provide and/or fund entrepreneurship programmes, and were conducted with the providers (typically the Programme Managers) and funders of the various entrepreneurship programmes. A total of eleven interviews were conducted in this study, each lasting approximately one and a half hours.

The Questionnaires

Participants in entrepreneurship training programmes were chosen to represent aspiring entrepreneurs. The particular individuals included in this study were selected because they were participating in the programmes already selected by the authors as cases in the comparative study and hence were readily accessible. (The actual profiles of the programme participants who took part in the study are presented in Chapter 7). Simple self-assessment type questions, designed to assess the participants' own perceptions of their entrepreneurial characteristics and skills, were chosen for this study for a number of reasons. Firstly, there is a plethora of tests and scales of a psychometric nature which purport to measure entrepreneurial attributes, and each test has its own particular administrative and interpretive difficulties. Secondly, there would appear to be a lack of consistency among these analytical instruments which, in turn, leads to overall disagreement about the emerging entrepreneurial profile (Kets de Vries, 1996). Thirdly, there is some doubt over their general reliability.

In addition, it has been argued that results derived from psychometric tests should not be considered in isolation and ought to be integrated with other analytical methods (Fowler, 1997). This is further justification for the use of a multi-method framework which incorporates several different sources of evidence.

The design of the first questionnaire, which was used to assess the participants prior to commencing entrepreneurship training, was informed by the literature, as well as the preliminary research described above. The purpose of this questionnaire was two fold: firstly, it helped to develop a profile of the aspiring entrepreneur or programme participant, and in this regard, it was administered to four groups (*n* = 102). Secondly, it represented stage one of the five part longitudinal study which tracked the progress of one particular group of programme participants (the treatment group) for the core part of the research. The questions dealt with the participants' background, business idea, and motivation for starting a business. Questions relating to the participants' perception of their entrepreneurial characteristics and business skills/abilities were also included. The individuals were also asked what they expected to gain by participating in their particular programme. After testing the questionnaire, it was personally administered to the participants when they arrived for the commencement of the entrepreneurship programme. This was the case with three of the four entrepreneurship programmes included in the profiling part of the study. Hence, the authors were able to provide the necessary instructions for its completion. However, in the case of the Dutch programme, the questionnaires were administered by mail for obvious logistical reasons. To help increase the response rate, the coordination of this part of the study was greatly assisted by a colleague based in the Netherlands.

The Longitudinal Study

With stage one of the longitudinal study completed through the initial self-assessment type questionnaires described above, stages two through five of the study adopted a narrower focus and concentrated on one particular group of aspiring entrepreneurs – the 35 individuals who participated in an all-Ireland, industry sponsored entrepreneurship programme – referred to as programme A, or the treatment group, and described in detail in Chapter 6. This particular programme was chosen for the longitudinal study because it was one of the largest single programmes (in terms of number of participants) in operation at the time of the study. Furthermore, programme A was in its pilot phase and a thorough evaluation was welcomed by both the providers and funders. In addition, for logistical reasons (i.e. the programme was based in Ireland) the programme data were readily accessible to the authors, and the participants were very willing to contribute to the research, which suggested that it would be easier to track the progress of this particular group over time.

While stage one of the study was conducted prior to the commencement of the entrepreneurship programme, stages two and three of the study were conducted at various points during programme A. The final two stages of the study were conducted at one year and two years post programme completion, respectively.

The first questionnaire (stage 1) was personally administered to the participants in programme A, however, the second and subsequent questionnaires were mailed. These questionnaires were sent out with cover letters explaining the objectives of the study and were relatively shorter than the first questionnaire. As would be expected in this type of research, the response rates fell as the study progressed, due to a combination of some of the participants dropping out of the programme and participants failing to return questionnaires. At stage one of the longitudinal study, the response rate was 35 (i.e. 100 per cent), and this reduced to 32 responses at stage 2 (half way through the programme), 25 at stage 3 (upon programme completion), 23 at stage four (1 year post-programme completion), and 23 at stage five (2 years post-programme completion). The response rates to those questionnaires that were mailed, were between 70 per cent and 97 per cent, rates that are typically considered to be good for postal questionnaires (Babbie, 1995).

The GET Assessment

In terms of the psychological aspects of the questionnaire, it was decided to supplement this simple self-assessment form with another more structured yet 'user-friendly' type of test, mainly because of its comprehensiveness and ease of administration and interpretation. The General Enterprising Tendency (GET) questionnaire was chosen for this purpose. The GET, developed by Durham University, is a structured pencil and paper assessment exercise where respondents rate predetermined test items which represent attitudes, preferences or habitual behaviours. The respondent is asked to rate him/herself on an agree/disagree basis against 54 predetermined test items (Caird, 1991, p. 179). The test measures enterprising tendency through the assessment of five enterprise characteristics, namely, calculated risk-taking, creative tendency, high need for achievement (nAch), high need for autonomy (nAut) and internal locus of control. For logistical reasons, this test was only administered to participants in programme A, the control group and the comparator group. (Details of the control and comparator groups used are provided below).

Data Analysis

Due to the small size of the survey groups, and the fact that the longitudinal study was conducted in several stages over a 3-year period, only limited statistical analysis was conducted. In terms of the paper-based questionnaires, for those questions dealing with quantitative data, the responses were recorded mostly on the basis of their frequency of occurrence, and the percentage of respondents answering in a particular category was also noted. For the more qualitative or open questions, where no particular type of response was prompted, the main responses were noted and the most popular and least popular responses were calculated on the basis of the percentage of overall respondents. The survey results were thus analysed more on a qualitative than on a quantitative basis, with tests of significance conducted where appropriate.

In terms of the interviews, the number of interviewees involved was also small and the questions were again of a qualitative, open nature. Thus, the interviews were analysed in terms of the most popular responses, with special attention paid to any emerging trends or commonalities in the opinions expressed by the funders and providers.

The Control and Comparator Groups

Two groups were identified against which the findings from the core study could be compared. The first group was a control group and consisted of 48 aspiring entrepreneurs who had a business idea at the pre-start-up stage. They had all expressed an interest in becoming entrepreneurs and had applied for a place on an entrepreneurship programme around the same time as the treatment group's programme (programme A) began. While the profiles of these individuals appeared to be broadly similar to those of the core group, they did not manage to secure a place on an entrepreneurship programme. In so far as the authors could tell, this appeared to be largely due to reasons of over subscription. This particular group was chosen because, in view of the difficulties associated with accessing suitable control groups for effectiveness studies, this appeared to be one of the 'purest' control groups available at the time. The fact that the two groups started from the same point with similar aspirations, and that their progress was examined at the same time, i.e. two years after completing programme A (or 3 years post the control group's original applications for places on one of the entrepreneurship programmes), adds to the validity of the comparison.

As a result of serendipity, the researchers had the opportunity to study another group of aspiring entrepreneurs. This group, which is referred to as a comparator group, consisted of 38 participants from one of the entrepreneurship programmes described in detail in the next chapter. This was an interesting group to study for comparison purposes because the individuals involved in this particular programme were facing a redundancy situation, and hence, were 'forced' to view self employment as a serious career option. The authors felt that comparing the progress of the treatment group – an entirely self-selected, voluntary group of aspiring entrepreneurs, with that of the redundancy group – a non-self-selected, involuntary group, could provide additional insights into effectiveness. Furthermore, this sort of comparison offered a good opportunity to test the real effects of entrepreneurship training when compared to the impact of displacement and/or the availability of resources as enabling factors and trigger mechanisms. This additional comparison would allow the effects and usefulness of entrepreneurship training programmes to be examined in two completely different situations, hence widening the debate surrounding the rationale for interventions of this nature. The comparator group was surveyed at the same time as stage 5 of the longitudinal study was conducted, i.e. around 18 months after their particular programme had been completed. The surveys for both the control and comparator groups focused mainly on economic outputs, the progress of the business idea and the general benefits that were derived, or could have been potentially derived, by the aspiring entrepreneurs.

Limitations of the Methodology

Despite its comprehensiveness, the methodology employed in this study has obvious drawbacks. In the first instance, the small group sizes and falling response rates over the duration of the longitudinal study, while not surprising, mean that the findings of this study must be viewed in context. The authors make no claim as to the generalisablility of the overall findings and conclusions presented in the chapters that follow, and fully appreciate that further research is required where programme outputs, costs and reported benefits can be compared on a broader scale.

In terms of the case studies, it would have been desirable to interview a greater number of individuals associated with each of the entrepreneurship programmes. However, as often happens with most entrepreneurship programmes, and mainly due to budgetary constraints, the operation of such programmes typically involves a very small team of people and it is normally the programme manager who can provide most of the information required.

In terms of the GET instrument, although it appears to be relatively simple to administer, it too has its limitations. It has been suggested that results derived from this test could apply not only to entrepreneurs but to enterprising people in general (Caird, 1991, p.182). Furthermore, the simple 'forced-choice' format may allow the respondent to consciously choose the more socially desirable responses, hence scoring highly (Caird, 1991, p.182). However, the test has been deemed valid by others, and suggestions have been made that further applications should be considered, particularly in terms of testing the discriminant and predictive validity of the instrument (Cromie and O'Donaghue, 1992). With this limitation in mind, the GET instrument has been used in this research as a support to the other self-assessed type analysis contained in the initial questionnaire.

Finally, while every effort was made to minimise bias in this study, it could be argued that the authors were too familiar with the actual programmes under investigation, particularly the Irish programmes. In fact, it could be said that the cases included in the study represented a convenience sample, which may have compromised the external validity of the research. While this may pose a difficulty in terms of the interpretation of findings, it had the benefit of providing access to documentation, programme participants, providers and funders that would not normally have been possible in the evaluation of other programmes.

Summary and Conclusion

This chapter has explained the research methodology used in this study, and has described how and why the particular cases were chosen. While the authors do not claim that this methodology is entirely new, its strength lies in the multi method approach adopted. In addition, the time scale over which the study took place, and the efforts to adopt a highly qualitative approach to programme evaluation, where the views of the programme participants themselves could be highlighted, add to the interest and validity of the research.

The following chapters discuss the findings of this study in terms of programme comparisons, participant analysis, and overall effectiveness from a longitudinal perspective.

Chapter 6

Entrepreneurship Training Programmes – A Comparative Analysis

Introduction

The debate concerning the merits and demerits of intervention has already been examined in Chapter 1. However, a subsequent debate concerns whether or not entrepreneurship can be taught. Even though there is much debate about which elements of entrepreneurship should be included within a programme (Timmons and Stevenson, 1985; Miller, 1987; Arzeni, 1992; Boussouara and Deakins, 1998), many commentators strongly support the view that entrepreneurship can be taught.

While entrepreneurship education programmes tend to be about enterprise and have awareness raising as their primary objective, entrepreneurship training courses are more concerned with providing instruction for enterprise (Jamieson, 1984). Such courses are, therefore, intended to help prepare the aspiring entrepreneur for the actual set-up of the business. As interest in the provision of structured intervention continues to grow, it becomes increasingly important that the fundamental question of why institutions choose to intervene in the entrepreneurial process is properly addressed. Focusing on the training aspect of structured entrepreneurship interventions provides a clearer picture of how effective or ineffective interventions of this kind really are.

Building on this theoretical foundation, this chapter considers the effectiveness of entrepreneurship training programmes by examining the outputs of eight such programmes in five European countries. It identifies both the benefits and shortcomings of entrepreneurship training programmes, investigating their overall impact in economic and non-economic terms.

The Cases – Eight Entrepreneurship Training Programmes

As described in Chapter 5, a multiple case study design was employed for the analysis of the eight entrepreneurship training programmes. The programmes included in the investigation were as follows:

- 4 programmes from Ireland:
  - an all-Ireland, industry sponsored programme   (Programme A)
  - a cross-border programme   (Programme B)
  - an industry-sponsored, redundancy programme (Programme C)
  - a Dublin based programme   (Programme D)
- 1 programme from The Netherlands   (Programme E)
- 1 programme from Sweden   (Programme F)
- 1 programme from Finland   (Programme G)
- 1 programme from Spain   (Programme H)

Data were gathered by means of analysis of documentary evidence (as described in Chapter 5) as well as from semi-structured interviews with both programme providers and funders. Although the interviews were designed primarily to determine the main reasons why the organisations provided and/or funded entrepreneurship training programmes, they also sought the views of interviewees concerning the perceived benefits derived by the participants from such training. Interviews were conducted with eleven individuals – four representatives from the funding bodies responsible for financing the training, and seven representatives from organisations providing the training. Those organisations which provided funding included: the Secretariat of the Council of Directors of the Institutes of Technology in Ireland – representing part of the European Social Fund (ESF), Dublin; the International Fund for Ireland (IFI); a large manufacturing company, Ireland; and Enterprise Ireland. Organisations providing training included: an incubation centre located on the campus of one of the Institute's of Technology in Ireland (two representatives interviewed); the University responsible for managing the Swedish programme; the Business Development Centre responsible for managing the Finnish programme; the universities responsible for the Spanish and Dutch programmes; and the Irish university responsible for the Dublin based programme.

Programme A: An All-Ireland, Industry Sponsored Programme

Programme Description Programme A was a joint initiative of a large manufacturing company and one of the Institutes of Technology in Ireland, and was designed to promote graduate entrepreneurship throughout the island of Ireland. The pilot programme was launched in January 1996 and targeted graduates of third level educational establishments, with the aim of encouraging and developing entrepreneurial talent through training. In order to qualify for entry, applicants had to hold a third level diploma, degree or higher qualification, and have a business idea at feasibility or pre-feasibility stage. The programme was designed as a part-time programme, hence, participants could be employed, unemployed or continuing their education on a full- or part-time basis. The budget for the total scheme, which included a prize fund, was around €126,974.

Structure and Content   This programme combined structured training with financial reward and a qualification, all within a competitive framework. It comprised a series of six intensive business training modules, individual assessment sessions and meetings with experienced mentors provided by Enterprise Ireland. The programme was normally delivered over a six-month period with participants having the opportunity to work towards a recognised qualification and compete for a prize fund of €22,855 at the time the research was carried out.

The training concentrated on what was identified by the UK Small Firms' Lead Body (1996) as the critical aspects of business planning, namely:

- Generating the business proposal
- Determining legal and financial requirements
- Planning the business operation
- Planning the market strategy
- Monitoring/controlling business operations and quality
- Planning the human resource development.

The topics were modelled on the 'Owner-Management Business Planning' Programme, a set of standards designed by the UK Small Firms Lead Body (1996) for those preparing to set-up, and be responsible for, the management of their own businesses. These standards, which have since been updated, were linked to the UK's NVQ (National Vocational Qualification) system and allowed participants to work towards the achievement of a Level Three qualification. The formal training sessions were delivered in a central location in Dublin, with the mentoring and assessment sessions provided on a regional basis to suit individual participants. Due to the wide geographical spread of participants, (applications were invited from all 32 counties in Ireland), the number of training sessions was minimised and a comprehensive training manual was designed as both a reference and distance learning support tool.   Thirty-five graduates were chosen to participate in the pilot scheme and these were selected solely on the basis of their business ideas, as described in their application forms.

Overall Effectiveness By the end of the programme, three of the 35 participants reported that their businesses had already reached start-up stage, with a further 15 stating that they intended to proceed to start-up, but that more work on product development and financial planning was necessary, particularly with regard to securing investors.

Exactly one year after completing the programme, participants were surveyed again to assess their progress. A self-complete questionnaire was mailed to the entrepreneurs to establish the number of businesses that had reached start-up. The responses received revealed that eleven of the original programme participants were in full-time employment, with a further three continuing their education at postgraduate level. Nine of the 35 original participants were self-employed, and eight of these had set-up their businesses based on the ideas developed through the scheme.

Programme B: An Irish Cross-border Programme

Programme Description Programme B was first developed in 1992 as a cross-border enterprise support programme designed to assist those with technology based product or service ideas. At the time of the investigation, it was jointly managed by one of the Northern Ireland Universities and an incubation centre based at one of the Institutes of Technology in Southern Ireland. The programme targeted both individual entrepreneurs and small existing companies seeking to develop new products or services in an effort to encourage the creation and growth of indigenous technology based businesses.

Structure and Content Two managers were responsible for the day-to-day running of the programme, one based in the North of Ireland and the other based in the South. A joint advisory Board monitored the overall progress of the programme and offered general strategic advice regarding the programme's development and fund raising. The programme had a total duration of 15 months and was structured in two stages. Stage one of the programme lasted for three months and was concerned with market feasibility. During this period participants were required to thoroughly research the market for their proposed product or service, to ensure that sufficient commercial potential existed before further resources were committed. At the end of stage one there was a formal review of progress which required participants to present their market research findings to an evaluation panel. Only those projects that showed greatest potential and commitment from their promoters were allowed to go forward to the next stage. Stage two lasted for up to twelve months, depending on the needs of participants, and it was during this time that the entrepreneurs focused on developing a prototype, determining an appropriate marketing strategy and completing a business plan. Formal periodic assessments were carried out to monitor participants' progress and identify early stage problems.

Those participating in this programme were provided with training, networking opportunities, access to marketing and technical consultancy, office facilities, secretarial support, access to the library, laboratories, computers and equipment. Thus, this particular scheme was an expensive programme, which at the time the research was being conducted, required an annual budget of around €222,200. In addition, participants were able to access some direct financial assistance through local grant aid schemes.

The formal training covered market research, marketing strategy, business management, production and quality, patenting and copyright, sales skills, finance/investment, presentation skills and developing a business plan. Business counselling and mentoring were also provided informally on a one-to-one basis every fortnight, by the programme managers and the local offices of the relevant

State agencies respectively. In addition, the programme had an arrangement with local companies for industry mentoring through which practising senior managers offered their time, expertise and their invaluable networks of contacts to help the aspiring entrepreneurs in the development and commercialisation of their products or services.

Overall Effectiveness During the first three rounds of the programme, a total of 30 technology projects were supported through the complete 15 month phase, resulting in the establishment of 26 new businesses. This represents an 86 per cent success rate in terms of new business creation. Collectively, these 26 new businesses were responsible for the creation of 56 new jobs.

Programme C: An Irish, Industry Sponsored, Redundancy Support Programme

Programme Description During the late 1990s, a large manufacturing company in Ireland announced a major redundancy programme. Those individuals facing redundancy were mostly long-serving employees with ten years' or more service and with expertise in the areas of production, quality, finance, human resources, training, distribution and general management. To mitigate the effects of these decisions, the company set up a special enterprise development programme aimed at encouraging and assisting individuals to set-up their own businesses as an alternative to unemployment.

Structure and Content Individuals were provided with an intensive three-day training programme covering the areas of marketing, finance and developing a business plan. The training sessions were delivered over a period of three weeks (one day per week). Representatives from local funding and grant agencies were also invited to the training sessions to meet with the group and to advise on the type and level of funding available. In addition, a training manual was provided for participants to use as a reference tool when drawing up their business plans. In the months that followed the training, the trainees were provided with a series of one-to-one mentoring/consultation sessions to help them develop their business plans into formal business propositions. The mentors met with the programme participants as required, and in this respect, the total programme duration was about six months.

In addition to the training and mentoring package, the manufacturing company also arranged for their redundancy group to have access to a special enterprise fund in the region, which would provide seed capital amounts of up to €12,700 to qualifying individuals. To avail of this funding, participants were required to complete the training programme and to submit a business plan that would be assessed by an evaluation panel. This funding could, where possible, be used to supplement grants or loans received from State agencies or banks. This particular programme had a total budget of around €11,500, excluding the seed capital funding. However, it must be noted that the seed capital element was an important part of the programme and a key motivating factor for participants in completing their business plans.

Overall Effectiveness By the end of the programme three of the 48 individuals who had participated had managed to set-up their businesses, with a further 15 stating that they intended to proceed but needed to do more research and preparation. Exactly one year after completing the programme, the participants were monitored and surveyed again to assess their progress. By this stage eight individuals had set-up their businesses and were trading. A further twelve expressed a strong intention to establish a business in the near future and had progressed their business ideas to the next stage. Unlike the other entrepreneurship programmes investigated, this was a 'one-off' programme, designed specifically for a redundancy situation, and as such, it is unlikely to be provided again by the particular employer, although, other companies facing redundancy situations may offer similar programmes in the future.

Programme D: An Irish, Dublin- Based Programme

Programme Description Programme D was managed by one of the Dublin based universities, and combined its own expertise and facilities with that of a local innovation centre to assist entrepreneurs in developing knowledge based enterprises. The programme targeted graduates who had proposals for innovative, knowledge-based products or exportable services, and participants were selected on the basis of their commitment and potential to create a new enterprise. The programme supported entrepreneurs in the development of their business ideas up to working prototype stage, and in managing the successful implementation of their business plans. It aimed to provide entrepreneurs with assistance in defining and developing their business ideas, in building multi-disciplinary teams and in preparing detailed business plans.

Structure and Content This programme was typically offered over a nine-month period to a maximum of 15 participants in every programme run. Workshops, seminars and consultancy sessions were combined to support the participating entrepreneurs in the development of their business ideas. This support package was designed to assist the promoters in analysing the strengths and weaknesses of the proposals, to improve efficiency and to identify opportunities for expansion. The end result aimed for was a realistic business plan for developing the new company that could be presented to a panel of experts. In addition, participants were linked with mentors who provided on-going advice and assistance on both the technological and business aspects of the projects. On completion of the programme, participants were required to present and defend their final business plans to an expert panel. Participants' achievements were recognised by means of a monetary or business consultancy prize, awarded for the project, which had made the most progress during the programme.

The training provided was of a practical nature and covered issues such as a range of legal matters and company formation, carrying out a feasibility study and conducting market research, sources of finance, approaching financial institutions and drawing up financial projections. This training was delivered to participants during monthly half-day workshops at the University and was designed to be both flexible and highly interactive. This particular programme cost around €127,000 with funding provided by the University itself and the local Innovation Centre.

Overall Effectiveness During its first year of operation, this programme supported eleven entrepreneurs. Seven of these had already established businesses when they joined the programme, although they were still in the very early stages of development. The results of a follow-up survey of the participants, showed that their general assessment of the programme was very good, with 33 per cent of the respondents rating the programme as 'excellent' and the balance rating it as 'very good'. The entrepreneurs felt that their specific requirements were either 'completely met' (55 per cent), or 'fairly well met' (45 per cent), with the level of subject treatment perceived as 'about right' by all respondents. The length and pace of the programme were also highly rated, again with 100 per cent of the respondents assessing these aspects as 'about right'. From the survey it was clear that all those who participated in the programme perceived it to be beneficial, with the interaction with other entrepreneurs/businesses being cited as the main benefit. Other benefits mentioned included mentoring, workshops, a focused business plan, better understanding of various issues, moral support from programme management and the opportunity to highlight the strengths and weaknesses of the business proposal. In total, four entirely new businesses were created by the eleven entrepreneurs trained under the programme, generating around 9 new jobs.

Programme E: A Dutch Programme

Programme Description Programme E was established by a Dutch University in 1984. Its primary objective was to encourage graduates of the University to set up their own knowledge-based businesses in the region. The catchment base grew over the years to include not only graduates, but also staff members of the university, as well as graduates from other universities and people outside the university with several years' industrial experience. During the programme year, the knowledge-based projects were located at the University. Thereafter, entrepreneurs normally moved their projects to the local Business Centre located on the University's campus. The entrepreneurs could then progress to their own premises within the University's Science Park as their businesses grew.

Structure and Content This programme was managed by the Industrial Liaison Office on the University campus. Through the programme, aspiring entrepreneurs were offered a wide range of support over a one-year period. This support included:

- Office space and facilities – where the entrepreneur was housed at the University and could avail of fax, telephone, computer and laboratory facilities as required.
- Training – while conducting research and tests on his/her business idea, the aspiring entrepreneur attended a course on 'Becoming an Entrepreneur' which was provided by the University's business school.
- Financing – participants each received an interest-free loan of €13,600 during the first year. This was a personal, rather than a company loan, which had to be repaid within five years.
- Mentoring – local experienced businessmen and women offered their time free of charge to support these entrepreneurs in a mentoring capacity.

To avail of the support outlined above, aspiring entrepreneurs had to have a business idea that matched the interests of one of the research groups at the university, and an outline business plan. Applications were accepted at any time of the year and were assessed by a committee that continued to offer guidance and support to entrepreneurs if they were successful in gaining entry to the programme. Unfortunately it was not possible to obtain an exact budget figure for this programme from the relevant literature. However, during the interview with the provider, a programme value of €100,000 per participant was mentioned, this being the 'value' placed on the total package of supports received through the programme by the participants. Based on 15 participants, this would have given an overall programme value of around €1,500,000 per year. Interestingly, though, an internal report on the programme referred to a total programme budget of €225,000 based on fifteen participants, (i.e. €15,000 per participant). Although there were obviously additional running costs, these would appear to have been absorbed into the University's own overheads, as is sometimes the case with such initiatives, making precise budget estimations difficult. In the first year of the programme, a large percentage of the funding was provided by the Dutch Government, through the Department of Economic Affairs. Since then, the programme was funded by the European Social Fund as well as a 'revolving fund' set up by the University itself. Many of the budget items were still covered by the University's own budget. For the purposes of the comparative analysis presented below, the authors took the stated budget figure of €225,000 as the actual programme cost since this was the officially documented figure.

Overall Effectiveness From its establishment in 1984 up to the end of 1997, 230 individuals had participated in this programme, resulting in the creation of 170 knowledge-based firms. A recent evaluation of the programme covering the same period, showed that 78 per cent of the companies established, still existed. These companies employed an average of nine people and covered a wide variety of industry sectors, including multi-media, mechanical engineering and microelectronics.

Programme F: A Swedish Programme

Programme Description Programme F was an initiative of a Centre for Innovation at a Swedish based University. It was targeted at individuals who had a viable business idea, and aimed to solve the problems that entrepreneurs often encounter when attempting to establish and manage a new firm.

Structure and Content This programme involved a number of workshops, during which the central themes of entrepreneurship and small business management were discussed. In parallel with the workshops, the participants developed business plans for the establishment of the new ventures, and some financial resources were made available to cover the costs of market research, surveys and associated travel. An important part of the programme was the mentoring carried out by existing networks of experienced businessmen and women. The programme management team worked in close co-operation with the local Science Park, which made its pre-incubator support facilities available to new firms. The programme was run on an annual basis and lasted for twelve months. It usually took place in the afternoons and evenings, thus it could easily be combined with study or work. It consisted of eight five-hour workshops and three counselling sessions, during which the entrepreneurs met their business counsellors to discuss the development of business plans and give feedback on the programme. In addition, programme participants were divided into groups which normally had two mentors who tended to be experienced entrepreneurs. The mentor meetings were not pre-scheduled, but were normally arranged directly between the groups and the mentors.

As part of the programme, participants were entitled to free membership of two local business networks. The programme was offered free of charge to participants and focused on the critical elements involved in starting a successful business. The various aspects of business planning were covered over the eight practical workshop sessions. In addition, participants were given project supervision and networking opportunities, and had use of incubation facilities. While there were no formal entry requirements, programme participants tended to be highly educated graduates, enterprise students or individuals with considerable industrial experience.

This particular programme was funded by NUTEK, the Swedish National Board for Industrial and Technical Development, and the Technology Bridge Foundation. The programme cost around €113,700 to operate, and supported at least 15 participants every year. According to the programme providers, the average cost per entrepreneur was around €4,500.

Overall Effectiveness This programme was first developed in 1993 and, during the following four-year period, 25 new firms were created across a wide variety of industry sectors. On completion of the programme, entrepreneurs could continue to avail of support from the Centre for Innovation in the form of business development, mentoring and networking programmes, depending on the specific requirements of each business. By the time the investigation was carried out in the late 1990s, this programme, together with other support programmes offered by the university in question, had been responsible for the creation of over 5,000 new jobs in their immediate geographical area, most of which were in the electronics sector.

Programme G: A Finnish Programme

Programme Description At the time of the authors' study, programme G was a joint venture between the scientific institutions, technical research centres, public authorities, financiers and the local business community. It was part of a wider range of enterprise support initiatives delivered through a Finnish Business Development Centre, which is based at one of the Technical Universities, and was managed by a privately owned science park company. The entrepreneurship training elements of this programme were financed by the Ministry of Trade and Industry, the Technology Development Centre (TEKES) and a Regional Centre of Expertise, and these funders were all represented on the programme's steering committee. The programme's main objectives were to foster the creation and growth of research based companies, to increase employment through these companies and to offer quality seed companies to venture capitalists. The programme targeted researchers, graduates and vocational school graduates working in scientific and technological areas, and helped them to develop their business ideas into new high-tech or knowledge-based companies in both the manufacturing and service-based sectors.

Structure and Content Programme G helped new entrepreneurs to identify the resources needed to develop their ideas into businesses or to license them to other companies. The programme also assisted entrepreneurs with estimating the profitability of proposed new ventures. Accordingly, the programme was structured in three phases. Phase one concentrated on project evaluation, whereby the entrepreneur's idea was assessed for its viability, future profitability and market potential. During this phase the entrepreneur conducted some market research and developed an outline business plan. The duration of the first phase appeared to be flexible, depending on the idea and the amount of research carried out before approaching the programme providers.

In phase two, entrepreneurs took part in a six-month business training and consulting programme, which focused on the further development of business plans, new venture management, economic issues, marketing and sales skills, and legal issues relating to licensing. Entrepreneurs had access to consultants and students to conduct market surveys and analyses. During this phase, business plans were re-evaluated, companies established and seed funding requirements were considered.

Phase three of the programme was aimed at those companies which, having completed phase two of the programme, were ready to develop their strategies for the international market. Further access to consultants and students for market research was also available during this phase. The Business Development Centre, which managed the programme, offered additional support mechanisms to companies developed out of this particular programme. These support mechanisms included seed capital, mentors to advise on growth strategies, incubation facilities, a centre of expertise for software projects and a networking club for participating entrepreneurs. Programme G cost around €505,000 and was funded by a variety of organisations, including the participants themselves, who were required to pay a small fee to join the programme. The Development Centre, which managed the programme, contributed around 15-20 per cent of the total budget costs.

Overall Effectiveness By the time the research was conducted, this particular programme had received more than 600 applications for the first phase (evaluation). Out of this phase, 230 proposals had been accepted, of which 170 had progressed through the programme and had been developed into new companies. About 20 per cent of companies created by the programme progressed to the international/growth stage of the programme. By 1998, these companies had created approximately 800 new jobs, with an additional 1,300 jobs generated indirectly. The majority of the companies created by this programme were mainly in the information/communications and health care sectors (55 per cent), with the balance in electronics, design, business services and energy sectors.

Programme H: A Spanish Programme

Programme Description Programme H is part of a wider initiative to promote employment in eastern Spain. It is managed by one of Spain's Polytechnic Universities and its main objectives are to introduce new employment opportunities to graduates, and support technology transfer through the creation of new firms. The programme also aims to create a favourable environment for the promotion of entrepreneurship within the University. This programme supports the incubation of new technology oriented firms created by the University's students and staff. At the time of the authors' study, the programme was offered with the support of the university rector and the local BIC (Business Innovation/Incubation Centre). It was funded by a local savings bank, a local SME support organisation, and the University itself, which collectively provided the €200,000 annual budget for the programme. The programme was managed by a small team based at the University's Technology Transfer Office.

Structure and Content This programme was structured in two parts. Part one involved the submission of a short proposal by aspiring entrepreneurs interested in participating in the programme. Selected applicants were then invited to submit a more detailed application, in the form of a simplified business plan. These plans were evaluated, and successful applicants were offered a place on part two of the programme.   Through this second part, which lasted for 10-12 months, participants were helped to develop a full business plan, offered finance for the development of their products or services, and provided with training in business administration. Participants in this part of the programme were also requested to undergo a series of psychometric tests, so that their areas of weakness could be identified and relevant training and support offered. These tests assessed the cognitive abilities, oral skills, creativity, ambition, confidence, self-discipline, interpersonal skills, organisational skills and motivation of the participants. In addition, aspiring entrepreneurs were provided with technical and business advice and a range of useful contacts. The programme ended with an awards ceremony, through which the best business proposals were rewarded with modest financial prizes. In terms of enterprise training, the content and format appeared to differ from year to year, depending on the needs of the participants. Some of the training was provided by the local BIC, and some by the University's Education Centre. The main topics covered were entrepreneurship, management, personal development and business planning.

The Spanish programme attributed its success to the following core principles:

- The staff's personal involvement with every entrepreneur
- An excellent business plan guide
- A system to evaluate entrepreneurial skills and abilities (the psychometric tests)
- Education to promote entrepreneurship
- Business consultancy.

Overall Effectiveness Programme H has been in operation since 1992 and, up until 1999, 528 applications had been received, of which 431 proposals were accepted for the programme following the technical evaluation phase. These proposals resulted in the development of 77 business plans, which in turn created 56 new businesses. The low output, in relation to the intake figures (i.e. 56 new businesses out of 431 accepted proposals over a seven-year period), appeared to be due to the high drop-out rate of participants who began the programme but did not progress to the business plan stage. However, further investigation revealed that, on a year by year basis, the completion rate for those participating in the programme had improved substantially in more recent years, with the completion rate rising from just under 10 per cent during the period 1992-1994 to over 18 per cent during 1996-1998. Despite this, the level of new business creation appeared to have dropped from 78 per cent during the period 1994-1996 to 65 per cent during 1998. There were no specific figures available for the survival or growth rate of the new businesses created. However, programme literature suggested that these new firms were low-tech, requiring modest investments and employed, on average, around four people.   Future plans for the programme included its extension to previous graduates of the University, the allocation of additional funds to the programme budget, the setting up of a Foundation to provide continuous funding, the creation of a bank of business ideas and the provision of incubation facilities.

Interviews with Programme Providers and Funders

Structured interviews were conducted with a total of eleven individuals with regard to the provision and funding of the eight programmes analysed above. Since it was not possible to directly access the funders of some of the programmes, a representative responsible for administering part of the ESF funding in Ireland was chosen for interview, as it was felt that some of her views could apply to ESF funded programmes in other parts of Europe. For ease of analysis and to facilitate comparison, the results of these interviews are divided into the responses given by the programme providers (seven in total) and those given by the programme funders (four in total).

Programme Providers

The seven providers interviewed represented the following organisations:

- The ILO (Industrial Liaison Office) at the particular Irish Institute of Technology responsible for programmes A, B and C (2 representatives interviewed)
- The ILO Office based at the Dublin University responsible for programme D
- The ILO Office based at the Dutch University responsible for programme E
- The Swedish University responsible for programme F
- The Business Development Centre in Finland responsible for programme G
- The Spanish University responsible for programme H.

Reasons for Providing Entrepreneurship Programmes

From all of the interviews conducted with the seven programme providers, promoting entrepreneurship and contributing to the economic development of their regions appeared to be a key part of their organisations' remits.   Providing entrepreneurship programmes was a means of complying with this remit.   The representative of the Finnish programme mentioned that her organisation provided entrepreneurship programmes in order to create knowledge intensive businesses and generate new 'healthy' jobs. This was also the focus of programmes D and H. Representatives of programmes H (Spain) and E (The Netherlands) also mentioned technology transfer as a key reason for providing entrepreneurship programmes, the Dutch representative hoped to develop joint R & D projects with some of their entrepreneurs in the future. For one of the providers interviewed (the Swedish representative), providing entrepreneurship programmes was an important way of enhancing the University's reputation and attracting students. From all seven interviews, it appeared that the providers believed they were responding to a need for more entrepreneurs and new business start-ups, particularly in the technology-based and knowledge-intensive sectors.

Objectives of Provision

The two Irish representatives interviewed (separately) at the Institute responsible for programmes A, B and C, mentioned the creation of new businesses as their organisation's main objective for providing entrepreneurship programmes. The businesses created would be technology based in the case of programme B, and in addition, the entrepreneurship programmes would help to generate new tenants for their business incubator. This was also an objective in the case of the Finnish programme, where generating 30-40 knowledge based companies every year in the region was an additional and more specific objective. While job creation appeared to be common to all seven organisations, the Swedish representative added 'competing with other universities' and 'building profile' as key objectives. There was also a particular focus on supporting graduate entrepreneurship in the cases of the Swedish, Dutch and Dublin based programmes.

The interviewees were asked whether they felt their objectives had actually been met by the programmes. This question yielded a mixture of general and specific responses. The Finnish representative was very specific, mentioning the large number of applications received (600), the number of these which had been developed into new businesses (170) and the number of new jobs created by the programme (800). The interviewee representing the Dublin based programme (programme D) was equally specific, quoting 36 new technology based businesses created since 1996, 90 per cent of which were still trading at the time of the interview. The Swedish representative mentioned that this programme had been more successful than had been anticipated, with at least twelve new businesses created each year, thereby enhancing the reputation of the University. The Irish Institute responsible for programmes A, B and C, together with the Dutch and Spanish representatives, all felt that their organisations' original objectives had been met by the respective programmes, and generally made positive comments regarding the extent of new business creation, jobs developed and the impact on the local area.

The Spanish representative, however, gave the most modest of the responses, stating that the organisation was pleased with the results achieved by the programme but realised they had a long way to go. With regard to the Dutch university, this respondent admitted that one key objective had not really been met by the programme – that of developing new R & D projects with the companies created.

Measures Used to Determine the Extent to which Objectives have been Met

In all seven of the interviews, key indicators such as the number of entrepreneurs applying, the number participating, the number of new businesses and new jobs created, were monitored on at least an informal basis. In the case of the Irish respondents for all four programmes (A - D) and the Finnish respondent, formal surveys were conducted by the providers themselves or by independent consultants. The Swedish respondent admitted that some of the outputs achieved were rather 'nebulous' in terms of available quantitative data, but there was a general feeling that the reputation and profile of the University had been raised.

Perception of Benefits Derived by Participants

Without exception, all of the interviewees felt confident that their organisations' programmes had been of real benefit to participants. In this respect, the representative of the Dublin-based programme (programme D), as well as the Finnish and Spanish respondents all gave quite specific responses. The respondent for the Dublin programme said that the programme had benefited participants by providing practical workshops, peer learning, expert advice and by offering them a step-by-step approach to developing their business ideas. It was claimed that the Finnish programme had increased the speed at which companies had been able to start their business activities, and had assisted in creating approximately 180 new companies. The respondent claimed that the programme helped aspiring entrepreneurs to 'cross the valley of death', organise finance and grow. The Spanish representative mentioned the more social aspects of the programme as key benefits, for example, opening the participants' minds to other possibilities, providing individual participants with employment, and giving them the opportunity to mature more quickly as human beings.

Concerning the Dutch University, the main perceived benefit accrued by those participating was the industry mentoring and the university work space and facilities. The Swedish interviewee stated that participants claimed their programme helped them to avoid costly mistakes and problems. The representatives of programmes A, B and C believed that their programmes benefited participants in terms of training, peer support and structure which, it was felt, encouraged participants to progress quickly. In the case of the programme B, the view was that participants benefited from having a business address, an office and a generally supportive environment in which to develop their business ideas. In the case of programme A, it was felt that the publicity afforded to the programme finalists was extremely beneficial for participants. The 'hand-holding' aspects of both programmes and the links with the Institute of Technology were also mentioned as aspects perceived as beneficial by the providers.

Measures Used to Determine Benefits Derived

In most cases, the measures used to determine whether programmes had benefited participants were those already cited above. In addition, the following were mentioned:

- The Dublin based programme used the individual consultation sessions during the programme and evaluation forms at the end.
- The Swedish programme employed informal direct feedback from participants and feedback from a past participants' network.
- The Finnish programme conducted annual studies to determine how their companies survived and compared their growth rates with those of other companies.
- The Spanish programme made use of questionnaires and personal tracking through the duration of the programme.

Difficulties Encountered with Programme Provision

Interestingly, all seven of the interviewees mentioned that their organisations had experienced some difficulties with the provision of their respective programmes. Three of the providers (representing programmes D, G and H) mentioned funding as their main difficulty. In most cases, funding appeared to be allocated on a year to year basis and seemed difficult to secure on a continuing basis. The respondent for programme D mentioned that this programme was 'seriously under funded' and the Finnish representative stated that additional funding was required to provide the sort of expert consultancy required for clients. The representatives of programmes A, B and C mentioned attracting sufficient high quality entrepreneurs from within their region as a main difficulty, as well as managing within budget constraints, and the time involved in reporting to the programme funders. The Dutch interviewee mentioned that difficulties had been experienced in matching entrepreneurs with suitable mentors, as well as finding space for programme participants to work in the University. Getting moral support and encouragement from within the University was the biggest difficulty for the Swedish programme, although the situation appeared to be improving.

Time and Resources Invested in Programme Provision

Most of the providers felt that their organisations had invested significantly more time and resources in the programmes than was originally anticipated. This certainly appeared to be the case with all of the Irish programmes, as well as the Dutch and Spanish programmes. Only the Swedish representative felt that the programme did not take up too much time, since it involved a number of outsiders as providers for some of the elements. The Finnish representative answered the question quite specifically, quoting the amount of money and man-years that the programme had cost – between €25,000 and €33,500, plus the equivalent of eleven man-years over a three-year period. The Spanish representative was specific too, and mentioned an investment of six full-time staff and €200,000 per year, while the figures quoted for Dublin-base programme (programme D) were 1000 man-hours and around €33,000. All of the Irish and Dutch interviewees indicated that it was difficult to put a figure on all the resources involved in their programmes, and it appeared that the investment in time particularly, was concentrated at certain critical points in the programme, such as the recruitment and completion phases. It was interesting that the Dutch representative commented on feedback from participants on his programme (programme E), which suggested that they believed the programme was worth around €100,000 in terms of their individual personal benefit.

Value for Money

Each of the providers interviewed stated that their organisations were definitely getting value for money from the programmes. However, the Irish respondents responsible for programmes A, B and C felt that more value could probably be derived from their programmes. Others commented that their organisations' involvement in entrepreneurship programmes brought additional benefits, such as better quality tenants for incubator units (programmes A, B, C and G). The representative for programme D – the Dublin-based programme felt that the wealth generated from programmes in terms of new businesses, jobs and turnover created, far exceeded the finances and resources invested. The Swedish interviewee commented that it was believed their funders were getting value for money too.

Future Plans for Programme Provision

Without exception, all of the providers interviewed stated quite clearly that their organisations intended to continue providing entrepreneurship training programmes. In all cases, however, this depended on the necessary funding being secured. The Dutch interviewee added that they had increased the academic value of their entrepreneurship programme so that it now carried more credit points than before.

In terms of changing the nature of the provision of the programmes, all seven of the providers interviewed stated that there was an intention to make some changes to the respective programmes. The representative for programme D – the Dublin-based programme, indicated that programmes were constantly under review, and the Dutch interviewee stated that there was a desire to add other elements to their programme. It seemed that a decision had already been taken to change the duration of the Swedish programme.

As indicated above, the providers seemed keen to make changes to their programmes. This appeared to be due both to their own experiences on the ground, and in consideration of feedback from the participants. One of the Irish respondents (representing programme A) felt that their programme would be better as an annual, instead of a bi-annual programme, as this would aid continuity. He highlighted the intention to add some extra training sessions and to include more experienced entrepreneurs as guest speakers. These were features considered desirable by participants. With regard to programme B, it was felt that there was possibly too much support given and that much of it was not availed of by the participants. Also, it was considered that the programme could be changed to accommodate both early stage inventor-types as well as actively aspiring entrepreneurs, since the programme attracted applications from both.

In the case the Swedish programme, the duration of the programme had just been shortened to seven months because the providers believed the participants tired when the programme lasted for twelve months. It was planned also to add sessions on intrapreneurship and exporting. The Swedish representative commented too, that their funders were not making any changes and would continue to support the programme.

The only change that the Spanish representative mentioned was that of starting up a Foundation to help with continued funding for the programme, as lack of such funding appeared to be a major problem. Securing funding on a continuing basis was a difficulty for programme D, and here it was planned to change the sources of funding sought, so that the programme could be continued and enhanced. In relation to the Finnish programme, concern over funding had led to the development of plans to seek private investment, in the form of venture capital and sponsorship. There was also a desire to expand the range of services, so that entrepreneurs could be supported at every stage of their 'life span'. Finally, the respondent from the Dutch programme indicated that he would like to add more elements to the programme, such as network meetings and summer schools to raise awareness and attract early stage entrepreneurs. This was envisaged as a 'pre-programme course' whereby participants could accumulate points toward participation in other programmes and courses.

Other Aspects

At the end of the interview, respondents were asked whether they wished to make any additional comments, but only a few of these were made. The Dutch representative commented that it was felt the monitoring and checking aspects of their programme were very useful to both the participating entrepreneurs and the programme manager. The Swedish and Dublin-based respondents considered that their particular programmes offered a good 'package' of supports to aspiring entrepreneurs which could be developed further. The representatives of programme A, B and C made a number of points about the drawbacks of some components of entrepreneurship programmes in general. These included the fact that most entrepreneurship programmes involved the completion of a business plan but that, in their experience, this was not an indicator of success. Some of their participants had completed a business plan but would never succeed. These representatives also commented that they were finding it increasingly difficult to get the necessary 'deliverables' from participants to fulfil programme requirements, since entrepreneurs were often quite secretive about their business ideas and did not like to document the details in a business plan.

Programme Funders

The four funders interviewed represented the following organisations:

- The Secretariat of the Council of Directors of the Institutes of Technology in Ireland, representing part of the European Social Fund – ESF (Dublin)
- The International Fund for Ireland – IFI
- The manufacturing company responsible for funding the 2 industry sponsored programmes (programmes A and C)
- Enterprise Ireland.

Rationale for Funding Entrepreneurship Programmes

All four representatives of the funding bodies interviewed stated that supporting entrepreneurship programmes was part of their organisations' overall mission or remit. In the case of the manufacturing company, the only private sector funder included in the study, their representative said that it was part of the company's 'Corporate Responsibility Programme' to become involved with initiatives to deal with unemployment. The ESF interviewee pointed out that funding entrepreneurship training programmes was a specific objective of one of the sub-measures of the R & D programme of the EU Community Structural Funds – to increase innovation and entrepreneurial development. The IFI respondent said that the funding of entrepreneurship programmes was a specific objective under their Business Enterprise Programme to assist economic development, while the Enterprise Ireland interviewee stated that their mission involved the creation of start-up businesses, so supporting entrepreneurship programmes helped to fulfil this objective.

Main Objectives

In terms of specific objectives, the industry representative stated that the company's main objective was to offer entrepreneurship training to graduates nationwide, with the aim of developing new businesses. Enterprise Ireland's objective was broadly similar, namely to support, encourage and develop enterprise in Ireland. The main objectives for IFI funding entrepreneurship programmes stemmed from those in their annual report, which included the promotion of economic and social advance, as well as the encouragement of dialogue and reconciliation between nationalists and unionists in Northern Ireland. It is also one of the specific objectives in their Business Enterprise Programme – 'encouraging people to progress their ideas into profitable businesses'. The ESF representative was more specific in her response, stating that their main objective was to provide the skills necessary for promoting enterprise and job creation. However, their own research indicated that, in Ireland, there had been too much focus on attracting overseas investment and there was now a clear need to support indigenous industry.

In terms of the extent to which objectives had actually been met, the ESF representative considered that, for the most part, the programmes funded by them had demonstrated good indications of success, although for some programmes it was too early to make a judgment. The IFI respondent believed that his organisation's objectives were satisfactorily met through the programmes they funded. He also indicated that the IFI was confident its support had actually helped to create new businesses. Both the Enterprise Ireland and the industry interviewees felt that the programmes which their organisations supported, had been successful and had met the funders' objectives very well. However, none of the funders interviewed was able to quote specific figures or results to support their claims, although the ESF representative did refer to a number of surveys that had been conducted on that organisation's behalf.

In terms of the actual measures used to determine whether or not objectives had been met, all four funding body representatives interviewed, stated that their organisations monitored various outputs from the programmes they funded, in at least an informal way. For example, Enterprise Ireland viewed the number of individuals who came to them for further support following the entrepreneurship programme, as a measure of how successful the programme had been, and of how well their objectives had been met. The company sponsor relied on the evaluation reports compiled by providers. However, the ESF and IFI appeared to be more thorough in measuring the extent to which their original objectives were met, using strict quarterly reporting from the providers (ESF) and independent evaluations conducted by consultants (IFI).

Benefits to Programme Participants

As with the programme providers, all four funder representatives interviewed, believed that the programmes their organisations supported, were of real benefit to participants. For the IFI, the main benefit claimed for the programme they funded (programme B), was the way in which it helped to make individuals' business ideas more realistic. It also reduced the risk involved for participants. The industry representative stated that the expert training given was the main benefit for participants as this, together with the mentoring, ensured a greater success rate. In their view, the facility to network with other participants also provided valuable support to those involved. As for Enterprise Ireland, it was the close association with a third level educational establishment, relevant to many of their programmes, and the networking between peers, which were perceived as the most beneficial aspects. The cross-border element in some of these programmes gave an added dimension in terms of widening the participants' geographical market and providing other sources of materials, skills and contacts. The response from the ESF representative was not as specific as the others. She felt that, due to the nature of the programmes funded, it was too early to determine how the participants had actually benefited. However, she considered there were already indications that they had benefited through acquiring the necessary entrepreneurial skills to set-up their businesses.

In terms of the actual measures used to determine the benefits derived by the participants, the funding organisations involved in the study, tended to use similar mechanisms to those outlined above by the providers. In the case of IFI, ESF and the industry sponsor, the initial source of information comprised the feedback and reports from relevant programme managers. IFI also had their programmes independently evaluated, and these evaluations normally involved interviews with programme participants to find out how beneficial they found the programme. Enterprise Ireland staff members were often involved in review panels for many of the programmes funded, and this gave them an opportunity to get some feedback from participants.

Difficulties Encountered in the Funding of Programmes

Three of the four funders interviewed claimed that their organisations had encountered no difficulties with the funding of their respective programmes. The ESF representative, however, indicated that her office had received the ESF funding very late and there was some uncertainty about when future funding might be received.

Time and Resources Invested by Funders

When asked about the time and resources they had invested in the programmes, the interviewees gave fairly specific responses. Most of them referred to the amount of money and staff time involved. In the case of the ESF, the amount invested in enterprise development programmes in Ireland through the Council of Directors, was around €457,000 per year, plus an administration input of one full-time manager and an evaluation committee. IFI had invested over €412,500 but administrative time was not mentioned. The industry representative revealed an investment of nearly €600,000, plus 1.5 full-time staff members, while Enterprise Ireland had invested over €63,000 plus some management and administrative time.

Value for Money

All four funding representatives interviewed believed their organisations were getting value for money from the particular programmes they supported. In the case of IFI, the interviewee added that the partnerships developed with programme providers had proved very beneficial. The ESF representative felt that value for money would become greater in the future, as participants completed their programmes and developed their business ideas through to start-up stage. The Enterprise Ireland interviewee considered that the real value for money from their perspective was that the entrepreneurship programmes they supported provided additional benefits for entrepreneurs which were not available from the funding organisation itself. The industry representative appeared to be completely satisfied that the programme their organisation funded, provided value for money.

Future Plans

All representatives of the funding bodies included in the study stated that their organisations intended to continue supporting entrepreneurship programmes. In the case of the ESF representative (the Council of Directors), it was indicated that their involvement in future programmes, while desirable and expected, would depend on the amount of funding made available to them at EU level. The IFI respondent mentioned that they were always looking for new ways to support SMEs, while the industry interviewee said that the company had already committed to funding a further two runs of programme A.

   None of the interviewees from the funding bodies reported plans to change the funding arrangements of their respective programmes. However, the funders were quick to add that, in most cases, their organisations were directly affected by the amount of funding available centrally, or by changes that might be made in the future regarding actual funding mechanisms. Therefore, while there were no specific plans to change funding arrangements, there was no guarantee that funding would be continued in the future. Funding was subject to applications being approved at Board level and was normally awarded on a year-to-year basis. In the case of IFI, for example, they normally funded projects (including entrepreneurship programmes) in the initial pilot stages only, and then other agencies were expected to take over. It was unlikely, therefore, that IFI would fund programme B again. The ESF representative stated that her organisation had no plans to change funding arrangements, but believed that funding in general would be reduced in the new millennium, and that this would obviously have an impact on which specific projects would be funded. Enterprise Ireland had just been restructured at the time of the interview, and it was unclear how this might impact upon funding arrangements in the future. While the industry sponsor had recently committed to funding further runs of programme A, the particular fund managed by the company was subject to continued approval by their head office which was overseas. Hence, while none of the funders planned to make any changes, it appeared that, in reality, changes were inevitable.

Other Aspects

At the end of the interviews, the funders were asked whether they wished to add anything to what they had already said. Only two of the funders had additional comments to make. The ESF representative mentioned that the Enterprise Development Programmes funded under the Operational Programme for Industry, were particularly good mechanisms for creating links with the educational system to increase entrepreneurship, innovation and R & D in Ireland. The IFI representative said that he felt the success of the programmes funded, depended very much on 'the people on the ground', in other words, the programme managers and support team.

Comparative Analysis of the Eight Entrepreneurship Training Programmes

Some problems were encountered in conducting the comparative analysis, since despite the apparent commonality in their overall aims and objectives, the programmes were all put together differently. In a number of cases, a breakdown of specific programme elements was not available, and often no distinction was made between formal training and practical workshops, or between mentoring and business counselling. Moreover, it was difficult in some instances to compare costs, since a number of programmes included grants in their budgets, while others dealt with this element separately and did not perceive it as part of the overall running costs. In addition, some programmes' budget costs were absorbed in the general overheads of the providing organisations, or were covered by other departments, an example of this being the Dutch programme. In spite of these constraints, it was possible to compare the programmes in several interesting ways. Table 6.1 compares the programmes by content, specifically in terms of training, mentoring, business counselling, office facilities, finance, access to grants and follow-up support.

It is interesting to note that all of the programmes included some sort of structured training or workshops, as well as mentoring and access to grants outside of the programmes provided. The training and workshop sessions covered a variety of subjects related to planning and setting up a new business, and in all cases this led to the completion of a business plan. All of the programmes, with the exception of programme C, included business counselling. A minority of the programmes (two) provided seed capital or a prize fund (programmes A and D), and only two (programmes B and E) provided incubation or office space for the participants.

Three of the programmes (programmes E, F and G, i.e. the Dutch, Swedish and Finnish programmes) provided follow-up support, although it was unclear what this involved. Overall, the Dutch programme appeared to be the most comprehensive scheme, as it included all of the elements investigated, with the exception of a prize fund or seed capital. However, the programme providers considered part of the low-interest loan, which has been categorised in Table 6.1 as a subsistence/living allowance (because it was normally paid monthly to entrepreneurs to cover their costs), to be seed capital for entrepreneurs.

Table 6.1 Comparative Analysis of Programmes by Content

	Irish Programmes				Mainland European Programmes			
	A	**B**	**C**	**D**	**E**	**F**	**G**	**H**
	Ireland	Ireland	Ireland	Ireland	Netherlands	Sweden	Finland	Spain
Training/workshops	√	√	√	√	√	√	√	√
Training/workshop topics	Bp, Dbi, Fin, Hr, Mr, Mk, O&P.	Bp, Dbi, Fe, Fin, Hr, Mr, Mk, O&P, P, S.	Bp, Dbi, Fin, Mk.	Bp, Cf, Fin, Im, Mk, Mnt, Mr, P, Pd.	Bp, E, Fe, Fin, Mr, Pd.	Bp, Cf, E, Fe, Fin, L, Mnt, P, Pr, Pt, Q, S.	Bp, Cf, D, Fe, Fin, Hr, L, Mk, Mnt, Pt, S.	Bp, E, Mnt, Per.
Mentoring	√	√	√	√	√	√	√	√
Business counselling	√	√	X	√	√	√	√	√
Office/incubation facilities	X	√	X	X	√	X	X	X
Subsistence allowance	X	√	X	X	X	X	X	X
Prize fund/seed capital	√	X	X	√	X	X	X	X
Access to grants	√	√	√	√	√	√	√	√
Qualification	X	X	X	X	√(credits)	√	√	X
Follow-up support	X	X	X	X	√	√	√	X

√ = this element is included in the Programme; X = not included in the programme. Training topics code: Ac=Accounting; Bp=Business plan; Cf=Company formation/legalities; Co=Computing; D=Distribution; Dbi=Developing the business idea; E=Entrepreneurship; Ec=Economics; Fe=Feasibility study; Fin=Financing; Hr=Human resources; Im=Internet marketing; Mk=Marketing; L=Leadership; Mnt=Management; Mr=Market research; O&P=Operations and production; P=Patenting; Pd=Product development; Per=Personal development; Pr=Pricing; Pt=Partnerships; Q=Quality management; S=Sales.

While there appeared to be strong similarities in the content of the structured training/workshop sessions, as Table 6.1 reveals, the Swedish programme (programme F) appeared to be the most comprehensive programme in terms of training content, covering a total of twelve business related topics, including pricing and quality management, topics not apparently included in the other programmes.   The Finnish programme had the next most comprehensive training content, with eleven topics, which is considerably higher than programme C (the Irish redundancy programme), which only had four topics, the least number in the eight programmes reviewed.   However, the exact breakdown of the training content was not always clear, as in the case of Spanish programme (programme H), which appeared to amalgamate a number of different topics under the heading of Entrepreneurship.   Similarly, in the Dutch programme literature, reference was made to a course on 'Becoming an Entrepreneur' which was the vehicle for the training input to the programme, but only a few specific topics were identified separately.   Interestingly, only programmes A, B and E provided some accreditation for the training element, with programme E (the Dutch programme) giving credits against other courses.

Table 6.2 draws further comparisons between the programmes in terms of quantitative measures, such as programme duration, number of participants, cost per programme, cost per participant, number of new businesses created, number of new jobs created and the average cost per new business and new job created.

In terms of duration, the longest programme appeared to be programme B, the Irish cross border programme, which lasted a total of 15 months, the shortest programme being programme C, lasting only 6 months.   The mean duration of the entrepreneurship programmes was 10.88 months.   It would seem that, in terms of participation, the Spanish programme attracted and supported the largest number of aspiring entrepreneurs, with an average of 150 participants per programme.   In contrast, the lowest number of participants supported was 15, and as this was the case in four of the programmes – programmes B, D, E and F – it represents the modal participation level for the eight programmes.

Table 6.2 Comparison of Programmes by Duration, Costs and Outputs

	A IRL	B IRL/NI	C IRL	D IRL	E NL	F SW	G FIN	H SPAIN
Total programme duration	12 mths	15 mths	6 mths	9 mths	12 mths	12 mths	9 mths	12 mths
Training/workshops	6 days	10 days	3 days	4.5 days	Varies	8 days	10-12 days	10 days +
Mentoring (no. of sessions[1])	3-4	3-5	3	9	Varies	6	Varies	Varies
No. of participants	35	15	38	15	15	15+	50+	150+
Cost[2] per Programme	€126,974	€222,204	€11,428	€126,974	€225,000	€113,713	€504,564	€200,000
Cost[2] per participant	€3,628	€14,814	€301	€8,465	€15,000	€4,549	€10,091	€1,333
Average no. of new businesses created (% success rate)[3]	8 (23%)	8.7 (58%)	8 (21%)	4 (27%)	12 (80%)	5+ (33%+)	21+ (42%+)	18+ (12%+)
Cost[2] per new business created	€15,872	€25,541	€1,429	€31,744	€18,750	€22,743	€24,027	€11,111
New jobs created	16	18	8	8.5	96	15	100	72
Cost[2] per new job	€7,936	€12,345	€1,429	€14,938	€2,344	€7,581	€5,046	€2,778

1. Mentoring sessions are between 1.5 and 3 hours duration
2. % success rate = the percentage of projects converted to new businesses based on the number of participants
3. All figures are on 'an average per programme' basis

Interestingly, the costs of running these programmes appeared to vary considerably, ranging from €11,428 (programme C) to €504,564 (programme G). In most cases, the differences in costs reflected differences in programme content and level of support provided. Therefore, in the absence of a breakdown of the various components included in each of the programme budgets, an exact comparison of costs is not possible. However, it can be noted that, based on the data available, the mean cost per participant was €7,273, with programme C (the Irish redundancy programme) having the lowest cost per participant (€301), and the programme E (the Dutch programme) having the highest cost per participant (€15,000).

In terms of economic effectiveness and the impact of the programmes on new business/new job creation, the Finnish programme appeared to contribute most to economic development, generating on average 21 new businesses and 100 new jobs per programme. However, the cost of each new business created was €24,027, with the cost of each new job amounting to €5,046. Neither of these figures is the lowest for the eight programmes. Overall, the average number of new businesses and new jobs created by the eight programmes reviewed, was 11 and 42, respectively, at an average cost of around €19,000 and €7,000, respectively. The Dutch programme seemed to have the best success rate, converting on average 80 per cent of the projects involved into new businesses. In contrast, the Spanish programme appeared to have the lowest success rate, converting only 12 per cent of participants' projects into new businesses.

These comparisons must be treated with caution, particularly with regard to costs. As previously stated, these entrepreneurship programmes all appeared to be put together and costed differently, hence it was difficult to determine exact budgets for each. Attention should be drawn in particular to the Dutch programme as the provider mentioned a notional programme value, which was significantly higher than the stated budget figure in the available documentation. Furthermore, many of the budget items in this programme appeared to be absorbed into the organisation's general overheads. This is not entirely unusual, since all of the programmes are run by divisions of larger organisations so there are supposedly some shared costs. In the case of the Dutch programme, however, the stated budget figure of €15,000 per participant would only just cover the individual loan or subsistence allowance, leaving little extra for the training, mentoring, office space and administration. In addition, the costs of programme C (the Irish redundancy programme) should also be viewed with caution, since the grants to which the participants had direct access, were not included. Although these grants were administered outside of the programme, they clearly had an impact on participation and completion levels, as well as on the number of new businesses created. The grants of up to €12,700 each were clearly viewed by the participants as an important part of the scheme.

In addition to comparing the content of the programmes and their various outputs, the opinions of the providers and funders of these programmes may also be compared. Although, overall, the responses from the providers were much more specific and quantifiable than those from the funders, there were several similarities in the answers given. For example, it was clear from the interviews that both the providers and the funders were involved in entrepreneurship programmes because it was part of their organisations' remit to do so. The primary objective in all cases was to promote economic development, through the creation of new businesses and new jobs. However, in relation to the providers, there appeared to be secondary objectives, which included generating tenants for their incubators and enhancing the reputation of the organisations as a whole. Both the providers and the funders felt that their objectives were met by the programmes in which they were involved, and that the participants benefited. A mixture of informal monitoring and formal evaluations were used to determine the degree to which objectives were met and the benefits derived by the participants. Interestingly, the programme funders seemed to rely quite heavily on feedback from the providers, with the providers appearing to monitor various aspects more closely. On the issues of value for money and whether they planned to continue their involvement in entrepreneurship programmes in the future, both the providers and funders were in agreement that they would continue to be involved in such programmes. There were, however, some differences between the opinions of the providers and those of the funders, and these appeared to be in two main areas. Firstly, with regard to the difficulties encountered, the providers mentioned that they had experienced a number of these, while the funders claimed they had experienced no difficulties. Secondly, regarding plans to change the nature of the provision or funding of the programmes, all of the providers appeared keen to make changes, but none of the funders had any plans to do so.

Summary and Conclusion

This chapter considered the overall effectiveness of entrepreneurship training programmes by presenting a detailed comparative analysis of eight such programmes offered by providers in five European countries. These programmes were investigated in terms of their objectives, structure, content, costs and overall effectiveness. In addition, structured interviews were conducted with a number of the providers and funders of these programmes to determine, among other things, their objectives in becoming involved in such support schemes, the extent to which they felt their objectives had been met, and their future plans for the programmes. From the analysis and the comparisons made, a number of conclusions may be drawn.   While there was considerable variety in the structure, content and objectives of the entrepreneurship training programmes investigated, there also appeared to be a number of similarities. These similarities related to the types of training topics covered and the provision of mentoring and business counselling. The main differences were quantitative in nature, and were evident in the different programme costs and outputs. While, as explained above, the between-programme comparisons must be treated with caution, nevertheless some appeared to be more effective than others in converting participants' projects into new businesses and jobs.

With regard to the interviews with the programme providers and funders, both groups were confident of the benefits accruing to participants from the programmes with which they were involved, although there were differences in the perceptions of these benefits, and the measures used to determine them. Among other things, this comparative analysis has enabled the authors to identify key elements of the seemingly most effective programmes. These elements, together with the findings from the longitudinal study, presented in the next chapter, combine towards the development of a set of useful practical guidelines for improving programme effectiveness.

Chapter 7

Profiles of the Programme Participants

Introduction

The extensive body of literature presented in Chapters 2 and 3 claims that entrepreneurs possess certain social, psychological and behavioural characteristics that distinguish them from other individuals. However, most of the empirical evidence to support these claims is based on an analysis of established entrepreneurs, and little attention has been paid to the aspiring entrepreneur, and to whether these characteristics are present in individuals at the pre-start-up and early development stages.

This part of the study, therefore, aims to address the question of what type of people participate in entrepreneurship programmes and to determine whether such individuals, i.e. aspiring entrepreneurs, actually possess the particular characteristics deemed in the literature to be critical for entrepreneurial success. With this in mind, participants from four of the eight entrepreneurship training programmes included in the comparative study presented in the previous chapter were chosen for analysis. These participant groups were from the Dutch programme (participants from various cohorts), and from three of the Irish programmes (participants from the 1996 and 1997 cohorts). These particular groups were chosen on a convenience basis for reasons of accessibility. A total of 121 individual participants were surveyed, of whom 102 provided useable responses. It is noted that four of the 102 respondents (one from programme B and 3 from programme E) had reached set-up stage with their businesses prior to joining the entrepreneurship programmes. However, these businesses were in the very early stages of the start-up process, hence, still fitted the authors' definition of aspiring entrepreneurs, as described earlier in this study. The findings from this part of the study are presented in this chapter. The actual survey groups are described and the social, psychological and behavioural characteristics of the group participants are examined.

Description of the Survey Groups and Response Rates

Survey Group 1 – Participants from Programme A (Ireland)

This survey group comprised the 35 individuals from programme A, each of whom completed the questionnaire as requested, and thus a 100 per cent response rate was achieved. These individuals were participating in an all-Ireland, industry sponsored entrepreneurship programme during 1996/1997. Each of these aspiring entrepreneurs was of Irish origin, with seven (20 per cent) of the individuals from Northern Ireland. All of the participants had a business idea at the feasibility or pre-feasibility stage, and had received a third level education to at least diploma standard. Most of the participants were single men, with women accounting for only 20 per cent of the group. Seven of the participants (4 men and 3 women) had children dependent upon them and two of the women were pregnant (each with their second child) at the time of commencing the programme. The business ideas proposed by the participants covered a wide range of industry sectors with some 86 per cent (30 business ideas) in manufacturing and the balance in the services sector.

Survey Group 2 – Participants from Programme B (Ireland)

This group consisted of 18 individuals participating in programme B, a cross-border programme, during 1997, 14 of whom (77 per cent) completed the questionnaire. Again, each of the individuals involved was of Irish origin and 12 (85 pre cent) were from Northern Ireland. All of the participants had a business idea at the feasibility stage, and one had already set-up his business prior to joining the programme and was in the very early stages of trading and business development. Although not a requirement for entry to the programme, eight of the participants (57 per cent) in this survey group had received a third level education and four (28 per cent) had followed postgraduate courses. The programme participants were mostly male (85 per cent), seven of the individuals were married and six had children dependent upon them. The business ideas appeared to be widely spread among the medical, electronics and agriculture/fisheries industry sectors (64 per cent), with the remaining ideas in the transportation, software, printing, plastics and training sectors.

Survey Group 3 – Participants from Programme C (Ireland)

The third survey group comprised the 38 individuals from programme C, all of whom completed the questionnaire. These individuals were part of a redundancy group who were offered enterprise training as part of a package of redundancy supports provided by their employer during 1997. Although there were no entry requirements to the programme (the individuals' employer decided who was eligible for the redundancy scheme), 68 per cent of the group (25 individuals) were university/college graduates. The majority of the group (63 per cent) was female, 76 per cent of the participants were married and 71 per cent had children dependant upon them. All but two of the individuals had a business idea at the feasibility or pre-feasibility stage and 32 per cent (12 ideas) of these were in training and consultancy, 26 per cent (10 ideas) in tourism and the balance (37 per cent, i.e. 14 ideas) in the food, crafts, retail and other sectors. Two individuals had no specific business idea in mind and were considering a range of options.

Survey Group 4 – Participants from Programme E (The Netherlands)

The final group surveyed consisted of 15 individuals from various cohorts of programme E, and who were all based in the Netherlands at the time of the survey. Questionnaires were mailed to 30 programme participants, from whom 15 useable responses were received. This was the target sample size as it represents the average number of individuals supported by this particular Dutch programme in any one year. Three of the participants in this particular group had already set-up their business prior to joining the programme, and were in the very early stages of trading and business development. The others had a business idea at the feasibility stage and all were graduates at degree, masters or PhD level. Most of the participants surveyed were married (73 per cent), all were male and 60 per cent had children dependent upon them. The business ideas proposed by this survey group were more 'high tech' than those in the other survey groups, with 53 per cent (8 business ideas) in the technical consultancy area, 26 per cent (4 ideas) in micro-filtration/science area, and the balance (21 per cent, i.e. 3 ideas) in the software and medical technology sectors.

Social Characteristics

Age

While there was no specific age limit laid down for any of the four programmes considered in this section, the criteria for entry to programme A required that applicants had to have graduated during or since 1990. The actual age of those selected to participate in that particular programme ranged from 20 to 35 years, with the bulk of participants (49 per cent) falling into the 25-29 age group and the balance split almost equally between the 20-24 and 30-35 age groups. The group from programme B was generally older by comparison, with most of the participants falling into the 41-45 age range (6 participants = 42 per cent). In contrast to this, the majority of the participants in the programme C group fell into the 31-40 age range. Most of the participants in the Dutch survey group (programme 4) were in the 31-35 age range (5 participants = 33 per cent), with 26 per cent (4 participants) falling into the 41-45 years age range.

Education and Work Experience

While only the participants in programmes A and E were required to have a third level qualification in order to participate, the qualification level of participants in the other programmes was, as indicated above, quite high. The areas of the qualification ranged from general business and marketing, to engineering and other technical areas. With regard to work experience, almost all of the participants, i.e. 97 of the 102 respondents (95 per cent) had worked for at least one year prior to joining the particular entrepreneurship programme, with 83 of these (81 per cent) having more than 3 years work experience. Forty of the participants (39 per cent) had experience at management level, 22 (21 per cent) had experience in sales, and almost half of the participants (48 per cent) had worked in an area directly related to the industry sector of their proposed business idea.

Venture Type and Role Allocation

As mentioned above, the types of business proposed by the participants covered a wide range of industry sectors. Table 7.1 shows the breakdown of the business ideas proposed by the 102 aspiring entrepreneurs who responded to the survey.

Table 7.1 Business Ideas/Industry Sectors

Idea type/industry sector ($n = 102$)	No. of ideas	Percentage of group
Education, training and consultancy (inc. technical consultancy)	22	22%
Tourism and leisure	19	19%
Food	8	8%
Textiles	6	6%
Agriculture/fisheries	5	5%
Engineering	5	5%
Pharmaceuticals	5	5%
Medical	4	4%
Software	4	4%
Electronics	4	4%
Plastics	2	1%
No specific idea	2	1%
Transportation	1	1%
Other*	15	15%
Total	102	100%

*includes ideas based on individual services such as secretarial, bookkeeping and furniture design. Percentages are rounded up to nearest 1%.

Although not illustrated in Table 7.1, exactly half of the business ideas (51) were manufacturing based, with the other half service based. With regard to the structure of the proposed venture, more than half of the participating aspiring entrepreneurs (57 individuals = 56 per cent) were developing their idea alone, with the remaining participants (45 individuals = 44 per cent) involved in a team based venture.

The participants were also asked to describe their role or proposed role in the business. Seventy five per cent of the respondents (76 individuals) described their role as that of managing director or business owner; 11 per cent described their role as being involved in the production or technical aspects of the proposed business; five per cent located their role in marketing; three per cent indicated that they would be working on the finances of the business, and 12 per cent felt that they would probably be doing 'everything', at least in the initial stages. Interestingly, despite the obvious importance of the sales function in any business, only seven per cent of the respondents felt that their role would be in actually selling their proposed product or service. However, further analysis of the proposed sales function for the businesses revealed that 58 per cent of the respondents believed that they would have the responsibility for sales, at least in the initial stages, 23 per cent had identified another person or agency who would deal with selling the product/service on their behalf, and 25 per cent had not yet determined who would be responsible for sales in the business. (Figures and percentages in this part of the analysis may not equal 100 (n=102) due to multiple answers and rounding.)

Motivation

In order to assess the various motives for setting up in business, the participants were asked to give their reasons for deciding to go into business for themselves. This question was not put to the participants in programme C, since their motivation was clearly linked to their imminent redundancy situation, and their participation in the entrepreneurship programme was prompted by their employer's initiative. The question was also inadvertently omitted from the Dutch survey group (programme E), and there was insufficient time to correct the omission with a second mailing. Hence, this question was asked of only two of the four groups, those participating in programmes A (35 responses) and B (14 responses). The responses from these 49 individuals are categorised in Table 7.2.

Table 7.2 Reasons for Wanting to Set-up in Business

Reason for wanting to set-up in business (n = 49)	No.*	%*
To be one's own boss and be independent	21	43%
To meet the challenge; for personal achievement/satisfaction	19	39%
To be successful and make money	10	20%
To have an opportunity to develop one's own ideas	5	10%
Frustration with current job	2	4%
To have a better lifestyle	2	4%
To be able to employ people	2	4%

*The frequency of response does not equal the total number surveyed (i.e. 49) and the percentages do not equal 100 due to multiple answers.

It was interesting that to be one's own boss and achieve personal satisfaction were the most frequently given reasons for the participants wishing to pursue an entrepreneurial career, rather than the desire to be successful and make money, which was only mentioned by 10 of the 49 respondents. Further analysis of all four groups of participants (102 individuals) revealed that, for the majority of participants, this was to be their first business venture, with only eighteen per cent (i.e. 19 individuals) claiming to have been involved in, or at least having attempted to set-up, a previous business. Some of these earlier entrepreneurial attempts had been modestly successful, and some had failed either before or shortly after start-up.

Expectations

In order to determine why individuals participate in entrepreneurship programmes, the participants from the four programmes were asked to list their main expectations from the programmes at the outset. Expectations ranged from gaining an opportunity to test the feasibility of their business ideas, to gaining new skills and knowledge in the general area of enterprise preparation. A summary of participants' main expectations is provided in Table 7.3.

Table 7.3 Participants' Expectations ($n = 102$)

Support and guidance on setting up and running a business	29%	Opportunity to compete for the prize fund/get funding	6%
Completion of Business Plan	25%	Networking and making new contacts	5%
To explore the feasibility aspects and develop the business idea	24%	Physical facilities and contact with the university or institute	5%
To gain new skills and knowledge	16%	Technical support	4%
Marketing/Business skills	12%	No expectations/no response	2%
An opportunity to focus on the business idea	8%	To gain experience	2%
Get help with financial planning and sourcing funding	7%	To get access to different experts	1%

Figures indicate frequency of response in terms of the percentage of participants stating a particular expectation. Percentages do not total 100 due to multiple answers.

While participants provided multiple responses to this part of the survey, it was clear that the most frequently mentioned expectation was that of 'getting support and guidance on setting up and running a business', with 29 per cent of the participants listing this as their main expectation from their entrepreneurship programme. The 'completion of a business plan' and 'being able to explore the feasibility aspects and develop the idea' were the next most frequently mentioned expectations, with 25 per cent and 24 per cent of participants listing these, respectively. Surprisingly, few participants (six per cent) listed the financial elements, such as a prize fund or actual grant aid/subsistence, as key expectations, even when these aspects were clearly marketed as part of the programme support.

Psychological Characteristics

In order to further analyse the type of individual taking part in the entrepreneurship programmes, the participants were asked to rate themselves against some of the key characteristics deemed in the literature to be critical to entrepreneurial success. Using a Likert scale of 1 to 5, where 1 is the lowest rating and 5 is the highest, the participants were asked to rate their level of enthusiasm, need for achievement, initiative taking, calculated risk taking, innovativeness, leadership, commitment and determination, confidence, communication and judgement abilities.

Overall, the amalgamated group (102 individuals) appeared to be quite confident in their entrepreneurial abilities. Most of the participants gave themselves very high ratings against all of the characteristics, with only a few individuals rating themselves lower than a 3. A summary of these ratings is presented in Table 7.4.

Table 7.4 Self-Ratings – Entrepreneurial Characteristics ($n = 102$)

Characteristics	Frequency of response (%) in each rating category						Mean rating
	?	1	2	3	4	5	
Enthusiasm	1%	0%	2%	5%	29%	65%	4.55
Need for Achievement	0%	1%	1%	7%	33%	58%	4.37
Taking Initiative	2%	0%	0%	13%	55%	31%	4.14
Calculated Risk Taking	1%	0%	5%	31%	39%	25%	3.80
Innovativeness	3%	%	1%	22%	43%	32%	4.04
Leadership	2%	1%	2%	27%	48%	20%	3.78
Commitment / Determination	3%	0%	0%	9%	36%	53%	4.40
Confidence	1%	1%	3%	17%	47%	32%	4.02
Ability to Communicate	2%	0%	1%	23%	57%	18%	3.89
Judgement	2%	0%	2%	26%	55%	16%	3.82

Note: Percentages may not total 100 due to rounding. ? = don't know or did not respond.

As Table 7.4 shows, the characteristics of enthusiasm and need for achievement attracted the highest number of top scores, with 65 per cent and 58 per cent of the participants rating themselves as a 5, respectively. The highest mean ratings were against the characteristics of Enthusiasm and

Commitment/Determination with mean ratings of 4.55 and 4.40, respectively. In contrast, the lowest scores were recorded against the characteristics of Leadership and Calculated risk-taking, with mean scores of 3.78 and 3.80, respectively. These two characteristics also attracted the highest number of lower scale scores (i.e. 3 or lower), with 36 per cent of the respondents rating themselves as a 3 or lower against Calculated risk taking, and 30 per cent of respondents rating themselves a 3 or lower against Leadership. Communication and Judgement abilities also attracted low scores, with mean scores of 3.89 and 3.82, respectively.

In order to determine whether the participants scored themselves independently against each characteristic, i.e. whether there was any significant relationship between their scores in one characteristic and another, further analysis was conducted on participants from just one of the survey groups – programme A (35 participants). Using the null hypothesis, i.e. the assumption that the scores were independent of each other, expected value tables were constructed. These were then compared with the observed scores of the participants against each of the characteristics relative to each other. This analysis showed that there appeared to be a tendency for individuals to score themselves similarly in Need for Achievement and Enthusiasm (Enthus.). In this case, 16 participants gave themselves a score of 5 in each. These results appear to have some significance, given that the expected value of such scores is 12. There are also a high number of zeros off the diagonal, as Table 7.5 shows.

Evidence of dependence was also present regarding Taking Initiative and Enthusiasm (11 paired '5' scores observed compared with 7.43 expected); Innovativeness and Enthusiasm (15 paired '5' scores compared with 9.71 expected); Taking Initiative and Need for Achievement (12 paired '5' scores compared with 7.80 expected); Innovation and Need for achievement (14 paired '5' scores compared with 10.20 expected); Innovation and Taking Initiative (10 paired '5' scores compared with 6.31 expected); Confidence and Leadership (5 paired '5' scores compared with 2.57 expected), with a greater number of participants than expected tending to score themselves highly in each case. However, despite this evidence, one could argue that there were insufficient results and too many score choices between 1 and 5 to be able to state these cases of dependence with confidence.

It was interesting to note that evidence of dependence was not as strong in the participants' self-ratings of Calculated Risk-Taking relative to other characteristics. For example, when paired with Enthusiasm, three people scored themselves low (2) on Calculated Risk-Taking and high (4) on Enthusiasm, compared to an expected result of 1.11. Similarly, in the Risk-taking and Need for Achievement relationship, two participants scored low (2) on Risk-Taking and high (4) on Need for Achievement. One individual scored 2 on Risk-Taking and 5 on Need for Achievement. This compares with expected values of 0.86 and 1.80 respectively.

Table 7.5 Observed and Expected Values – Entrepreneurial Characteristics (Participants from Survey Group 1 – Programme A)

n=35		OBSERVED					
		Need for Achievement					
		1	2	3	4	5	Total
Enthus.	1	**0**	0	0	0	0	0
	2	0	**0**	0	0	0	0
	3	0	0	**1**	1	0	2
	4	0	0	3	**5**	5	13
	5	0	0	0	4	**16**	20
	Total	0	0	4	10	21	35
		EXPECTED					
		Need for Achievement					
		1	2	3	4	5	Total
Enthus.	1	**0.00**	0.00	0.00	0.00	0.00	0
	2	0.00	**0.00**	0.00	0.00	0.00	0
	3	0.00	0.00	**0.23**	0.57	1.20	2
	4	0.00	0.00	1.49	**3.71**	7.80	13
	5	0.00	0.00	2.29	5.71	**12.00**	20
	Total	0	0	4.01	9.99	21	35

However, there appeared to be a relationship between participants' scores in Risk-Taking and Innovation, with ten individuals scoring 4 in each and 7 scoring 5 in each, as compared to respective expected values of 6.43 and 4.37. Hence, it would seem that those individuals who rated themselves highly on Risk-Taking also rated themselves highly on Innovation.

Behavioural Characteristics

In order to assess the participants' preparedness for setting up in business, and to determine their actual development needs, the 102 individuals were asked to rate their skills and knowledge in a number of key business areas. Once again, a Likert rating scale of 1 to 5 was used and the results of this analysis are presented in Table 7.6.

Table 7.6 Self-Ratings – Business Skills and Knowledge (*n* = 102)

Business skills and knowledge	Frequency of response (%) in each rating category						Mean rating
	?	1	2	3	4	5	
Raising finance	1%	5%	18%	47%	57%	9%	3.10
Sales management	3%	9%	18%	45%	22%	4%	2.90
Managing cash flow	1%	7%	18%	33%	32%	10%	3.17
Managing staff	1%	9%	8%	28%	35%	19%	3.40
Business legal issues	2%	31%	31%	23%	8%	6%	2.24
Health and safety legislation	3%	23%	27%	28%	15%	5%	2.48
Employment legislation	3%	23%	34%	28%	9%	4%	2.33
Stock control	4%	15%	12%	31%	23%	16%	3.10
Work planning and scheduling	1%	4%	6%	31%	43%	15%	3.52
Quality control	0%	6%	16%	24%	27%	25%	3.36
Quality standards	1%	8%	14%	28%	28%	21%	3.34
Market research and planning	0%	7%	22%	40%	31%	5%	3.14

Note: Percentages may not total 100 due to rounding. ? = don't know or did not respond.

It was interesting to note that the participants did not rate themselves as highly on business skills/knowledge as they did on entrepreneurial characteristics. In fact, the mean rating registered in the business skills section was 3.00, with most of the respondents giving themselves ratings of 3 or less against almost all of the skills listed. This compares with an average rating of 4.08 in the entrepreneurial characteristics analysis where most of the participants rated themselves as 4 or higher against the majority of the characteristics listed.

The lowest scores in the business skills/knowledge section appeared in the legal areas (i.e. business legal issues, health and safety legislation and employment legislation), with mean ratings of between 2.24, 2.48 and 2.33, respectively). Skills such as raising finance, cash flow management and sales management also attracted low ratings with mean scores of 3.17 and 2.90, respectively.

Summary and Conclusion

This chapter has considered the results of the analysis undertaken on the programme participants of four of the eight entrepreneurship programmes described in the previous chapter. A general description of each of the survey groups was provided, and the various social, psychological and behavioural characteristics of the participants were analysed. Based on the programmes studied, it can be concluded that a wide range of individuals participate in entrepreneurship training programmes but that many of them share certain characteristics. Such characteristics include having a third level qualification, which is normally to degree standard, being mostly male, having work experience and being over 30 years of age. The participants surveyed appeared to be quite confident about their entrepreneurial characteristics but less confident with regard to their business skills and knowledge. Hence, the most popular reason for participating in the entrepreneurship programmes was to get support and guidance on setting up and running a business.

Chapter 8

Entrepreneurship Education and Training – Assessing Effectiveness

Introduction

In Chapter 4 it was concluded that even though there has been much debate as to whether or not entrepreneurship can be taught, most commentators believe that at least some of the elements of the subject can be developed and/or enhanced via education and training. However, while research in the area of entrepreneurship education and training is growing, one aspect into which little research has been conducted is that of assessing the impact of educational and training initiatives. It was noted that this was surprising, given the fact that the development and running of courses and programmes is potentially expensive in terms of time and money, both to participants and sponsors. Indeed, many training initiatives do not actually appear to address the real needs of entrepreneurs.

This chapter seeks to contribute to the literature in this area by presenting and discussing an in-depth, five-part longitudinal study of one of the entrepreneurship training programmes reviewed in Chapter 6. The particular programme chosen as the core focus of the study, can be described in Jamieson's (1984) terms as 'education for enterprise', a programme that focuses on the preparation of aspiring entrepreneurs for a career in self-employment with the specific objective of encouraging participants to set-up and run their own business. This study, one of the few longitudinal studies conducted in this field, tracks the progress of 35 aspiring entrepreneurs over a three year period, and provides a more qualitative insight into the effectiveness of such programmes.

The Five Part Longitudinal Study

In recognition of the limitations associated with evaluating the impact of entrepreneurship training programmes (as discussed in Chapter 4), a longitudinal approach, comprising the participants from programme A – the treatment group, as well as two other groups – a control group and a comparator group, was adopted. The use of a longitudinal approach allowed the research team, on the one hand, to fully determine the effectiveness of the core entrepreneurship programme studied and, on the other, to ascertain whether there was any change in how effectiveness was perceived over time (Fleming, 1996). Of particular importance in assessing the impact of entrepreneurship programmes is ensuring the validity of the methodology adopted. As discussed in Chapter 4, the most common approach to evaluating programmes is a subjective one, in which participants are asked for their views. While McMullan et al (2001) suggest that this is acceptable for determining participant satisfaction, objective measures should also be employed in order to assess the performance outcomes of a programme. Examples of such measures include the use of control samples and performance adjustments according to participants' subjective evaluations.

In this longitudinal study, as mentioned above, three groups were involved, and these were as follows:

• The Treatment Group – the core survey group which comprised the 35 participants from programme A, as described in Chapter 6.

• A Control Group – a group of 48 individuals who had a business idea and had applied for a place on an entrepreneurship programme around the same time as programme A began, but were not selected for participation, as explained in Chapter 5. Hence, this group received no entrepreneurship training (also referred to as the 'unexposed' group in this chapter).

• A Comparator Group – the 38 participants from programme C, as described in Chapter 6, who were facing a redundancy situation and who were provided with entrepreneurship training as part of a package of supports organised by their employer (also referred to as the 'redundancy' group in this chapter).

The additional measure of employing a control group and a comparator group would allow the effects and benefits of entrepreneurship training programmes to be examined in two completely different situations, hence widening the debate surrounding the rationale for interventions of this nature. In this longitudinal study the impact of the entrepreneurship training programme was measured from the participants' point of view through an investigation of the benefits derived by the individuals involved, an examination of their entrepreneurial development, and gauging whether the participants' perceptions of the programme changed over time. The economic outputs from the programmes, in terms of the number of new businesses created and the number of new jobs generated, were also analysed in an effort to supplement the sparse empirical evidence on effectiveness.

The longitudinal study, which was conducted over a three year period, was set up to run in parallel with, and beyond, the treatment programme (programme A), and involved the questioning of participants pre, during and post their participation in the programme. Thus, paper based questionnaires were designed and administered to the programme participants at the following stages:

Stage 1: Pre-programme
Stage 2: Half way through the programme
Stage 3: Upon completion of the entire programme

Stage 4: After 1 year post programme completion
Stage 5: After 2 years post programme completion (i.e. almost 3 years after joining the programme).

The objective of the first part of the study was to analyse the social, psychological and behavioural characteristics of the programme participants, and to investigate their reasons for joining the programme. These findings were included with the analysis of other participant groups presented in Chapter 7. This background information helped to provide a frame of reference against which the progress of the participants could be measured as they worked through the programme. For ease of reference, Table 8.1 has isolated key characteristics of the participants in the treatment group from the aggregated data reported in Chapter 7.

Table 8.1 Summary of the Characteristics of Participants in the Treatment Group (Programme A)

Table a): Social Characteristics (n =35)	
Nationality	All Irish: 80% (28) from ROI; 20% (7) from NI.
Sex	Male: 80% (28)
	Female: 20% (7)
Age	20-24 years: 26% (9)
	25-29 years: 48% (17)
	30-35 years: 26% (9)
Education	All educated to at least third level diploma standard
Educational Area	Business/Marketing: 40% (14)
	Engineering: 14% (5)
	Other: 46% (16)
Work Experience	Some experience: 97% (34)
	More than 3 years: 70% (25)
	Experience directly related to business idea: 44% (16)
Employment Status	Employed: 86% (30)
	Self-employed: 0% (0)
	Unemployed: 6% (2)
	Studying full-time: 8% (3)
Business Idea Type	All at feasibility/pre-feasibility stage
	Manufacturing based: 86% (30)
	Service based: 14% (5)

Figures in brackets indicate number of individuals.

In terms of their psychological characteristics, the participants in programme A appeared to be fairly confident individuals, giving themselves the highest rating in most areas, particularly in need for achievement, enthusiasm and innovativeness. Interestingly, their lowest scores were in judgement and risk taking, with a small number of respondents giving themselves a score of only 2 on the scale of 1 - 5.

With regard to the self-assessment of their business skills, the participants appeared to be less confident about their abilities, giving themselves a low rating against most of the skills listed, particularly against employment law, safety legislation and raising finance. Overall, the group's average rating against each of the business skills listed was much lower than that registered against the psychological characteristics.

The second part of the study, carried out half way through the programme, and following the formal training sessions, sought to evaluate the impact of the programme itself in terms of how the participants perceived the overall quality of the training received, what benefits had been derived, what skills had been learnt and whether they had made any useful contacts through the programme. In addition, the participants were asked to indicate whether they felt there were any gaps in the programme and suggest areas for improvement. Furthermore, having completed the formal training element of the programme, participants were again asked to rate their knowledge of key business skills so that a comparison could be made with the responses they had given prior to commencing the programme.

The third part of the study sought to evaluate other specific elements of the programme, such as the mentoring, assessment, qualification (National Vocational Qualification – NVQ) and competitive elements. In this respect, questionnaires were administered upon completion of the entire programme with the intention of gauging participants' overall opinions of the support they had received, and to determine whether there had been any change in their perceptions. By this stage, the mentoring and assessment sessions, the NVQ work, the business plan and the competition for the prize fund had all been completed. The group was asked to comment on the amount of work and time commitment required during the programme, and to assess whether this was more or less than had been expected. The participants were also asked how they felt the programme had impacted upon the development of their business ideas, on their entrepreneurial abilities and on their own personal development. Finally, the group was asked once again for their suggestions for improving the programme.

The fourth part of the study was administered just over one year after the participants had completed the programme, and was designed as a tracking process aimed at determining the number of participants who had set-up their businesses and the nature and employment levels of the new ventures created. With regard to those individuals who had not yet reached set-up stage, the survey sought to determine their employment status, whether they intended proceeding with their original or another business idea, and what further work was required to bring the business idea to start up stage. Once again, the participants were asked how they felt the programme had benefited them in an effort to determine whether their perceptions of the benefits gained had changed over time.

The fifth part of the study was undertaken just over two years after the participants had completed the entrepreneurship programme. This part of the research sought to determine whether there was a change in the number of new businesses set-up by the programme participants, as well as the nature of the businesses and their employment levels. Once again, with regard to those individuals who had not progressed with their business idea, the survey sought to determine the reasons for this and whether the participants were planning to develop the idea at some point in the future. The question of benefits was also raised, in order to determine once again whether there was any change in the participants' perceptions over time. In addition, the participants were asked for their suggestions for improving the programme and whether they felt personal confidence in their entrepreneurial ability had changed as a result of their participation.

The response rates at each stage of the study were reasonably high. Not surprisingly, the response rates for the first part of the study were the highest with the rate decreasing over time. In stage one a 100 per cent response rate was obtained, with all 35 of the individuals surveyed responding. By the time the second part of the survey was administered, two of the participants had dropped out of the scheme for work related reasons, leaving 33 to be surveyed, and of these, 32 useable responses were received. The third part of the survey yielded 25 responses out of the 33 surveyed, with the fourth part yielding 23 useable responses. The fifth and final part of the survey initially yielded a 52 per cent response rate (i.e. 17 responses) out of a total survey size of 33. However, with follow-up calls and reminder letters, the response rate for the fifth part of the study was increased to 70 per cent (i.e. 23 useable responses). The findings of this five part study, excluding those derived from the first part, which were included in Chapter 7, are presented below according to each stage.

Findings From Stage 2: Half Way Through the Programme

Completion of the formal training elements marked the halfway point of the programme, and at this stage, participants were asked for their general, overall opinion of the programme thus far. Responses were solicited in terms of the programme being 'very poor', 'poor', 'satisfactory', 'good' or 'excellent'. Fifty-six per cent of the respondents (18 participants) stated that they felt the programme was 'excellent', with the balance indicating that they felt the programme was 'good'. None of the respondents had a 'satisfactory', 'poor' or 'very poor' opinion of the programme. The individuals were also asked whether they felt their original expectations of the programme had been met. Over 90 per cent of the respondents stated that their expectations had been met, even at the half way stage of the programme, with the balance stating that they were 'unsure'.

In addition, participants were asked to describe the benefits they felt they had derived from the programme (see Table 8.2 below). Just under one third of the participants mentioned contact with other entrepreneurs as being the main benefit gained, with about 19 per cent stating that business training was a key benefit. Gaining a better understanding of general business operations and a knowledge of marketing and legal aspects were the next highest rated benefits. When asked what they felt was the single most important benefit that they had gained from the programme, the programme participants cited contact with other entrepreneurs and the production of a business plan.

Table 8.2 Benefits of the Programme (n=32)

Contact with other aspiring entrepreneurs	29%	Networking	6%
Business training	19%	Practical advice	3%
Knowledge of marketing & business legal issues	16%	Testing the business idea	3%
Better understanding of business operations	16%	Access to information	3%
Personal development	13%	Stimulation	3%
Knowledge from trainers	13%	Meeting experts in different fields	3%
Insight into business success factors	13%	In depth training & assessment	3%
Motivation	10%	Support	3%
Working to a schedule	6%	Various business techniques	3%

* Percentages do not total 100 due to multiple answers.

In order to investigate the extent to which the individuals networked within the programme, participants were asked whether they had made any valuable new contacts as a direct result of participating. About three-quarters of the participants said that they had made valuable new contacts, ranging from potential customers for their proposed products, to suppliers and contacts in foreign markets. In addition, it was interesting that the trainers and guest speakers contributing to the programme were also mentioned as useful new contact points for the entrepreneurs.

Participants were asked about the new skills and knowledge they had gained by taking part in the scheme (see Table 8.3). Responses ranged from marketing and financial skills, through to quality control. Marketing was the most common response, with over half of the group listing it as an important area in which they had gained new skills/knowledge.

Table 8.3 New Skills and Knowledge Gained (*n* = 32)

Marketing	52%	Unsure	3%
Finance	23%	Awareness of funding sources	3%
Business planning	19%	Production management	3%
HR management	10%	Ability to seek new networks	3%
Legal aspects	10%	Entrepreneurial skills	3%
Better understanding of start-up business requirements	6%	Assertiveness	3%
Better judgement	3%	Analytical techniques	3%
Information and training	3%	Communications	3%
Quality control	3%	Improved research methods	3%

* Percentages do not total 100 due to multiple answers.

In addition, the participants were asked to say what they felt was the single most important new skill or knowledge they had gained by participating in the programme. Although not shown in Table 8.3, business planning and marketing were the highest rated skills.

When asked whether they felt there were any gaps in the programme, half of the respondents in the programme indicated that there were. When asked to identify those gaps, the participants' responses ranged from 'not enough individually focused sessions', 'not enough information on finance, marketing and patenting', to 'not enough group sessions'. Surprisingly, while only 16 respondents had identified gaps in the programme, 25 respondents made suggestions for improving the programme. The most frequently mentioned recommendations were 'include more group work and practical sessions', 'adjust the time scale of the programme to cover more training over a longer period', and 'include more one-to-one sessions'.

In an effort to determine whether these aspiring entrepreneurs perceived the entrepreneurship programme as impacting upon the success of their proposed business ventures, the participants were asked how they felt the programme would facilitate the set-up of their businesses. Most of the respondents indicated that they felt the programme would have a 'significant impact' on their ability to reach set-up stage. Three of the respondents said that they felt the programme would have a 'minimum impact' on the set-up of their business, with the remaining respondents perceiving the programme to have a 'medium impact' in terms of helping them to reach set-up stage.

Given that the formal training part of the programme was completed at this stage of the study, it was important to determine which of the training elements were considered to be the most beneficial and which the least so. The marketing and legal training sessions were listed as the most beneficial. Those sessions perceived to be the least beneficial included human resource management and operations management.

The participants were also asked to indicate whether they felt there had been any improvement in their business skills and knowledge as a result of participating in the programme. In this regard, following completion of the training sessions, they were asked to rate themselves again against key business skills. The participants were not given a copy of their original ratings, and it was clear from the analysis that, overall, their mean ratings at the end of the training sessions had appeared to improve in every area. The areas where most improvement seemed to occur included employment legislation and business legal issues, with 1.07 and 1.01 points improvement level (on the original scale rating of 1-5), respectively, when compared to participants' original mean ratings. In order to determine whether this improvement was statistically significant, a paired sample test was undertaken on the raw data (individual scores) to further compare the participants' ratings before and after the training. The results of this test are shown in Table 8.4.

Table 8.4 Results of Paired Sample Test – Improvement in Business Skills and Knowledge (for the Treatment Group – Programme A)

Skill/Knowledge Area	Mean Difference	Standard Deviation Difference	Valid Cases	*t*-Test Statistic
Raising finance	0.44	1.3664	32	1.822
Sales management	0.41	1.0115	32	2.293
Managing cash flow	0.66	1.2854	32	2.905
Managing staff	0.39	1.2296	31	1.766
Business legal issues	1.06	1.2365	31	4.773
Health and safety legislation	1.06	1.4591	31	4.045
Employment legislation	1.09	1.2011	32	5.134
Stock control	0.69	1.4013	32	2.785
Work planning and scheduling	0.22	1.2374	32	1.006
Quality control	0.41	1.2916	32	1.796
Quality standards	0.56	1.2936	32	2.449
Market research and planning	0.66	1.0035	32	3.721

($n = 32$, with 31 in some cases, as indicated. Alpha value = 0.05).

The null hypothesis was that there would be no increase in the participants' ratings after the training. The figure of 1.645 was taken from the *t* tables with an alpha value of 0.05. Therefore, if in the calculation the critical value is less than 1.645, then the null hypothesis cannot be rejected. As Table 8.4 shows, the test statistic was greater than 1.645 in all but one case (work planning and scheduling). These results provide enough evidence to reject the null hypothesis, indicating that the training programme made a significant positive impact on the participants' business skills and knowledge. The fact that most of the participants also felt that the programme had a 'significant (positive) impact' on their own personal development provides further evidence supporting the point that entrepreneurship programmes yield measurable benefits for participants. The participants' perceptions that their own entrepreneurial abilities had improved as a result of their participation in the programme, a point highlighted in Caird's study (1989), helps to strengthen this conclusion.

Findings from Stage 3: Upon Completion of the Programme

During the second half of programme A, participants received a series of mentoring and assessment sessions on a one-to-one basis. At the end of these, the group was asked to rate these elements of the programme in terms of neutral, beneficial and very beneficial (see Table 8.5).

Table 8.5 Ratings of Mentoring and Assessment Sessions ($n = 25$)

Rating	Mentoring Sessions	Assessment Sessions
Neutral	24%	20%
Beneficial	36%	36%
Very Beneficial	32%	40%
Didn't attend these sessions	8%	0%

It was significant that over two thirds of the participants found the mentoring and assessment sessions to be either beneficial or very beneficial, since this relates to their wish for more one-to-one sessions.

Part of programme A also involved the completion of work towards an NVQ qualification at Level 3. All 33 of the participants who completed the programme were offered the opportunity to obtain this qualification, and of these, 23 submitted evidence for assessment. Twenty of these candidates managed to achieve NVQ certification for various units of the course, with the remaining three not providing sufficient evidence within the time scale for the NVQ award.   At the very end of the programme, the participants were asked how beneficial they felt the NVQ accreditation was to their project. Forty per cent of the group rated it as being 'beneficial' to their project, with 24 per cent rating it as 'very beneficial', and the balance rating it as being of 'neutral benefit'. In terms of the work required to obtain the qualification, as well as the time scale allowed in which to complete it, all those who responded to this part of the survey felt that the work-load was more than anticipated and that not enough time was given for its completion. However, more than half of the participants surveyed felt that it was important for aspiring entrepreneurs to gain certification for work completed in the area of business preparation and planning (Henry et al, 1997).

In order to determine if there had been any change over time with respect to the perception of benefits derived from the programme, participants were asked for their views in this regard. The 'training sessions' and the 'completion of a business plan' were each mentioned by 40 per cent of the respondents as being the most beneficial aspects of the programme, with the prize fund listed by 28 per cent as the least beneficial aspect. It was surprising to note that the mentoring sessions were mentioned by 20 per cent of respondents as the next least beneficial part of the programme, when 68 per cent of the respondents had rated these as either 'beneficial' or 'very beneficial' in a previous question (see Table 8.5). Furthermore, in stage two of the study, some of the participants had indicated their preference for more individually focused sessions, which would normally take the form of mentoring sessions. However, five participants also stated that all elements in the programme were beneficial. One of the participants even commented that he felt 'special' participating in the programme.

With all aspects of the programme completed, the aspiring entrepreneurs were again asked to what degree they felt their original expectations had been met. Using a Likert scale, where a rating of 1 equated to 'not at all' and 5 equated to 'very well', 80 per cent of respondents registered a 4 or higher, with 36 per cent (nine individuals) registering a 5 on the scale.

In order to further test the impact of entrepreneurship training, participants were asked whether they felt they would have developed their business idea to its current stage without the help of the programme. Almost two thirds of the respondents (64 per cent) stated that they would possibly not have developed their business idea to its current stage without the help of the programme. So as to determine how the group benefited in terms of their own personal development as a result of taking part in the training scheme, the participants were asked to rate the programme's impact in this respect. Using a Likert scale of 1 - 5, where 1 represented 'no real impact' and 5 represented 'significant impact', 72 per cent of respondents registered a 4 or higher. In addition, the participants were asked to state whether their confidence in their own entrepreneurial abilities had improved as a direct result of the programme. Again using a scale of 1 - 5, where 1 implied 'no more confident than before' and 5 implied 'significantly more confident', 52 per cent of the participants registered a 4 or higher. It was also interesting to note that, by the end of the programme, three of the participants reported that their businesses had already reached set-up stage. Fifteen of the survey respondents said that they intended to proceed to set-up stage but needed to do more work on product development and finding investors.

Now that all elements of the programme had been completed, participants were again asked whether they felt there were any gaps in the programme. While in general, most of the participants surveyed stated that there were no significant gaps in the programme, most offered at least one recommendation for improvement. The four main recommendations offered comprised the need for more group sessions in the programme, the inclusion of more 'real' entrepreneurs, and the provision of more one-to-one mentoring sessions, as well as allowing more time for the completion of the business plan and NVQ work. Other suggestions included offering more discussion with participants about their individual ideas, and providing more training sessions.

Findings From Stage 4: One Year Post Completion

The two main foci of this stage of the study were on economic outputs and ascertaining to what stage the participants had progressed since completing the programme. Thus participants were asked whether their business idea had reached set-up stage. Eight of the respondents claimed that they had now set-up their business, generating a total of 16 new jobs. The mean number of jobs generated per new business created from the programme was two. With regard to those participants who had not reached set-up stage (15 respondents), they were asked whether they intended proceeding with their business idea and whether the idea had changed significantly since their participation in the programme. Three individuals stated that they did not intend proceeding with their idea, with the remaining twelve respondents stating that it was their intention to proceed. Of those who expressed their intention to continue working on their business ideas, eight individuals stated that their idea had changed significantly from their original one as a result of participating in the programme. In most cases, the participants viewed funding and R & D as the main ingredients they now needed to bring their ideas to the implementation stage. At this stage in the study over half of the respondents were employed, while three were continuing their education on a full-time basis.

So as to determine whether there had been any change in the participants' perception of the benefits they derived from the programme over time, respondents were asked to specify those aspects they perceived to be most useful (see Table 8.6).

Table 8.6 Benefits Perceived After One Year ($n = 23$)

Benefit	Frequency of response
Business advice and training	41% (9)
Provide a structure and helped with planning	27% (6)
Helped to access funding	18% (4)
Other (various)	18% (4)
Contacts and networking	14% (3)
Prestige – beneficial when dealing with banks/agencies	14% (3)
General support and guidance	9% (2)
Gave confidence	5% (1)
Helped in getting a job	5% (1)
Mentors	5% (1)

Multiple responses given. Figures in brackets represent the number of respondents.

Findings From Stage 5: Two Years Post Completion

Stage five of the study sought to determine the participants' level of progress two years after completing the programme in terms of their employment status, business idea and personal development. In addition, the objective was to determine whether there had been any change in the perceived benefits over time and to compare any changes with findings from earlier parts of the study. The participants were again asked about their employment status in order to determine whether there had been any change since the last study one year previously. This part of the study revealed that 14 of the respondents were employed and a further 8 were self-employed. It was interesting to note that only one of the respondents was continuing his/her education on a full-time basis, and none was unemployed.

The fact that the majority of the survey respondents in programme A had not actually gone on to set-up their businesses subsequent to their participation in the programme is another interesting finding of this research, and one that might actually be viewed as an important, positive outcome. Helping individuals to realise that their business ideas may not be viable, or that significant further development is required, is one of the often overlooked roles of entrepreneurship training programmes.

As it was more than two years since the programme had been completed, the participants were asked whether they had continued to work on their business ideas. Thirteen of the respondents stated that they had continued to work on their business ideas, and eight of these had now set-up their business, collectively employing a total of 40 people. The mean number of employees per new business was five.

For those who had not continued working on their ideas, it appeared that this was mainly due to the individual concerned having taken a full time job, losing confidence in their ideas or realising that the proposed venture was not feasible. Losing interest, a lack of finance and feeling that the project was too time consuming were among other reasons given by the participants for not continuing work on their business idea after the programme. Seven of these respondents stated that they did not intend continuing with their business idea in the future, mostly because they realised that there was no market for the product or that they would need too much capital investment. One participant felt that there was too much risk involved and another claimed that a competitor had copied her idea. In contrast, six of the respondents who had not continued working on their idea after the programme, stated that they did intend proceeding at some point in the future but required finance, additional market research, production facilities and a good financial plan. These individuals anticipated that they would set-up their business within a four-year period. The other individuals could not say when they might be in a position to start their business.

As in previous parts of the study, the question of benefits was raised once again in order to determine whether there had been any change in the participants' perceptions of the programme benefits over time. The main benefits perceived by respondents were training and completing a business plan, which corresponds to those outlined at the end of stage four.

In terms of the least beneficial aspect of the programme, the prize fund, networking and the mentoring and assessment sessions were the main elements mentioned. Seven respondents could not say which was the least beneficial aspect, as they were either unsure, or felt that all of the elements were of benefit.   The group was also asked whether, at this stage, they would recommend any improvements to the programme.   While there were several different individual suggestions, providing follow-up support and including more mentoring sessions in the programme, were the main recommendations offered.

It was interesting to note that, in terms of the respondents' perceptions of their own entrepreneurial ability, 12 individuals stated that they now felt *more confident* in their entrepreneurial ability than before. Six individuals stated that they felt *considerably more confident* than before, and five individuals indicated that they perceived *no change* in their entrepreneurial ability.

Changes over Time

Table 8.7 indicates the employment status of the participants in programme A at the beginning, at the end, and at one and two years post programme completion. It is interesting to note that there was a small positive change in the number of individuals who had been unemployed, with none of the respondents indicating that he/she was unemployed one or two years after the programme, compared with two individuals being unemployed at the beginning and at the end of the programme.   The most significant change in the employment status of the respondents was in the number of individuals starting their own businesses and thus being termed self-employed.

Table 8.7 Change in Employment Status (Treatment Group – Programme A)

Overall Change - (*n* = various, as indicated)				
Status	At the beginning (*n* =35)	At end (*n* =25)	After 1 year (*n* =23)	After 2 years (*n* =23)
Employed (E)	30 (86%)	18 (72%)	12 (52%)	14 (61%)
Self-employed (SE)	0 (0%)	3 (12%)	8 (35%)	8 (35%)
Unemployed (UE)	2 (6%)	2 (8%)	0 (0%)	0 (0%)
Studying full-time (SFT)	3 (8%)	2 (8%)	3 (13%)	1 (4%)

Figures in brackets indicate percentages.   The figures relating to the beginning of the programme were taken from the individuals' application forms.

Since the response rated varied at each part of the survey, as indicated in Table 8.7, it is clear that the same individuals did not respond at each part of the survey (i.e. some individuals responded to the survey at the end of the programme but not to the survey after 1 year). Thus, to further investigate the change in employment status of the participants in programme A, those individuals ($n = 15$) who consistently responded to each part of the survey were identified, and the specific change in their employment status was tracked over the three year period (see Table 8.8).

As Table 8.8 indicates, while there was no change in the employment status of four of the individuals (participants 004, 005, 010 and 032), there was a positive change in the status of most of the other individuals following completion of the programme, with a move from unemployed, employed or studying full-time status, to either employed or self-employed. Two of these individuals (participants 025 and 031) set-up their own businesses and moved to a self-employed status for a year, before returning to full-time, traditional employment. Two other individuals (participants 017 and 019) returned to full-time education as postgraduate students one year after completing the programme, and then took up full-time jobs once their courses were finished.

Table 8.8 Specific Tracking of Programme Participants in the Treatment Group (Programme A)

($n = 15$)	At the beginning	At end	After 1 year	After 2 years
004	E	E	E	E
005	E	E	E	E
006	SFT	SFT	E	E
008	E	SE	SE	SE
010	E	E	E	E
013	SFT	E	E	E
014	E	SE	SE	SE
017	E	E	SFT	E
019	E	E	SFT	E
021	UE	UE	E	SE
025	E	E	SE	E
027	E	E	SE	SE
031	E	E	SE	E
032	E	E	E	E
035	SFT	SFT	SFT	E

E = Employed; SE = Self-employed; UE = Unemployed; SFT = Studying full-time.

As already mentioned, none of the participants in the treatment group had set-up his/her business prior to joining the programme. The survey conducted one year after programme A had been completed revealed that eight of the participants had set-up their businesses employing a collective total of 16 people with a mean employment level of two per business. By the time the final part of the study had been completed one year later (i.e. at two years post programme completion) the collective total employment level had risen to 40, with a mean employment level of five people per business.

In order to determine whether there had been a change in the perception of the benefits derived by the participants, it was important to consider the participants' original expectations prior to commencing the programme. Most of the participants had listed *support and guidance on setting up a business* and *completing a business plan* as their main expectations from the programme, with twelve and eleven participants mentioning these, respectively. The *opportunity to test the feasibility of the business idea* and *being able to gain new skills and knowledge* were among the least mentioned expectations, with two and four participants mentioning these, respectively. When the participants were asked about benefits half way through the programme, *contact with other entrepreneurs* and *training* were the most frequently mentioned benefits, with the *opportunity to test the feasibility of the idea* being the least mentioned benefit. At the end of the programme, there had been a slight change in the participants' perceptions of the benefits derived by them, with training and completing a business plan being mentioned more frequently by participants as the main benefits. Surprisingly, at this point the mentoring was mentioned as the least beneficial aspect of the programme.

One year after completing programme A, the responses from the participants were more or less similar to those given at the end of the programme, with training once again being the most frequently mentioned benefit and mentoring being the least mentioned. Two years after completing the programme, most of the participants were still listing training as the key benefit, while completing the business plan was highlighted by six of the respondents. Surprisingly, at this point, the opportunity to test the feasibility of the business idea was the least frequently mentioned benefit, despite this being included as one of the participants' original expectations at the outset. This would imply that the programme did not provide sufficient opportunity for participants to do this.

In terms of personal development, there appeared to be a significant difference in how the participants felt about their entrepreneurial abilities between the end of the programme and two years later. Upon completion of the programme 52 per cent of the participants indicated that they were either *more* or *significantly more* confident about their entrepreneurial ability than before. In the survey conducted two years later (stage 5 of the longitudinal study) this figure had risen to 78 per cent of respondents.

Although the satisfaction level with the programme appeared to be high at every stage, the participants made a number of different suggestions for improvement at the various stages of the study. Half way through the programme participants recommended including more group sessions, more one-to-one sessions and allowing more time to complete the programme. At the end of the programme, these were still the main recommendations offered by the participants. Two years later at the final part of the study, the provision of follow-up support and the inclusion of more one-to-one and mentoring sessions were the most frequently mentioned recommendations for improvement. It is noteworthy that the participants consistently mentioned the desire for more one-to-one sessions when they had rated these as the least beneficial aspect of the programme.

Comparisons with the Control and Comparator Groups

Since there had not been the same degree of contact with the control group (i.e those individuals who had not received entrepreneurship training) as there had been with the other two groups (i.e. the treatment group – participants from programme A, and the comparator group – the redundancy group from programme C), no psychological self analysis had been conducted on this particular group. Therefore, it was felt that this would be a good opportunity to include such a test. The General Enterprising Tendency (GET) test was chosen, as described in Chapter 5, and this was administered to all three groups (the treatment group, the control group and the comparator group). This was done to facilitate comparison and to further supplement the self-analysis conducted in both the treatment and the comparator groups in the early stages of the study. From the treatment group, 16 useable test scores were received. There were 12 useable test scores received from the control group, and 10 received from the comparator group (see Table 8.9). It is interesting to note that, if the overall GET scores of both the control and comparator groups are compared with those of the treatment group, there does not appear to be a significant difference. The comparator group had the highest mean overall GET score at 38.2, compared to 36.5 in the control group and 37.69 in the treatment group. In fact, the highest mean scores for need for achievement, internal locus of control and calculated risk taking were all registered in the comparator group, with the control group and the treatment groups registering higher mean average scores in only need for autonomy and creative tendency, respectively.

Table 8.9 Mean GET Scores for the Treatment, Control and Comparator Groups

GET Score Categories	Treatment Group (A) (*n* =16)	Control Group (*n* =12)	Comparator Group (C) (*n* =10)
Overall GET	37.69	36.5	38.2
Need for Achievement	8.56	8.7	9.7
Need for Autonomy/Independence	3.69	3.83	3.2
Internal Locus of Control	8	8.42	9
Creative Tendency	8.5	7.67	7.3
Calculated Risk Taking	8.94	7.83	9

It was also interesting that, in total, only 15 of the 38 individuals who completed the GET in the three groups, scored over the GET mean score of 41.04. This is the figure identified by Caird (1991) as significant, in her study, in determining the enterprising tendency of business owner-managers. Of these, six were in the treatment group, four in the control group, and five in the comparator group.

While this study provides insufficient evidence that aspiring entrepreneurs actually possess the key psychological characteristics required for entrepreneurial success, it does provide sufficient evidence to suggest that aspiring entrepreneurs perceive themselves to possess such characteristics. In contrast, and perhaps understandably, the aspiring entrepreneurs surveyed in this study were less confident about their business skills and knowledge, suggesting that many individuals participate in entrepreneurship programmes to develop such skills.

In order to further investigate the possibility of statistically significant differences between the GET scores, a non-paired *t* test was conducted to analyse the differences between the means in each group. Based on the null hypothesis that there was no significant difference, i.e. that the mean difference would be equal to zero, the *t*-test was conducted, and the results are presented in Table 8.10.

Since in all cases the test statistic was not greater than the critical value, it can be concluded that there are no significant differences between the groups' mean GET scores.

Table 8.10 Results of Non-paired *t*-Test to Compare GET Scores

		NAch	NAut	Locus	Create	Cal Risk	Total
Treat.[1]	Mean 1	8.56	3.69	8	8.5	8.94	37.69
Ctrl[2]	Mean 2	8.75	3.83	8.42	7.67	7.83	36.5
	N1	16	16	16	16	16	16
	N2	12	12	12	12	12	12
	S1	2.2500	1.5800	1.8300	2.1300	2.4600	8.0600
	S2	2.2600	1.5300	2.1100	2.3500	2.3300	6.6500
	S^2	5.0816	2.4306	3.8156	4.9539	5.7882	56.1885
	Test stat	-0.2207	-0.2351	-0.5630	0.9765	1.2082	0.4157
	Dof	26	26	26	26	26	26
	Crit value	2.056	2.056	2.056	2.056	2.056	2.056
Treat.[1]	Mean 1	8.56	3.69	8	8.5	8.94	37.69
Comp[2]	Mean 2	9.7	3.2	9	7.3	9	38.2
	N1	16	16	16	16	16	16
	N2	10	10	10	10	10	10
	S1	2.2500	1.5800	1.8300	2.1300	2.4600	8.0600
	S2	1.7000	1.9900	1.8900	2.1100	2.2100	7.4100
	S^2	4.2478	3.0453	3.4326	4.5051	5.6138	61.1928
	Test stat	-1.3721	0.6966	-1.3389	1.4025	-0.0628	-0.1617
	Dof	24	24	24	24	24	24
	Crit value	2.064	2.064	2.064	2.064	2.064	2.064
Ctrl[1]	Mean 1	8.75	3.83	8.42	7.67	7.83	36.5
Comp[2]	Mean 2	9.7	3.2	9	7.3	9	38.2
	N1	12	12	12	12	12	12
	N2	10	10	10	10	10	10
	S1	2.2600	1.5300	2.1100	2.3500	2.3300	6.6500
	S2	1.7000	1.9900	1.8900	2.1100	2.2100	7.4100
	S^2	4.1097	3.0695	4.0561	5.0408	5.1837	49.0310
	Test stat	-1.0945	0.8398	-0.6726	0.3849	-1.2002	-0.5670
	Dof	20	20	20	20	20	20
	Crit value	2.086	2.086	2.086	2.086	2.086	2.086

A number of other areas were examined in the control and comparator groups, and comparisons were then made with the treatment group. The comparisons between these groups were made at the same time that stage 5 of the longitudinal study was conducted. These comparisons, which focus mainly on economic outputs, the progress of the business idea and the benefits derived, are presented in Table 8.11.

Table 8.11 Group Comparisons

Survey Question Area	Treatment Group (A)	Control Group	Comparator Group (C)
Survey size	$n=33$	$n=48$	$n=38$
Response rate	23 (70%)	18 (38%)	19 (50%)
Employment status:			
- Employed	14 (61%)	11 (61%)	6 (32%)
- Self-employed	8 (35%)	3 (17%)	9 (47%)
- Unemployed	0 (0%)	3 (17%)	4 (21%)
- Studying full-time	1 (4%)	2 (11%)	0 (0%)
Continued working on business idea:			
- Yes	13 (57%)	5 (28%)	13 (68%)
- No	10 (44%)	13 (72%)	6 (32%)
New businesses created	8	3	9
Total of new jobs generated	40	19	9
Mean employment level per new business	5	6	1

Figures in brackets indicate the percentage responses.

It was interesting to note that, in the control group, the group where the individuals received no entrepreneurship training, less than one third of the respondents actually continued working on their business idea after applying for a place on the entrepreneurship programmes. Not surprisingly, all of those who participated in the treatment and comparator group programmes (excluding the two participants who dropped out half way through the treatment group programme) continued working on their business ideas for at least the duration of the programmes, and over half of these continued working on their ideas after completing the programmes.

In terms of those individuals who did not continue working on their ideas, there appeared to be several reasons for this. For those in the comparator group, the main reasons given were that the individual was offered a full time job, that the other partner involved pulled out of the project, or it was concluded that the idea was either not viable or not suited to them. For the control group (the group which received no entrepreneurship training), the reasons given included the individual being offered a full time job, not being picked for participation in one of the programmes, or lacking confidence, time or commitment.

The Control Group

Since most of the individuals in the control group did not continue working on their business idea after being turned down for the entrepreneurship training programmes, few sought further help. Two of the respondents were offered and accepted a place on another entrepreneurship programme, and another secured a small grant for his project. At the time of the survey, (i.e. around 3 years after applying for the entrepreneurship programmes), four of the respondents indicated that they intended proceeding with their business idea at some point in the future. However, to achieve this aim they indicated that a number of issues would have to be addressed first. Two respondents indicated that further research was needed, one needed to secure capital investment, one respondent felt that he/she needed to obtain proper advice, while another had to prepare a business plan. Although one of the respondents in this category indicated that he/she expected the business to be set up within one year, the others gave no indication of an anticipated start date. Of the five respondents who did not intend proceeding with their ideas, two stated that this was because they preferred full time employment.

These respondents were also asked to state how they thought the entrepreneurship programme would have helped them, had they participated. Although the responses were varied, the respondents stated that the entrepreneurship programme would have provided them with the necessary business skills and knowledge, given them access to advice on starting up a business, helped them to realise the amount of time and work required, provided them with a financial foundation, offered networking opportunities, motivated them to reach set-up stage and given them confidence. Two of the respondents said that they did not know how the programme might have helped them, and one said that he was certain the programme would have helped but he was unable to indicate how.

The Comparator Group

Of those individuals in the comparator group (the redundancy group) who had not already set-up their business, only one stated that he intended proceeding with his idea in the future. This particular respondent claimed that no further resources would be required in order to reach set-up stage. Of the eight individuals who did not intend proceeding with their business proposals, this appeared to be mainly due to having taken a full time job, their proposed business partner having pulled out of the project, requiring high capital investment or the individual losing interest in the project. In terms of the actual training and support received, programme C (redundancy group) participants rated the training on marketing, sources of funding and how to develop the business idea as the most beneficial aspects of the programme. In contrast, the least beneficial aspects of the programme were cited as those sessions facilitated by bankers, as well as the finance/cash flow sessions.

The participants in the comparator group were also asked whether they felt their confidence in their entrepreneurial ability had changed as a result of the programme. Eight of the respondents said that they felt *no change* in this regard, and six respondents said that they felt more confident in their entrepreneurial ability than before. Interestingly, two of the respondents said that they actually felt *less confident* than before, and three respondents did not state whether there had been any change.

Suggestions were also sought from the comparator group for improving their particular entrepreneurship programme. The recommendations offered included inviting real entrepreneurs as guest speakers, providing case studies of real successful businesses, allowing more time for each training session, providing more financial planning, introducing small group sessions, and providing individual training focused on each type of business idea.

Assessing the Impact of Entrepreneurship Training

In attempting to determine the impact of the core entrepreneurship programme in this study, i.e. programme A, the employment status of the participants in this group (the treatment group), as well as those in the comparator group (the redundancy group – programme C), was determined prior to the commencement of the programmes as well as after their completion. At the start of programme A, 30 participants were employed, two were unemployed, three were in full-time study and none was self-employed (see Table 8.7 for further details). On completion of the authors' longitudinal study, 14 of the participants in this group were employed, eight had started their own business and one was engaged in full-time study. In terms of the comparator group (programme C participants), all of the respondents in that group, although employed at the beginning of the study, were facing a redundancy situation. After the participants had completed programme C, of those who responded to the survey, six were employed, nine were self-employed, four were unemployed and none was engaged in full-time study.

Comparisons were also drawn with the respondents in the control group, i.e. those who had not received any entrepreneurship training. The original employment status of the 18 individuals in the control group was 14 individuals employed and four in full-time study. None was self-employed or unemployed. When stage 5 of the longitudinal study was completed, of those who responded to the survey, eleven were employed, three were self-employed, three were unemployed and two were studying full-time.

Even though there was not a 100% response rate from all three groups, it can be concluded that there was a more noticeable positive change in the employment status of the two groups that were *exposed* to the entrepreneurship training (the treatment and comparator groups), when compared to the *unexposed* group (the control group). Furthermore, there were significantly more new businesses created in the treatment and comparator groups than in the control group. The increase in the number of those becoming employed, as well as the decrease in the number of those originally unemployed, bearing in mind the imminent redundancy situation facing the comparator group, reinforces the point that the non-exposed group (the control group) fared less well than the other two groups, and further underlines the benefits of the entrepreneurship training.

Drawing Conclusions from the Longitudinal Study

From this in-depth analysis it may be concluded that the participants' perceptions of the programme were quite positive, with several benefits being highlighted. Most of the participants felt more confident in their entrepreneurial ability after the programme than before, and they also felt that their business ideas had progressed significantly since joining the programme. The economic benefits of the programme were also evident in the positive change in employment status, the number of new businesses created, and the number of new jobs generated following the programme. In this respect, it was clear that the two groups of individuals who actually participated in an entrepreneurship programme and received training (i.e. the treatment group – participants from programme A, and the comparator group – participants from programme C – the redundancy programme) fared better than the control group (i.e. those who had received no entrepreneurship training). One of the most significant findings of this part of the research was that the participants perceived the entrepreneurship programmes to have made a significant positive impact on the level of their business skills and knowledge, and to have positively facilitated the set-up of their businesses. In addition, one of the main benefits of the entrepreneurship programmes, as revealed by this research, was the opportunity for the participants to network with other aspiring entrepreneurs. Despite this, however, a number of gaps were identified in the programmes and several recommendations for improving them were advanced by the participants.

Entrepreneurship Training Programmes – A Framework

Despite an increase in the amount of research conducted in the area of entrepreneurship education and training, there is little consensus with respect to how best to design and develop appropriate courses and programmes. Indeed, great diversity exists with regard to determining the learning outcomes, content, structure, delivery mode and target audience of entrepreneurship education and training programmes. Given the lack of uniformity in this area, as highlighted in Chapter 4, and on the basis of the conclusions drawn from each stage of the empirical research reported in this monograph, the authors have proposed a framework for informing the development of future entrepreneurship training programmes. The particular focus of such a framework is on programmes which support *aspiring* rather than *established* entrepreneurs; programmes which have the primary objective of assisting participants to set-up and run their own businesses – what Jamieson (1984) terms *education for enterprise* and what Garavan and Ó Cinnéide (1994) describe as *education and training for small business ownership.* As has been highlighted previously, assessing the effectiveness of entrepreneurship education and training programmes is a complex issue due to the number of variables which have to be taken into consideration. With reference to the available literature to date, the authors developed a research methodology to attempt to ascertain the impact of a number of entrepreneurship programmes. Based on the empirical research subsequently conducted, a number of elements were identified as being important to consider when designing and developing future programmes. Thus, the various components of the seemingly most effective programmes, in terms of structure, duration, training, content and outputs, as highlighted in Chapter 6, have been incorporated into the framework proposed by the authors.

Part of the rationale for this approach is that the programmes reviewed by the authors currently exist, and their impact has actually been established. In particular, the Dutch programme and the Irish cross-border programme (programme B) appeared to have the highest success rates in terms of converting participants' proposals into new businesses. Moreover, the Finnish programme appeared to contribute most to economic development, with the highest levels of new business and new job creation per programme. In addition, it was interesting to note that the Spanish programme, although not one of the most successful programmes, was the only one which *tested* participants prior to their participation, not to determine who was most suitable, but rather, to identify weaknesses which could be addressed in the training. The inclusion of such a test should be considered in any framework aimed at improving the training and educational opportunities for aspiring entrepreneurs. However, such a framework would be incomplete without considering the type of individual who actually participates in entrepreneurship programmes, as well as their expectations, opinions and recommendations.

From the surveys conducted, it was clear that many aspiring entrepreneurs tend to have received a third level education to at least diploma standard, with a high proportion having completed primary or postgraduate degrees. Furthermore, most of those surveyed had at least one year's work experience, with most having more than three years' experience. Their experience was varied, however, almost half of those surveyed had worked in an area directly related to their proposed business venture. This profile of the aspiring entrepreneur – the individual who is considering becoming an entrepreneur – must be considered when developing a framework, since it impacts on what the programme participants expect. From the research conducted, it would appear that participants in entrepreneurship programmes have four main expectations, which include support and guidance on setting up and running a business, completing a business plan, exploring the feasibility aspects and developing the business idea and gaining new skills and knowledge.

Furthermore, in terms of profile, most aspiring entrepreneurs perceive themselves to be enthusiastic, innovative, initiative takers, committed/determined and confident, with a high need for achievement. However, this study also indicated that the programme participants surveyed did not rate themselves as highly in areas such as risk taking, leadership, communication and judgement abilities. In terms of their skills and knowledge, they perceived their main weaknesses to be in the areas of sales management, business and legal issues, health and safety, and employment legislation. Hence, it would appear appropriate to include these elements in an entrepreneurship training programme.

The five-part longitudinal study indicated that the main benefits derived by the participants included training sessions, business advice, the completion of a business plan, and networking. In addition, participants mentioned the opportunity to test the feasibility of the business idea as a key benefit. The mentoring and assessment sessions also received favourable feedback when evaluated separately. Overall, the participants mentioned the marketing and legal training sessions as the most beneficial. Recommendations for improvement included the provision of more group sessions, more one-to-one sessions, incorporating more real entrepreneurs as guest speakers and allowing more time to complete the programme. The inclusion of follow-up support was suggested in a later part of the survey.

As well as including the recommendations and opinions of programme participants, it was felt that, in order to obtain as holistic a perspective as possible, the experiences and views of the programme providers and funders should be included. In the interviews with these individuals, it was felt that the comments about the benefits to the participants and the difficulties encountered, as well as any changes planned, were those most relevant for inclusion in such a framework. With regard to benefits, the providers' views appeared to correspond with those of the programme participants in that they felt the practical workshops, expert advice, peer learning, the step-by-step approach to developing the business idea and the hand-holding, were the key benefits for participants. In addition, the funders believed that the training, the opportunity to provide a 'reality check' on the feasibility of the business ideas, the reduction of risk, as well as the association with a third level educational establishment, were the main benefits to the participants.

The only difficulties encountered were those of the programme providers, which concerned funding, and thus impacted on the amount of expert consultancy available to participants. With regard to changes to the programmes, again, only the providers had any plans in this respect, suggesting the inclusion of more training sessions, more entrepreneurs as guest speakers, a wider range of services, access to venture capital and a pre-programme session for aspiring entrepreneurs to raise awareness of existing courses. The Irish Institute of Technology that was responsible for programmes A, B and C also mentioned their concern over the excessive focus on the business plan and the increasing difficulty of getting *deliverables* from participants.

Summary and Conclusion

This chapter has presented the findings from the authors' in-depth, five-part longitudinal study which focused on one of the entrepreneurship training programmes reviewed in the previous chapter (programme A) and, for analytical purposes, mainly referred to in this chapter as 'the treatment group'.

The findings from this part of the study have helped to highlight the benefits derived by the programme participants, as well as the new skills and knowledge they gained. The changes in the participants' perceptions of the programme benefits from one stage of the survey to the next were also noted, and the overall economic outputs in terms of new businesses and jobs created were calculated.

The progress of the treatment group was also compared to the progress of two other groups – a *control* group consisting of individuals who had business ideas but did not participate in any of the entrepreneurship training programmes, and a *comparator* group which consisted of a group of individuals who were facing a redundancy situation and were provided with entrepreneurship training (through programme C) as part of a support package offered by their employer. Findings from this part of the research further highlighted the seemingly positive impact of entrepreneurship training on aspiring entrepreneurs.

On the basis of this empirical research, a number of issues for consideration by both researchers and providers of entrepreneurship training courses and programmes have emerged. These will be discussed in more detail in the next chapter.

Chapter 9

Conclusion

Introduction

This study began with a discussion on the role and importance of entrepreneurship and new business creation to both the economy and society in general. There is strong evidence to show that entrepreneurship is not only important, but also critical to the development and growth of a healthy economy. The expansion in the small firms sector is particularly important because, as many have noted, not only has there been a significant increase in the number of small businesses, but there has also been an increase in their share of employment. The fact that most companies in the European Union are SMEs, and account for around two thirds of total employment, and over 60% of business turnover, serves to further underline the importance of the small firms sector.

Given the above, there is a powerful argument in support of intervention. However, since a great deal of time and money is involved in supporting new business development, and in view of the difficulties associated with determining the effectiveness of support mechanisms, the debate surrounding intervention will no doubt continue. That said, one cannot overlook the fact that intervention exists, and that intervention policy already receives considerable attention. This is demonstrated by the constantly changing enterprise policies of countries such as Ireland, as well as the extensive range of interventions currently in existence in the UK, as discussed in Chapter 1.

The main aim of this study was to investigate the nature and effectiveness of entrepreneurship education and training, and to make a particular contribution in the area of entrepreneurship training. Having reviewed the theoretical foundation in Part I, a comprehensive study was presented in Part II and this comprised of a comparative analysis of eight entrepreneurship training programmes from five European countries, as well as a longitudinal study which tracked the progress of a group of 35 aspiring entrepreneurs over a three year period. In addition, the characteristic variables of a total of 102 programme participants were analysed in an attempt to build a profile of the aspiring entrepreneur. The case studies were selected mainly on the basis of accessibility and represented typical examples of entrepreneurship training programmes managed by universities or third level institutes. The core group of 35 aspiring entrepreneurs was selected because it appeared to be the largest entrepreneurship programme (in terms of number of participants) in operation at the time, and was accessible to the authors.

This chapter presents a framework for aiding the development of entrepreneurship training programmes, derived from a synthesis of the information generated by the constituent elements of the study; summarises the main conclusions that can be drawn from the study overall, and discusses the implications for entrepreneurship programme design, provision and effectiveness.

A Framework for Entrepreneurship Training

If the elements identified in the previous chapter are drawn together, then a framework for aiding in the development of entrepreneurship training programmes might take the following format (see Figure 9.1).

Stage 3 – Post Programme:
- Testing of participants
- Programme evaluation
- Offer of follow-up support
- Offer of networking opportunities
- Participant tracking

Stage 2 – During Programme:
- Training and workshop sessions
- Successful entrepreneurs as speakers
- Business counselling
- Mentoring
- Monitoring by programme manager
- Office incubation facilities
- Subsistence allowance
- Access to seed capital

Stage 1 – Pre-Programme:
- Pre-programme workshop
- Application process/proposal evaluation
- Pre-programme testing of participants (business skills and entrepreneurial characteristics audit)

Figure 9.1   A Framework for the Development of Entrepreneurship Training Programmes

Stage 1 – the pre-programme stage – might include an interactive workshop of about a half to one day's duration to raise awareness, encourage participants and explain what is involved in the programme. This could be followed by the application process, where the aspiring participants' applications are evaluated by the programme management team and an expert enterprise panel, including successful entrepreneurs. Finally, once the participants are selected, they could be asked to take part in a skills audit to determine their specific training needs.

Stage 2 – during the programme – might include the elements listed above as core components over a 12-month period. Around 10 days of normal training or workshop sessions throughout the programme would appear to be appropriate, covering, at the very least, the key topics of business planning, marketing and finance, as mentioned by the programme participants. Successful entrepreneurs and past participants could be included as guest speakers, where possible. While linking the training to a qualification may or may not be beneficial to the participants, depending on the group type, linking the training to a set of standards, such as NVQ (National Vocational Qualification) or MBA module standards, as indicated earlier, might provide a useful training framework for the providers to follow. Funding and other support agencies, as well as potential investors, could also be introduced to the programme participants through the workshops. Throughout the programme, the participants should be given the opportunity of testing the feasibility of their business ideas and getting constructive feedback.

Stage 3 – the post programme stage – could include a test of participants' business skills and knowledge to determine the immediate impact of the training. In addition, a thorough evaluation should be conducted where both the economic outputs and the participants' viewpoints are taken into consideration. Follow-up support, a missing element in many of the programmes reviewed in this research, and an element requested by the participants, should be offered where possible. Unfortunately, from the investigation undertaken in this study, it would seem that the absence of follow-up support is due mainly to the lack of funding. Finally, in an attempt to continually assess the impact of the training received, it is important to track programme participants over time, to determine the longitudinal value of the programme and to continue to advise on other support mechanisms available.

Profiling the Aspiring Entrepreneur

Chapters 2 and 3 considered the extensive literature on the entrepreneurial personality and presented the psychological, social, behavioural and various other approaches to studying the entrepreneur. Even at the outset, there were difficulties with defining the term *entrepreneur* and differentiating between *entrepreneurship* and *enterprise*. In this regard, the literature reveals that while an *entrepreneur* can be *someone who bears risks and aims to make profits by setting up a business, an enterprise* can simply represent a *state of mind*. For the purposes of this particular study, the authors have adopted the more traditional definition of entrepreneurs as *individuals who set up a business*, and aspiring entrepreneurs as *individuals who are considering doing just that, and who may be at varying stages of the preparation phase*. In this study, entrepreneurship programme participants were chosen to represent aspiring entrepreneurs.

Despite the vast amount of literature on the entrepreneurial persona, and the various personality tests that exist, it can be concluded that one is really no closer to defining who or what is an entrepreneur. There is little agreement in the literature on the exact profile of the entrepreneur, with a vast range of requirements being deemed critical for entrepreneurial success. In many ways, it would appear that the hunt for the 'heffalump' (Kilby, 1971) continues!

Notwithstanding the above, a number of core entrepreneurial traits, on which most researchers tend to agree, can be identified from the literature, and these were applied by the authors in their attempts to build a profile of the aspiring entrepreneur.

Background

While the ages of aspiring entrepreneurs can vary, they tend mostly to be between 31 and 40 years of age. Based on the raw data, this particular study found that the typical participant in an entrepreneurship programme is 34 years (mean age), with the youngest participant being 19 and the oldest 54. In addition, those who participate in entrepreneurship programmes tend to be mostly male (68% of respondents), with about half of the participants being married with children. Most programme participants will be educated to at least degree standard, some may even have specialist qualifications at postgraduate level, and the majority will have had at least three years work experience.

Business Ideas and Expectations

While the business ideas proposed by programme participants in this study tended to cover a wide range of industry sectors, education, training, tourism, leisure and related consultancies were the most popular choices, although there appeared to be an even split between manufacturing and service based projects. Surprisingly, despite the current opportunities in the technological field, there is still a lack of business proposals in this sector, and the non-technical entrepreneur is still very much in vogue.

There would appear to be some evidence to suggest that those who participate in entrepreneurship programmes and aspire to becoming entrepreneurs have not fully considered what is actually involved in setting up and developing a new business. For example, while most aspiring entrepreneurs will normally have a particular business idea in mind before joining an entrepreneurship programme, the amount of development work they will have done prior to applying for participation on the programme will vary greatly and, in many cases, the proposal will only be at the concept stage. Furthermore, this particular study revealed that less than half of the participants on the entrepreneurship programmes had gained experience of working in an area directly related to the industry sector of their proposed business ideas, and most had not been involved in a previous business venture. In addition to the above, there appears to be a preference for individual rather than team-based ventures. Revelations such as the fact that many aspiring entrepreneurs want to be their own boss, that most see themselves as the managing director/owner of the business, and that a considerable number of them have not identified how the sales or marketing function will be handled, provides further, albeit disappointing, evidence of the naivety of the aspiring entrepreneur.

This study has shown that individuals participate in entrepreneurship programmes in order to learn how to complete a business plan, and to set-up/run a business. Furthermore, for many participants, entrepreneurship programmes are seen merely as testing grounds for potential business ideas. If this is the case, then the expectations of programme providers regarding business creation levels, may need to be revised, since one can expect to create very few new business ideas within the programme timeframe from proposals which are clearly very early stage or even just pure concepts deriving from inexperienced, naive promoters.

The above would seem to support the suggestion for some type of pre-programme workshop prior to the programme proper. Such a workshop would not only give the programme providers an opportunity to improve their applicant screening process, it would also give participants an insight into what is actually involved in setting up and running a business, as well as a chance to get some feedback on their ideas, possibly begin some of the feasibility work, and draft an outline business plan. In this way, aspiring entrepreneurs would enter programmes better prepared, with a clearer idea of the work involved in small business development, and a more realistic picture of their own strengths and weaknesses. Undoubtedly, this would in turn improve the overall effectiveness of programmes and provide better value for money for the providers and funders.

Key Characteristics

Notwithstanding their apparent naivety, this study indicates that aspiring entrepreneurs are extremely confident individuals, who rate themselves highly on key entrepreneurial characteristics, including enthusiasm, need for achievement and locus of control. However, the GET scores showed that, while there was a marginal difference in the mean scores for need for achievement, need for autonomy, internal locus of control, creative tendency and calculated risk taking between the aspiring entrepreneurs and Caird's (1991) established entrepreneurs, the overall GET mean scores were lower in both groups of aspiring entrepreneurs than in Caird's study. While this study provides insufficient evidence that aspiring entrepreneurs actually possess the key psychological characteristics required for entrepreneurial success, it does suggest that these individuals perceive themselves as possessing such characteristics. In contrast, and perhaps understandably, the aspiring entrepreneurs surveyed were less confident about their business skills and knowledge, suggesting that most individuals participate in entrepreneurship programmes to develop such skills.

The Provision and Funding of Entrepreneurship Training Programmes

Rationale

The interviews conducted with the programme providers in this study indicated that most organisations are involved in entrepreneurship programmes because they want to promote entrepreneurship and contribute to the economic development of their region. In this context, the development of new businesses and the creation of jobs, appeared to be the main reasons for providing such programmes. It was clear that the providers also had some secondary objectives for their involvement in programmes, and these included the promotion of graduate entrepreneurship, enhancing the profile and reputation of their organisation and attracting more students to their university. Although there did not appear to be any evidence that providers' objectives differed significantly from programme to programme or from country to country, it is not surprising that some of the more technology-oriented organisations/programmes focused more on the creation of knowledge-intensive or technology-based businesses. Furthermore, those organisations with incubation centres had the additional objective of generating new tenants for these. It would appear that the promotion of economic development through new business and new job creation is also the main reason why funders get involved in entrepreneurship programmes. However, most funding bodies appeared to have a broader yet more rigid set of objectives and the funding of entrepreneurship programmes neatly fits into the enterprise-oriented ones. Although the objectives of the funding organisations were all phrased differently in the official documentation, i.e. annual reports, and so on, there was essentially no evidence to suggest that these objectives differed from funder to funder. In basic terms, these organisations either supported economic development or they did not. In other words, if it was part of the particular organisation's remit to fund such initiatives then proposals for funding were considered; if it was not, then these types of initiatives were not considered in the first place.

While the interviews conducted by the authors revealed that most organisations invest in entrepreneurship programmes to create new businesses and generate new jobs, it would appear that such objectives are normally built into the particular organisation's remit from the outset. Furthermore, since the mission statements or remits of many support organisations are often directly influenced, and indeed determined, by government policy, then obligation would appear to be the driving force behind the provision of entrepreneurship programmes, as opposed to an established need or demand.

While there was evidence in the findings of this study to suggest that some support organisations have secondary objectives for getting involved in such programmes, the core objectives of the organisations surveyed did not appear to differ significantly between programmes or between providers. However, it is understandable that specialist entrepreneurship programmes tended to focus more on one particular aspect, such as the promotion of technology-based businesses.

Programme Objectives

From the authors' study, it would appear that entrepreneurship programmes are actually attempting to create new businesses in the particular region of the providers, and generate sustainable new jobs. In this respect, both the providers and the funders believe that their programmes have been successful. Overall, the providers of entrepreneurship programmes would appear to be able to measure programme success in quite specific, and mainly economic, terms, normally expressed by the number of participants completing the programme, the number of new businesses created and the resulting level of job creation. The funders, on the other hand, appear to be less specific about the success of the programmes they fund, relying mostly on the programme providers for progress reports.

Programme Costs

Chapter 6 provided a comparison of the costs associated with entrepreneurship programmes in terms of the overall programme budget, the cost per participant, the cost per new business created and the cost per new job generated. While, as indicated, the issue of comparing costs is problematic, there is evidence to suggest that the typical cost of running an entrepreneurship training programme is currently around €190,000, or just over €7,000 per participant, with each new business and new job created costing on average nearly €19,000 and €7,000 respectively. For the most part, the Irish entrepreneurship programmes cost less to run than programmes operating in other parts of Europe. Chapter 6 also underlined the differences in costs between countries, by comparing the Irish programmes with their other European counterparts. When the mean figures are considered, it would appear that the other European programmes cost almost twice as much as the Irish programmes. Hence, the costs associated with entrepreneurship programmes would appear to differ significantly from provider to provider, and from country to country.

Programme Content

Despite the variety in entrepreneurship programmes, this study has shown that they share a number of common elements. All of the programmes reviewed included some sort of structured training or workshop sessions, mentoring and access to grants. Although the actual topics covered within the training were not always itemised in the programme literature, the basic topics of business planning, finance, marketing, and feasibility testing appeared to be common to all. However, none of the Irish programmes included follow-up support, while almost all of the other European programmes did. With regard to duration, most programmes would appear to last around 11 months (mean duration), with the most popular (modal) duration being 12 months. The modal number of participants per programme appears to be 15. However, this figure varied greatly from programme to programme with the participant level reaching 150+ in one of the programmes (the

Spanish programme) and the mean number of participants being 41.6 across the eight programmes analysed.

The indication from this study that most organisations get involved in entrepreneurship programmes for similar reasons, i.e. to create new businesses and generate new jobs, demonstrates the commonality of their overall aims and objectives. Furthermore, the fact that the organisations interviewed tended to measure their success in terms of the number of new businesses and jobs created, as well as their percentage conversion rate of proposals to businesses created, is evidence that their objectives are mainly quantitative in nature.

While there would appear to be several differences in entrepreneurship programmes, the trend in diversity among programmes, which was mentioned in the review of other studies and presented in Part I, does not appear to be continuing. In fact, a number of elements that are common to most programmes can be identified. Such elements include training, mentoring and grant aid, as discussed above. Furthermore, this study has indicated that the main differences between programmes operating in Ireland and those operating in the rest of Western Europe are in terms of costs and the number of participants supported, rather than in structure, content or duration.

Effectiveness

This study indicates that entrepreneurship programmes achieve a variety of results. From Chapter 6 it can be concluded that at least some of these achievements are clearly quantifiable and can be measured in economic terms. Collectively, the eight programmes reviewed by the authors were responsible for training 333 participants in various aspects of entrepreneurship, creating 85 new businesses and generating 334 new jobs, all within a single run of each programme. Overall, based on the mean figures, it would seem that a typical entrepreneurship programme can train 42 individuals, help to create 11 new businesses and generate 42 new jobs. Naturally, such outputs come at a cost. Furthermore, these outputs appear to differ from programme to programme and from country to country, as indicated in Chapter 6. When the entrepreneurship programmes operating in Ireland are compared with those in other European countries, it can be concluded that the Irish programmes, while, for the most part, costing less to run, tend to yield fewer new businesses and create fewer new jobs. However, it must also be noted that the Irish programmes overall, have fewer participants to begin with, hence both costs and outputs are lower. Obviously, a direct comparison of costs is difficult when programme structures, duration, content, participant levels and budgets vary so much. However, it would appear that, based on the authors' study, other the European countries are investing considerably more in entrepreneurship training than Ireland, and they are achieving better results, with an overall success rate, in terms of conversion of participant proposals to new businesses, of 41.8% compared to Ireland's 32.3%.

Benefits to Participants

Over 90% of the participants in the Irish programme A – the core treatment group in the authors' longitudinal study – felt that their original expectations had been met by the programme, and most of them felt the programme would have a 'significant impact' on their ability to reach set-up stage with their business idea. Findings such as these demonstrate the types of general benefits derived by the participants. The more specific benefits included making new contacts, gaining new skills and making progress with the business idea. However, the clearly measurable benefits were underlined by the participants' improvement in skills and knowledge (evidenced by the paired sample test in Chapter 8), the number of new businesses/jobs created and the employment status of the individuals when compared with the control group. These benefits would probably not have been readily observed without the type of longitudinal, qualitative and quantitative study undertaken by the authors.

This study has also confirmed that entrepreneurship programmes yield certain direct benefits for their participants, and, while these are mostly of a qualitative nature, they are measurable. For example, in general terms, even half-way through the programme when the formal training aspects had been completed, it was clear that the participants' opinions of the core entrepreneurship programme included in the longitudinal study (programme A) were very positive. All of the participants rated the programme as 'excellent' or 'good', and over 90% stated that their original expectations had been met. In addition, most of the participants felt that the training programme would have a 'significant' impact on their ability to reach set-up stage with their business idea. In more specific terms, it was also clear that the participants believed they had gained a number of measurable benefits from the programme. These benefits included making useful new business contacts, acquiring new skills and knowledge in the area of setting up and running a business, and making significant progress with their business ideas.

The participants also seemed to gain several different types of business skills/knowledge, with marketing, finance and business planning being the skills most frequently mentioned by the participants surveyed. The benefits derived in terms of business skills/knowledge are further underlined in Chapter 8, where the participants' self-ratings before and after the training are compared. It can also be concluded from the paired sample test carried out on these results that the programme had made a significant positive impact on the participants' business skills and knowledge in almost every area. The fact that most of the participants also felt that the programme had a 'significant (positive) impact' on their own personal development provides further evidence to support the conclusion that entrepreneurship programmes yield measurable benefits for the participants. The participants' perception that their own entrepreneurial abilities had improved as a result of their participation in the programme, a point supported by one of Caird's studies (1989), strengthens this conclusion.

Change in Perception of Benefits

Chapter 4 uncovered some evidence to suggest that participants' perceptions of the benefits of entrepreneurship programmes change over time (Caird, 1989; Fleming, 1996). In order to determine whether there had been a change in the perceptions of the benefits derived by the participants in this study, their original expectations of the programme were considered. *Support and guidance on setting up a business* and *completing a business plan* were listed as the participants' main expectations of the programme at the outset. However, at stage 2 of the longitudinal study, the actual benefits that appeared to have been derived by the participants were primarily *contact with other aspiring entrepreneurs* and *training*. Stage 3 of the study showed a slight change in the participants' perceptions of the benefits they had derived, with *training* and *completing a business plan* being mentioned as the main benefits. There did not appear to be any significant change in the participants' perceptions of the general benefits derived at stages 4 and 5 of the study, i.e. at one and two years post programme completion. However, there seemed to be a significant difference in how the participants felt about their entrepreneurial abilities between stages 3 and 5 of the study. Upon completion of the programme (stage 3), 52% of participants indicated that they were either *more confident* or *significantly more confident* about their entrepreneurial abilities than before the programme. Two years after completing the programme (stage 5), this figure had risen to 78%.

There also appeared to be a significant change over time in the progress of the participants' business ideas. One year after completing the entrepreneurship programme (stage 4 of the study), eight of the participants had set up their businesses, employing a collective total of 16 people. The collective employment figure had subsequently risen to 40 when the final part of the study was completed one year later. There was also a small positive change in the participants' employment status over the various stages of the study. The most significant changes in this respect were the increase in the number of participants who were self-employed two years after the programme, and the reduction in the number of those who had been unemployed.

As mentioned in Chapter 8, the finding from the longitudinal study that the majority of the survey respondents in the treatment group (15 individuals or 65% of respondents) did not set-up their businesses subsequent to receiving entrepreneurship training is not a totally negative outcome. If an entrepreneurship programme helps an individual to realise that his/her business proposal is not viable, then this benefits the individual by saving him/her from devoting time and money to an idea which will probably fail. This can also save the State, banks and other support institutions from providing unnecessary funds for business proposals with a low probability of success. However, a pre-programme screening stage may help prevent this situation from arising.

The conclusions that are drawn from the longitudinal study can be reinforced to some degree by the comparison with the control and comparator groups. It was clear that the control group (those who had a business idea but received no entrepreneurship training) 'performed' less well when compared to the other two groups. Fewer people in the control group continued working on their business idea following their unsuccessful application for a place on the entrepreneurship programmes, and overall, there were fewer people employed, fewer new businesses created and fewer new jobs generated in this group than in the other two. These findings are further reinforced when the original employment status of the various individuals are taken into consideration. While the authors recognise that there were significant differences between the control group and the comparator group, the progress of the comparator group (the redundancy group) provides additional evidence of the benefits of entrepreneurship training in this respect. These findings also support those of Adams and Wilson (1995) who showed that entrepreneurship programme participants found it easier to get salaried employment than non-participants.

Thus, it can be concluded that, not only are there clear benefits for the participants of entrepreneurship programmes, but also that aspiring entrepreneurs appear to benefit more with entrepreneurship training than without it. Indeed, the cumulative findings of the authors' study suggest that entrepreneurship programmes are indeed effective in supporting and developing aspiring entrepreneurs, and that they yield several measurable benefits for the participants, which are both qualitative and quantitative in nature.

This study has shown that entrepreneurship programmes can help create new businesses and generate new jobs. More specifically, such programmes can assist aspiring entrepreneurs by providing useful new business contacts and by teaching them a range of skills and knowledge relevant to setting-up and running a business. Furthermore, the findings of this research indicate that entrepreneurship programmes also help the aspiring entrepreneur to become more confident in his/her entrepreneurial abilities, and to test the feasibility of his/her business idea and determine whether or not it is commercially viable. It would appear that entrepreneurship programmes can also improve one's employability.

This study has also demonstrated that programme participants will gain new skills and knowledge relevant to setting up and running a business; develop a network of other aspiring and practising entrepreneurs, trainers and consultants; test the feasibility of their business ideas, and in some cases, make significant progress with their development; increase their confidence in their entrepreneurial abilities; improve their employability; and, very possibly, set up their own businesses.

Implications for the Design of Entrepreneurship Training Programmes

The findings from the study help to provide a 'profile' or set of expectations for the typical entrepreneurship programme, representing a benchmark against which programme performance can be measured. The provision of such a programme 'profile', indicating typical costs and outcomes, will help programme funders to understand what they can expect to achieve by funding an entrepreneurship programme.

Furthermore, the findings from the analysis of the 102 programme participants from four different entrepreneurship programmes have helped to provide a much-needed profile of the *aspiring* rather than the *established* entrepreneur. The provision of such a profile, in terms of the aspiring entrepreneur, may benefit programme providers as it will allow them to understand the needs of programme participants from the outset and gear their programmes accordingly. Programme managers may gain greater understanding of the type of individual they are dealing with in entrepreneurship programmes, what these individuals expect and why they participate. The realisation that not all programme participants will actually go on to set up their business should help programme providers to be more realistic about the outcomes they may expect. In short, a profile of the aspiring entrepreneur is critical to the understanding of the needs of programme participants, and crucial to the design of any entrepreneurship support programme.

Probably the most valuable output from this study has been the development of a framework for entrepreneurship training. It was a combination of the case study analysis, the interviews with the programme providers and funders, and the 5-part longitudinal study, which led to the development of this framework. An understanding of the type of individual who participates in entrepreneurship programmes, i.e. the aspiring entrepreneur, was also critical to the development of such a framework.

While the literature suggests several different structures for entrepreneurship training, the framework presented by the authors is different because it is comprehensive and is based on research which combines theory with practice. It is also a highly qualitative framework, directly informed by the opinions of the programme participants. While the framework proposed in this chapter still requires testing in its entirety, it is based on core elements derived from the seemingly most successful programmes analysed in the authors' study. For example, much of the actual programme content, suggested in stage two of the framework, has already been tested within the various programmes studied by the authors, and has been further augmented by the incorporation of the opinions of the programme funders, providers and participants surveyed.

Such a framework for entrepreneurship training programmes would be of benefit to designers, providers and funders of entrepreneurship programmes. For example, first time programme providers could implement this framework in the absence of their own. In addition, experienced programme providers could compare the authors' framework with their own and make amendments accordingly. The framework suggested by the authors is a comprehensive one, which incorporates pre, during and post programme elements, with built-in programme evaluation. The inclusion of a pre-programme workshop, as suggested by the authors, will significantly improve the quality of application received by the programme providers, and will give the programme applicants an indication of how they can expect to benefit from the programme. In addition, the pre-programme testing of participants will help to identify specific training needs. This training needs analysis will not only help programme providers to adjust the programme content accordingly, but will be of particular benefit to the providers of industry specific or high tech programmes, where specialist training or consultancy requirements need to be identified.

One of the most novel aspects of the framework developed from this research is the much-needed post-programme follow-up support. While this is often excluded from most programmes due to budget restraints, such follow-up support need not be expensive. This study has suggested that even the provision of networking opportunities, where programme participants could meet following completion of the programme, would be of benefit.

Provided that account is taken of the particular economic environment, it would appear that the framework proposed by the authors could be applied on a European scale. It is believed that, collectively, the framework developed by the authors, together with the profile of the aspiring entrepreneur, and the set of expectations regarding outputs and costs for the typical entrepreneurship training programme, offer an invaluable support package to entrepreneurship programme designers, providers and funders throughout Europe.

The Need for Evaluation

The focus of this study has been on the effectiveness of entrepreneurship training programmes. Evidence has been presented which confirms that such programmes can be effective and yield significant benefits for aspiring entrepreneurs. The study has also demonstrated that the effectiveness of entrepreneurship training programmes can be improved to the benefit of the providers, funders and participants. However, it must be remembered that a significant amount of public funds are used in the provision of entrepreneurship programmes, and that there are a number of difficulties associated with conducting effectiveness studies. Therefore, the authors accept that there is a need for continued research in this particular area. More effectiveness studies which use control groups and include longitudinal designs are needed so that findings from research such as this can have greater external validity. In addition, issues such as the impact on effectiveness of different pedagogical methods used to deliver entrepreneurship programmes, as well as the particular entrepreneurial experience of the trainers involved, also need to be considered.

A major objective of this investigative study has been to contribute to the arguments in favour of intervention in the entrepreneurial process, and to demonstrate that structured interventions can and should be improved. While the framework developed by the authors has been designed to aid such improvement, this study illustrates that the need for evaluation continues.

Bibliography

Adams, A.V. and Wilson, S. (1995). 'Do Self Employment programs Work?', *Finance & Development*, September, 32: 3, pp.16-19.

Aitken, H.G. (1965). *Exploration in Enterprise*, Harvard University Press: Cambridge, Mass.

Ajzen, I. (1991). 'The Theory of Planned Behaviour', *Organisational Behaviour and Human Decision Processes*, 50, pp.179-211.

Ajzen, I. and Fishbein, M. (1980). *Understanding Attitudes and Predicting Social Behaviour*, Prentice-Hall: Englewood Cliffs, N.J.

Aldrich, H. (1999). *Organizations Evolving*, Sage Publications: London.

Aldrich, H. and Martinez, M. A. (2001). 'Many are Called, but Few are Chosen: an evolutionary perspective for the study of entrepreneurship', *Entrepreneurship Theory and Practice*, 25: 4, pp. 41-56.

Arzeni, S. (1992). 'Encouraging the Entrepreneur', *OECD Observer (Organisation for Economic Co-operation and Development countries)*, Feb-March, 174, pp.19-22.

Atherton, A., Gibb, A. and Sear, L. (1997) 'Reviewing the Case for Supporting Business Start-ups: a policy overview of current thinking on business start-ups', Durham University Business School, Durham.

Atherton, A. and Hannon, P.D. (1996). 'Competitiveness and Success: how the owner-managers of small firms perceive success in a turbulent external environment', *Proceedings of the 19th Institute of Small Business Affairs - National Small Firms Conference*, Birmingham, pp. 400-416.

Audit Commission. (1989). 'Urban Regeneration and Economic Development: the government dimension', HMSO: London.

Autio, E; Keeley, R; Klofsten, M. and Ulfstedt, T. (1997). 'Entrepreneurial Intent Among Students: Testing an intent model in Asia, Scandinavia and the USA', Helsinki University of Technology, Helsinki.

Babbie, E. (1995). *The Practice of Social Research*, Wadsworth Publishing Company: California.

Bannock, G. and Daly, M. (1990). 'Size Distribution of UK Firms', *Employment Gazette*, May, pp. 255-258.

Bannock, G. and Peacock, A. (1989), as cited in Storey, D.J. (1994), *Understanding the Small Business Sector*, Routledge: London.

Barclays Bank. (1995). 'Start-Ups Head Towards Half-a-Million Landmark', *Barclays Small Business Bulletin*, 4.

Barkham, Richard J. (1989). 'Entrepreneurship, New Firms and Regional Development', PhD Thesis, University of Reading.

Barnes, L.B. and Hershon, S.A. (1976). 'Transferring Power in the Family Business', *Harvard Business Review*, July-August, 54: 4: pp.105-114.

Baron, R. A. and Markman, G. D. (2000). 'Beyond Social Capital: how social skills can enhance entrepreneurs' success', *The Academy of Management Executive*, 14: 1, pp.106-116.

Barrow, C. and Brown, R. (1996). 'Training to Help Small Businesses Grow', *Proceedings of the 19th Institute of Small Business Affairs - National Small Firms Conference*, Birmingham, pp.1062-1078.

Baumol, W.J. (1968). 'Entrepreneurship in Economic Theory', *American Economic Review*, 58: 2, pp. 58-60.

Beaver, G. and Jennings, P. (1996). 'Managerial Competence and Competitive Advantage in the Small Business: an alternative perspective', *proceedings of the 26th European Small Business Seminar*, Vaasa, pp.181-196.

Begley, T. M. and Boyd, D. P. (1987). 'Psychological characteristics associated with performance in Entrepreneurial firms and smaller businesses,' *Journal of Business Venturing*, 2, pp. 79-93, cited in Lee, D Y and Tsang, E W K 2001 'The Effects of Entrepreneurial Personality, Background and Network Activities on venture Growth', *Journal of Management Studies*, 38: 4, pp. 583-602.

Bell, J. (1991). *Doing Your Research Project: a guide for first-time researchers in education and social science*, Arrowsmith: Bristol.

Bennett, R. (1977). 'SMEs and Public Policy: present dilemmas, future priorities and the case of business links', *proceedings of the National Small Firms Policy and Research Conference*, Belfast. (Copy available from the author, Department of Geography, University of Cambridge, Cambridge).

Bennis, W. G. and Nanus, B. (1985). *Leaders: The strategies for taking charge*, Harper and Row: New York.

Bhide, A. (1994). 'How Entrepreneurs Craft Strategies That Work', *Harvard Business Review*, March-April, 72: 2, pp.150-161.

Bhide, A. (1996). 'The Questions Every Entrepreneur Must Answer', *Harvard Business Review*, Nov-Dec, 74: 6, pp.120-130.

Binks, M., and Vale, P. (1990). *Entrepreneurship and Economic Change*, McGraw-Hill: London.

Birch, D. (1994). Cited in Storey, D.F. (1994). *Understanding the Small Business Sector*, Routledge: London.

Bird, B. (1988). 'Implementing Entrepreneurial Ideas: the case for intention', *Academy of Management Review*, 13: 3, pp. 442-453.

Birley, S. and Westhead, P. (1994). 'A Comparison of New Businesses Established by Novice and Habitual Founders in Great Britain', *International Small Business Journal*, 12: 1, pp. 38-60.

Blair, A. (1997). 'Owners in the Driving Seat (common qualities of company founders)', *Management Today*, September, pp. 44-48.

Block, Z. and Stumpf, S.A. (1992). 'Entrepreneurship Education Research: Experience and Challenge', in Sexton, D.L. and Kasarda, J.D. (eds), *The State of the Art of Entrepreneurship*, PWS-Kent Publishing Company, USA, pp.17-42.

Bolton, B. and Thompson, J. (2000a). *Entrepreneurs: Talent, Temperament, Technique*, Butterworth-Heinemann: Oxford.

Bolton, B. and Thompson, J. (2000b). 'A Breed Apart', *Director*, 53: 10, pp. 54-57.

Bolton Committee. (1971). 'Report of the Committee of Inquiry on Small Firms (Bolton Report)', HMSO: London.

Boussouara, M., and Deakins, D. (1998). 'Learning, Entrepreneurship and the High Technology Small Firm', *proceedings of the Enterprise and Learning Conference*, University of Aberdeen.

Boyd, N.G. and Vozikis, G.S. (1994). 'The Influence of Self-efficacy on the Development of Entrepreneurial Intentions and Actions', *Entrepreneurship Theory and Practice*, 18: 4, pp. 63-77.

Braden, P. (1977). *Technical Entrepreneurship*, Ann Arbor: University of Michigan.

Brazeal, D. and Herbert, T.T. (1999). 'The Genesis of Entrepreneurship', *Entrepreneurship Theory and Practice*, 23:3, pp. 29-45.

Brennan, Z. and Waterhouse, R. (1999). 'Escape to Dot.Com', *Sunday Times*, (Focus section), 19th December, p.14.

Bridge, S., O'Neill, K. and Cromie, S. (1998). *Understanding Enterprise, Entrepreneurship & Small Business*, Macmillan Publishing: London.

British-Irish Agreement Act. (1999). www.irlgov.ie/bill28/acts/1999.

Brockhaus, R. H. (1975). 'I-E Locus of Control Scores as Predictors of Entrepreneurial Intentions', *proceedings of the Academy of Management Conference*, pp. 433-435.

Brockhaus, R.H. (1980). 'Risk Taking Propensity of Entrepreneurs', *Academy of Management Journal*, 23: 3, pp. 509-250.

Bruyat, C. and Julien, P.A. (2000). 'Defining the field of research in entrepreneurship', *Journal of Business Venturing*, 16: 2, pp.165-180.

Burke, A.E. (1995). 'Enterprise and Employment Creation in Ireland: data regularities and issues for research', *paper presented at the first Irish Entrepreneurship Research Conference*, University College Dublin.

Bygrave, W. D. (1989). 'The Entrepreneurship Paradigm (II): chaos and catastrophes among quantum jumps', *Entrepreneurship Theory and Practice*, 14:2, pp.-30.

Bygrave, W. D. and Hofer, C. W. (1991). 'Theorising about Entrepreneurship', *Entrepreneurship Theory and Practice*, 16: 2, pp. 3-22.

Caird, S. (1989). 'Self Assessment of Participants on Enterprise Training Courses', *British Journal of Education and Work*, 4: 3, pp. 63-80.

Caird, S. (1991). 'Testing Enterprising Tendency in Occupational Groups', *British Journal of Management*, 2, pp.177-186.

Caird, S. (1992). 'What Support is Needed by Innovative Small Business?', *Journal of General Management*, 18: 2, pp. 45-68.

Cantillion, R. (1755). *Essai sur la Nature du Commerce en Général*, H. Higgs (ed.), (1931), Macmillan, London.

Carland, J. W., Hoy, F., Boulton, W. R, and Carland, J. A. (1984). 'Differentiating Entrepreneurs from Small Business Owners: a conceptualization', *Academy of Management Review*, 9, pp. 354-359.

Carney, M. and Turner, D. (1987). 'Education for Enterprise', Counselling and Career Development Unit, University of Leeds, Osmosis Publishing.

Carson, D., Cromie, S., McGowan, P. and Hill, J. (1995), *Marketing and Entrepreneurship in SMEs - an innovative approach*, Prentice Hall: London.

Carter, S. and Jones-Evans, D. (2000). 'Enterprise and Small Business - Principles, Practice and Policy', *Financial Times*, Prentice Hall: Essex.

Cassidy, J. (2002). 'After the gold rush', *The Times*, 23rd January, pp. 4-5.

Casson, M. (1982). *The Entrepreneur: An Economic Theory*, Martin Robertson: Oxford.

Chell, E. (1985). 'The Entrepreneurial Personality: A Few Ghosts Laid to Rest', *International Small Business Journal*, 3: 3, pp. 43-54.

Chell, E., Haworth, J. and Brearley, S. (1991). *The Entrepreneurial Personality - Concepts, Cases and Categories*, Routledge: London.

Churchill, N. C. and Lewis, V. L. (1986). 'Entrepreneurship Research', in Sexton, D L and Smilor, R W (eds), *The Art of Entrepreneurship*, Ballinger: Cambridge, MA, pp. 333-365.

Clark, R.W., Davis, C.H. and Harnish, V.C. (1984). 'Do courses in Entrepreneurship aid in New Venture Creation?', *Journal of Small Business Management*, 22: 2, pp. 26-31.

Cole, A.H. (1965). 'An Approach to the Study of Entrepreneurship', in Aitken, H.G. (ed.), *Explorations in Enterprise*, Harvard University Press, Cambridge, Mass, pp. 30-44.

Collins, O., Moore, D. and Unwalla, D. (1964). *The Enterprising Man*, Ann Arbor: University of Michigan.

Collins, O. and Moore, D. G. (1970). *The Organization Makers*, Appleton: New York, cited in Sharma, P. and Chrisman, J. J. (1999), 'Toward a Reconciliation of the Definitional Issues in the Field of Corporate Entrepreneurship', *Entrepreneurship Theory and Practice*, 23: 3, pp.11-27.

Connor, J., Dawes, F., and Haydock, W. (1996). 'Management Learning Frameworks and Small Business Growth: a challenging role for Business Schools', *proceedings of the 19th Institute of Small Business Affairs - National Small Firms' Conference*, Birmingham, pp.1289-1300.

Cooney, T. and O'Connor, A. (1995). 'Perceived Barriers to Innovation of SMEs in Ireland', paper presented at *the First Irish Entrepreneurship Research Conference*, University College Dublin.

Cooper, A.C. (1971). 'The Founding of Technological-Based Firms', Centre for Venture Management: Milwaukee, WI.

Cox, L. W. (1996). 'The Goals and Impact of Educational Interventions in the Early Stages of Entrepreneur Career Development', *proceedings of the Internationalising Entrepreneurship Education and Training Conference*, Arnhem.

Cramer, J. J. (1999). 'The Top 10 Internet Myths', Paper presented at the *Goldmans Sachs International Tech Conference*, London, 23rd September.

Crane, D. (2001). 'People are new economy's biggest resource', *The Toronto Star*, 12th May.

Cromie, S. (1994). 'Entrepreneurship: The Role of the Individual in Small Business Development', *IBAR - Irish Business and Administrative Research*, 15, pp. 62-75.

Cromie, S. and Johns, S. (1983). 'Irish Entrepreneurs: Some Personal Characteristics', *Journal of Occupational Behaviour*, 4, pp. 317-324.

Cromie, S. and O'Donaghue, J. (1992). 'Assessing Entrepreneurial Inclinations', *International Small Business Journal*, 10: 2, pp. 66-71.

Culliton Committee. (1992). 'A Time for Change: Industrial Policy for the 1990s – Report of the Industrial Policy Review Group (Culliton Report)', Government Stationery Office, Dublin.

Culson-Thomas, C. (1999). *Individuals and Enterprise – creating entrepreneurs for the new millennium through personal transformation*, Blackhall Publishing: Dublin.

Curran, J. (2000). 'What is small business policy in the UK for? Evaluation and assessing small business policies', *International Small Business Journal*, 18: 3, pp. 36-50.

Curran, J. and Stanworth, J. (1989). 'Education and Training for Enterprise: Some Problems of Classification, Evaluation, Policy and Research', *International Small Business Journal*, 7: 2, pp.11-23.

Curran, J. and Storey, D.J. (2002). 'Small Business Policy in the United Kingdom: the inheritance of the Small Business Service and implications for its future effectiveness', *Environment and Planning C: Government and Policy*, 20, pp.163-177.

Dalton, G.W. and Holdaway, F. (1989). 'Preliminary Findings - Entrepreneur Study', working paper, Brigham Young University.

Daly, M. (1991). 'Job Creation 1987-1989: the contribution of small and large firms', *Employment Gazette*, 99: 11, pp. 589-594.

Davids, L.E. (1963). 'Characteristics of Small Business Founders in Texas and Georgia', The United States Small Business Administration: Washington D.C.

Davidsson, P. (1995). 'Determinants of Entrepreneurial Intentions', *proceedings of the 9th RENT Workshop in Entrepreneurship Research*, Piacenza, Italy.

Davies, L.G. and Gibb, A.A. (1991). 'Recent Research in Entrepreneurship', *proceedings of the 3rd International EIASM Workshop*, Gower: London.

Deakins, D. (1996). *Entrepreneurship and Small Firms*, (1st edition), McGraw-Hill: London.

Deakins, D. (1999). *Entrepreneurship and Small Firms*, (2nd edition), McGraw-Hill: London.

DeCarlo, J. F. and Lyons, P. R. (1979). 'A comparison of selected personal characteristics of minority and non-minority female entrepreneurs', *Journal of Small Business Management*, 17: 4, pp. 22-29, cited in Lee, D. Y. and Tsang, E. W. K. (2001), 'The Effects of Entrepreneurial Personality, Background and Network Activities on Venture Growth', *Journal of Management Studies*, 38: 4, pp. 583-602.

De Faoite, D.; Van der Sijde, P. and Henry, C. (2002). 'Training and Finance for Small Firms - a comparative study between Ireland and the Netherlands', *proceedings of the High Technology - Small Firms Conference*, Enschede, June.

Dermer, B. (1997). *Management Planning and Control Systems: advanced concerns and cases*, Richard Irwin: Homewood IL.

DfEE – Department for Enterprise and Employment. (2001). 'Opportunity for All in a World of Change', White Paper, DTI Publications/The Stationery Office, Publications Centre, London.

Diesling, P. (1971). *Patterns of Discovery in the Social Sciences*, Aldine-Atherton: Chicago.

Domegan, C. and Fleming, D. (1999). *Marketing Research in Ireland, Theory and Practice*, Gill and MacMillan: Dublin.

Douglass, M. (1976). 'Relating Education to Entrepreneurial Success', *Business Horizons*, 19: 6, pp. 40-44.

Drucker, P. (1985). *Innovation and Entrepreneurship*, Pan Books Ltd: London.

DTI. (2002). Dti.gov.uk/enterpriseact.

Dunsby, B.L. (1996). 'Small Firms Policy Proposals - Meeting the Needs of Start-ups and Micro-Businesses', *proceedings of the 19th Institute of Small Business Affairs – National Small Firms' Conference*, Birmingham, pp. 51-72.

During, W.E., Kerhof, M., Woolthuis, R.J.A. and Smitt, J.M.J. (1997). 'Entrepreneurship and Small Business Management in a Dutch Environment', in H. Landstrom, H. Frank and J.M. Veciana (eds), *Entrepreneurship and Small Business Research in Europe*, Avebury: Aldershot, pp. 200-225.

Dyer, W.G. and Handler, W. (1994). 'Entrepreneurship and Family Business: Exploring the Connections', *Entrepreneurship: Theory and Practice*, 19: 1, pp. 71-83.

Economist. (1998). 'Entrepreneurs to Order', *The Economist*, 14th March, 346: 8059, pp. 29-33.

Eisenhardt, K.M. (1989). 'Building Theories From Case Study Research', *Academy of Management Review*, 14:4: pp. 223-244.

Enterprise Bill. (2002). dti.gov.uk/enterpriseact.

European Commission and Eurostat. (1994). 'Enterprise in Europe: the third report', Office for Official Publications of the EC, Luxembourg.

European Commission. (1995). 'Small and Medium Sized Enterprises – A Dynamic Source of Employment, Growth and Competitiveness in the European Union', Report presented by the European Commission for the Madrid European Council, Brussels.

European Commission. (1996). *Journal of the European Communities*, No. 107/6, Brussels.

European Commission. (2001). 'Creating an Entrepreneurial Europe - the activities of the European Union for SMEs', March, Brussels.

European Observatory for SMEs. (1993). 'First Annual Report', EIM Small Business Consultancy, The Netherlands.

European Observatory for SMEs. (1994). 'Second Annual Report', EIM Small Business Consultancy, The Netherlands.

European Observatory for SMEs. (1995). 'Third Annual Report', EIM Small Business Consultancy, The Netherlands.

European Observatory for SMEs. (1997). 'Fifth Annual Report', EIM Small Business Consultancy, The Netherlands.

Fiet, J. O. (2000a). 'The Theoretical Side of Teaching Entrepreneurship Theory', *Journal* of *Business Venturing*, 16: 1, pp. 1-24.

Fiet, J. O. (2000b). 'The Pedagogical Side of Entrepreneurship Theory', *Journal of Business Venturing*, 16: 2, pp. 101-117.

Filley, A. C. and Aldag, R. J. (1978). 'Characteristics and Measurement of an Entrepreneurial Typology', *Academy of Management Journal*, 21: 4, pp. 578-591.

Fleming, P. (1994). 'The Role of Structured Interventions in Shaping Graduate Entrepreneurship', *IBAR - Irish Business and Administrative Research*, 15, pp. 146-164.

Fleming, P. (1996). 'Entrepreneurial Education in Ireland: a longitudinal study, *Academy of Entrepreneurship Journal*, (European edition), 2: 1, pp. 95-119.

Florida, R. (2000). 'Place and the New Economy', paper presented at *the Champions of Sustainability Lecture Series*, 27th August, Pittsburgh.

Florida, R. (2001). 'The Entrepreneurial Society', paper presented at the *Conference on Entrepreneurship and Public Policy*, Kennedy School of Government, Harvard University, 10th April.

Flynn, A. and Hynes, B. (1999). 'High-Tech Entrepreneurial Teams – Managing the Challenges of Growth', *proceedings of the Institute of Business Advisers' Cross-Border Conference*, May, Enniskillen.

Forfás. (2000). 'Enterprise 2010 – a new strategy for the promotion of enterprise in Ireland in the 21st century', Forfás: Dublin.

Fothergill, S. and Gudgin, G. (1979). 'The Job Generation Process in Britain', Centre for Environmental Studies, Leicester University.

Fowler, A. (1997). 'How to Select and Use Psychometric Tests', *People Management*, 3: 20, 25th September, pp. 45-46.

Frank, H. and Landström, H. (1997). 'Entrepreneurship and Small Business in Europe – economic background and academic infrastructure', in H. Landström, H. Frank and J.M. Veciana (eds), *Entrepreneurship and Small Business Research in Europe: an ECSB Survey*, Aldershot: Avebury, pp.1-13.

Gable, C.G. (1994). 'Integrating Case Study and Survey Methods: an example in information systems', *European Journal of Information Systems*, 3: 2, pp.112-126.

Gallagher, C. and Miller, P. (1991). 'New Fast Growing Companies Create Jobs', *Journal of Long Range Planning*, 24: 1, pp. 96-101.

Gallagher, C. and Robson, G. (1996). 'The identification of High Growth SME Firms', *proceedings of the 19th Institute of Small Business Affairs - National Small Firms Conference*, Birmingham, pp. 18-28.

Garavan, T. N. and Ó Cinnéide, B. (1994). 'Entrepreneurship Education and Training Programmes: a review and evaluation', *Journal of European Industrial Training*, part I – 18: 8, pp. 3-12, part II – 18: 11, pp. 13-21.

Garavan, T.N., Ó Cinnéide, B. and Fleming, P. (1997). *Entrepreneurship & Business Start-Ups in Ireland*, Oak Tree Press: Dublin.

Gartner, W. B. (1989). 'Who is an Entrepreneur? is the wrong question', *Entrepreneurship Theory and Practice*, 13: 4, pp. 47-68.

Gartner, W.B. (2001). 'Is there an elephant in entrepreneurship? Blind assumptions in theory development', *Entrepreneurship Theory and Practice*, 25: 4, pp. 27-39.

Gartner, W. B., Mitchell, T. M., and Vesper, K. H. (1989). 'A Taxonomy of New Business Ventures', *Journal of Business Venturing*, 4: 3, pp. 169-186.

Gasse, Y. (1990). 'An Experience in Training in the area of Entrepreneurship and Starting a business in Quebec: the project *Become an Entrepreneur*', in Donckels, R. and Miettinen, (eds), *New Findings and Perspectives in Entrepreneurship*, Avebury: Aldershot, pp. 99-114.

Gasse, Y., and Théoret, A. (1980). 'L'innovation dans les PME au Québec et en Belgique: une étude empirique', *Ensenement et Gestion*, 15.

Gibb, A.A. (1987a). 'Education for Enterprise: Training for Small Business Initiation – Some Contrasts', *Journal of Small Business and Entrepreneurship*, 4: 3, pp. 42-47.

Gibb, A.A. (1987b). 'Enterprise Culture – Its meaning and implications for education and training', *Journal of European Industrial Training*, 11: 2, pp. 1-38.

Gibb, A.A. (1993a). 'Do We Really Teach Small Business in the Way We Should?', *proceedings of the Internationalising Entrepreneurship Education and Training Conference*, Vienna.

Gibb, A.A. (1993b). 'The Enterprise Culture and Education: Understanding Enterprise Education and its Links with Small Business Entrepreneurship and Wider Educational Goals', *International Small Business Journal*, 11: 3, pp. 11-34.

Gibb, A.A. (1997). 'Small Firms' Training and Competitiveness. Building Upon the Small Business as a Learning Organisation', *International Small Business Journal*, 15: 3, pp. 13-29.

Gibb, A.A. (2000). 'SME policy, academic research and the growth of ignorance, mythical concepts, myths, assumptions, rituals and confusions', *International Small Business Journal*, 18: 3, pp. 13-35.

Gibb, A.A. and Cotton, J. (1998). 'Entrepreneurship in Schools and College Education – Creating the Leading Edge', background paper to the conference on *Work Futures and the Role of Entrepreneurship and Enterprise in Schools and Further Education*, December, London.

Gibb, A.A. and Ritchie, J. (1981). 'Influences on Entrepreneurship: A Study over time', in *Bolton Ten Years on, Proceedings of the UK Small Business Research Conference*, Polytechnic of Central of London, pp. 20-21.

Gibb, Y.K. and Nelson, E.G. (1996). 'Personal Competences, Training and Assessment: A Challenge for Small Business Trainers', *proceedings of the European Small Business Seminar*, Finland, pp. 97-107.

Glaser, B. and Strauss, A.L. (1967). *The Discovery of Grounded Theory: strategies of qualitative research*, Wiedenfeld and Nicholson: London.

Global Entrepreneurship Monitor (GEM) Report. (2001). Reynolds, P.D., Camp, S.M., Bygrave, W.D., Autio, E., Hay, M., Babson College, MA.

Gorman, G., Hanlon, D. and King, W. (1997). 'Some Research Perspectives on Entrepreneurship Education, Enterprise Education and Education for Small Business Management: a ten year literature review', *International Small Business Journal*, 15: 3, pp. 56-78.

Gould, L.C. (1969). 'Juvenile Entrepreneurs', *American Journal of Sociology*, 74: 6, pp. 710-719.

Greenberg, J. and Baron R. A. (2000). *Behavior in Organizations*, 7th edition, Prentice-Hall: New Jersey.

Greenfield, S.M. and Strickon, A. (1986). *Entrepreneurship and Social Changes*, pp. 4-18, University Press of America: Los Angeles.

Greiner, L. (1972). 'Evolution and Revolution as Organisations Grow', *Harvard Business Review*, 50: 4, pp. 37-46.

Griffith, V. (2001). 'How the fittest survived the dotcom meltdown', *FT.com*, 27th August.

Groot, W., Hartog, J. and Oosterbeek, H. (1994). 'Costs and Revenues of Investment in Enterprise-related Schooling', *Oxford Economic Papers*, October, 46: 4, pp. 658-675.

Guest, D. (1992). 'Right Enough to Be Dangerously Wrong: An analysis of the In Search of Excellence phenomenon', in Graeme Salaman (ed.), *Human Resource Strategies*, (Open University Course Reader), Sage Publications: London, pp. 5-19.

Hagen, E. (1962). *On the Theory of Social Change*, The Dorsey Press: Homewood, IL.

Hammersley, M. (1985). 'From Ethnography to Theory: a programme and paradigm for case study research in the sociology of education', *Sociology*, 19: 2, pp. 187-211.

Harré, R. (1979). *Social Being*, Basil Blackwell: Oxford.

Harrison, R. and Leitch, C. (1995). 'Entrepreneurship and the Learning Company: from concepts to practice', paper presented at *the First Irish Entrepreneurship Research Conference*, University College Dublin.

Hatch, J. and Zweig, J. (2000). 'What is the Stuff of an Entrepreneur?' *Ivey Business Journal*, 65: 2, pp. 68-72.

Hay, M., Verdin, P., and Williamson, P. (1993). 'Successful New Ventures: Lessons for Entrepreneurs and Investors', *Journal of Long Range Planning*, 26: 5, pp. 31-43.

Henry, C. (1998). 'The Effects of Enterprise Training - a comparative practical study', *Proceedings of the Research Conference*, Dundalk Institute of Technology, May.

Henry, C. and Titterington, A. (1996). 'The Effects of Enterprise Support Programmes on the Success of Small Business Start-ups: the experiences of the Technology Enterprise Programme', *proceedings of the Internationalising Entrepreneurship Education and Training Conference*, Arnhem, The Netherlands, June.

Henry C. and Titterington, A. (1997). 'The Use of Enterprise Training Programmes as a Mechanism for Determining Entrepreneurial Suitability', *Proceedings of the 20th Institute of Small Business Affairs – National Small Firms Conference*, Belfast, pp. 1395-1413.

Henry, C. and Titterington, A. (2001). 'The Use of Enterprise Training Programs as a Mechanism for Assessing Entrepreneurial Suitability', in *Entrepreneurship Education – A Global View*, Brockhaus, R.H., Hills, G.E., Klandt, H. and Welsch, H. (eds), Ashgate: Aldershot.

Henry, C., Titterington, A., and Wiseman, K. (1997). 'Encouraging Innovative Enterprise – The Role of Enterprise Training', *Proceedings of the Dublin City University Innovation Conference*, Dublin, September.

Henry, C., Hill, S. and De Faoite, D. (2001). 'Encouraging Innovative Start-ups: in search of the technology based entrepreneur', *proceedings of the European Small Business Seminar*, Dublin, September.

Herron, L., Sapienza, H.J. and Smith-Cooke, D. (1991). 'Entrepreneurship Theory from an interdisciplinary perspective: volume 1', *Entrepreneurship Theory and Practice*, 16:2, pp. 7-12.

Hill, S. and Ó Cinnéide, B. (1998). 'Entrepreneurship Education - Case Studies from The Celtic Tiger', *proceedings of the Enterprise and Learning Conference*, University of Aberdeen, September.

Hills, G.E. (1988). 'Variations in University Entrepreneurship Education: An Empirical Study of An Evolving Field', *Journal of Business Venturing*, 3: 1, pp.109-122.

Hills, G.E., Romaguera, J.M., Fernandez, L., Gonzalez, C., Hamilton, L.C., Perez, C. and Rollman, R.J. (1996). 'Entrepreneurship Curriculum Innovation: The University of Puerto Rico Case', *Proceedings of the Internationalising Entrepreneurship Education and Training Conference*, Arnhem.

Hirschmeyer, J. (1964). *The origin of entrepreneurship in Meiji, Japan*, Harvard University Press: Cambridge, MA.

Hisrich, R.D. (1988). 'The Entrepreneur in N. Ireland: Characteristics, Problems, and Recommendations for the Future', *Journal of Small Business Management*, 26: 3, pp. 32-39.

Hisrich, R.D. and Brush, C.G. (1994). 'The Woman Entrepreneur: Management Skills and Business Problems', *Journal of Small Business Management*, 32: 1, pp. 30-37.

Hisrich, R.D. and Ó Cinnéide, B. (1985). 'The Irish Entrepreneur: Characteristics, Problems and Future Success', University of Limerick.

Hisrich, R.D. and Peters, M.P. (1985). *Entrepreneurship* (1st edition), Irwin McGraw-Hill: Boston, MA.

Hisrich, R.D. and Peters, M.P. (1995). *Entrepreneurship* (3rd edition), Irwin McGraw-Hill: Boston, MA.

Hisrich, R.D. and Peters, M.P. (1998). *Entrepreneurship* (4th edition), Irwin McGraw-Hill: Boston, MA.

Hornaday, J.A. and Aboud, J. (1971). 'Characteristics of Successful Entrepreneurs', *Journal of Personnel Psychology*, 24: 1, pp. 141-153.

Hornaday, J.A. and Bunker, CS. (1970). 'The Nature of the Entrepreneur', *Journal of Personnel Psychology*, 23: 1, pp. 45-54.

Howell, R.P. (1972). 'Comparative Profiles: Entrepreneurs Versus the Hired Executive: San Francisco Peninsula Semiconductor Industry', in A.C. Cooper and J.L. Komives (eds), *Technical Entrepreneurship: A Symposium*, Center for Venture Management: Milwaukee, pp. 47-62.

Hull, D., Bosley, J. and Udel, G. (1980). 'Reviewing the Hunt for the Heffalump: Identifying Potential Entrepreneurs by Personality Characteristics', *Journal of Small Business Management*, 18: 1, pp. 11-18.

Hunt, D. (1995). 'Telematic SMEs and the Ephemeral Economy', paper presented at *the First Irish Entrepreneurship Research Conference*, University College Dublin.

Investni – Invest Northern Ireland. (2002). www.investni.com.

IPPR - Institute of Public Policy Research. (1998). Gavron, R., Cowling, M., Holtham, G. and Westhall, A. 'The Entrepreneurial Society', London.

Jack, S.L. and Anderson, A.R. (1998). 'Entrepreneurship Education within the Condition of Entreprenology', *Proceedings of the Conference on Enterprise and Learning*, Aberdeen.

Jamieson, I. (1984). 'Schools and Enterprise', in A.G. Watts and P. Moran, (eds), *Education for Enterprise*, published by CRAC, Ballinger, Cambridge, UK, pp. 19-27.

Jennings, P.L. and Hawley, D. (1996). 'Designing Effective Training Programmes', *proceedings of the 19th Institute of Small Business Affairs – Small Firms' National Conference*, Birmingham, pp. 1301-1326.

Johannisson, B. (1991). 'University training for entrepreneurship: Swedish approaches', *Entrepreneurship and Regional Development*, 3, pp. 67-82.

Johannisson, B. and Landstrom, H. (1997). 'Research in Entrepreneurship and Small Business – state of the art in Sweden', in H. Landstrom, H. Frank and J.M. Veciana (eds), *Entrepreneurship and Small Business Research in Europe – an ECSB survey*, Aldershot: Avebury, pp. 276-295.

Johnson, A.T. and Sack, A. (1996). 'Assessing the Value of Sports Facilities: the importance of non-economic factors', *Economic Development and Quarterly*, 10: 4, pp. 369-381.

Johnson, S., Sear, L. and Jenkins, A. (2000). 'Small Business Policy, Support and Governance', in S. Carter and D. Jones-Evans (eds), *Enterprise and Small Business*, Pearson Education Limited: Essex.

Jones, F. F., Morris, M. H., and Rockmore, W. (1995). 'HR Practices that Promote Entrepreneurship', *Human Resources Magazine* (US), 40: 5, pp. 86-90.

Jones-Evans, D. (1987). 'Entrepreneurship Research and the Emerald Isle – a review of small business studies in the Republic of Ireland' in, H. Landstrom, H. Frank and J.M.

Veciana (eds), *Entrepreneurship and Small Business Research in Europe – an ECSB survey*, Avebury: Aldershot, pp. 152-174.

Kailer, N. (1990). 'Further Training in Small and Medium-sized Enterprises (Austria), *Journal of Small Business Management*, 28:1, pp. 60-63.

Kantor, J. (1988). 'Can Entrepreneurship be taught? – A Canadian Experiment', *Journal of Small Business and Entrepreneurship*, 5: 4, pp. 12-19.

Kaufmann, P. J. and Dant, R. P. (1999). 'Franchising and the Domain of Entrepreneurship Research', *Journal of Business Venturing*, 14: 1, pp. 5-16.

Keats, R., and Abercrombie, N. (eds). (1991). *Enterprise Culture*, Routledge: London.

Kets de Vries, M.F. (1970). 'The Entrepreneur as a Catalyst of Economic and Cultural Change', unpublished doctoral dissertation, Harvard University, Graduate School of Business Administration.

Kets de Vries, M.F. (1977). 'The Entrepreneurial Personality - A Person at the Crossroads', *Journal of Management Studies*, 14: 1, pp. 34-57.

Kets de Vries, M.F. (1996). 'The Anatomy of the Entrepreneur: clinical observations', *Journal of Human Relations*, 49: 7, pp. 853-884.

Kilby, P. (1971). 'Hunting the Heffalump', in P. Kilby (ed.), *Entrepreneurship and Economic Development*, Free Press: New York; Collier-MacMillan: London, pp. 27-35.

Kinnear, T.C. and Taylor, J. (1996). *Marketing Research: An Applied Approach*, McGraw-Hill: New York.

Kinni, T.B. (1994). 'Leadership up Close: effective leaders share four major characteristics', *Industry Week*, 20th June, 243: 12, pp. 21-23.

Kinsella, R.; Clarke, W., Storey, D.J.; Mulvenna, D. and Coyne, D. (1994). 'Fast Growth, Small Firms: An Irish Perspective', Irish Management Institute, Dublin.

Kirby, D.A and Mullen, D.C. (1990). 'Developing Enterprise in Graduates: the results of an experiment', in *Frontiers of Entrepreneurship Research*, Babson College: Wesley, MA, pp. 603-604.

Kirzner, I. M. (1978). *Competition and Entrepreneurship*, University of Chicago Press: Chicago, IL.

Klofsten, M. (1998). *The Business Platform: Entrepreneurship & Management in the Early Stages of a Firm's Development*, published by TII (Technology Innovation Information): Luxembourg.

Knight, F.H. (1940). *Risk Uncertainty and Profit*, Houghton – Mifflin: Boston.

Kolb, D. (1984). *Experiential Learning*, Prentice Hall:Englewood Cliffs, N.J.

Kruegel, N.F. and Brazeal, D.V. (1994). 'Entrepreneurial Potential and Potential Entrepreneurs', *Entrepreneurship: Theory and Practice*, 18: 3, pp. 91-105.

Kurder, F. (1968). 'General Manual, Occupational Interest Survey', Science Research Associates: Chicago.

Lau, T. and Chan, K.F. (1994). 'The Incident Method - An Alternative Way of Studying Entrepreneurial Behaviour', *IBAR - Irish Business and Administrative Research*, 15, pp. 48-61.

Laukkanen, M. (2000). 'Exploring alternative approaches in high-level entrepreneurship education: creating micro-mechanisms for endogenous regional growth', *Entrepreneurship and Regional Development*, 12, pp. 25-47.

Lee, D. Y. and Tsang, E. W. K. (2001). 'The Effects of Entrepreneurial Personality, Background and Network Activities on Venture Growth', *Journal of Management Studies*, 38: 4, pp. 583-602.

Leibenstein, H. (1968). 'Entrepreneurship and Development', *American Economic Review*, 58, pp. 72-83.

Le Roux, E. and Nieuwenhuizen, C. (1996). 'Small Business Management Education and Training: an innovative approach to the reconstruction and development of the new

South Africa', *proceedings of the Internationalising Entrepreneurship Education and Training Conference*, Arnhem.

Levinson, H. (1971). 'Conflicts that Plague Family Business', *Harvard Business Review*, 49: 2, pp. 90-98.

Levenson, H. (1974). 'Activism and Powerful Others: Distinctions within the concept of internal-external control', *Journal of Personality Assessment*, 38: 4, pp. 377-383.

Lightfoot, G. (1998). 'Financial Management and Small Firm Owner-Managers', unpublished PhD thesis, Kingston University.

Litzinger, W.D. (1965). 'The Motel Entrepreneur and the Motel Manager', *Academy of Management Journal*, 8: 4, pp. 268-281.

Low, M. (2001). 'The adolescence of entrepreneurship research: Specification of purpose', *Entrepreneurship Theory and Practice*, 25: 4, pp. 17-25.

Low, M and MacMillan, I. (1988). 'Entrepreneurship: Past research and future challenges', *Journal of Management*, 35, pp. 139-161.

Lumpkin, G. T. and Dess, G. G. (1996). 'Clarifying the Entrepreneurial Orientation Construct and Linking it to Performance', *Academy of Management Review*, 21: 1, pp. 135-172, cited in Sharma, P. and Chrisman, J. J. (1999), 'Toward a Reconciliation of the Definitional Issues in the Field of Corporate Entrepreneurship', *Entrepreneurship Theory and Practice*, 23: 3, pp. 11-27.

Lussier, R.N. (1995). 'Start-up Business Advice from Business Owners to Would-be Entrepreneurs', *SAM Advance Management Journal*, 60: 1, pp. 10-13.

Macrae, N. (1976). 'The Coming Entrepreneurial Revolution', *The Economist*, Christmas edition, London.

Mahlberg, T. (1996). 'Evaluating Secondary School and College Level Entrepreneurial Education - Pilot Testing a Questionnaire', *proceedings of the Internationalising Entrepreneurship Education and Training Conference*, Arnhem.

Mahoney, M. (2001). 'New Economy – The End or just the Beginning?', *E-Commerce Times*, 16th May.

Malinen, P. and Paasio, A. (1997). 'Entrepreneurship and Small Business Research in Finland', in H. Landstrom, H. Frank and J.M. Veciana (eds), *Entrepreneurship and Small Business Research in Europe – an ECSB survey*, Avebury: Aldershot, pp. 69-85.

Mazzarol, T., Volery, T., Doss, N. and Thein, V. (1999). 'Factors influencing small business start-ups', *International Journal of Entrepreneurial Behaviour and Research*, 5: 2, pp. 48-63.

McCabe, D. (1998). 'Building an Enterprise Culture in Northern Ireland and the Border Counties - the *en* framework', Centre for Innovation and Entrepreneurship, N. Ireland.

McCarthy, B. (2000). 'Researching the Dynamics of Risk-Taking and Social Learning: An Exploratory Study of Irish Entrepreneurs', *Irish Marketing Review*, 13: 1, pp. 46-60.

McClelland, D.C. (1961). *The Achieving Society*, D. van Nostrand Company: Princeton.

McClelland, D.C. (1965). 'Achievement Motivation Can Be Developed', *Harvard Business Review*, 43: 6, pp. 6-24 and 178.

McClelland, D.C. (1987). 'Characteristics of Successful Entrepreneurs', *Journal of Creative Behaviour*, 21: 3, pp. 219-233.

McClelland, D.C. and Winter, D.G. (1969 and 1971). *Motivating Economic Achievement*, The Free Press: New York.

McGovern, G. (2001). 'Always Make Mistakes'. Paper presented at the *Web Intellect – Advantage Seminar Series Online Survival conference*, Dublin, 17th October.

McMullan, C.A. and Boberg, A.L. (1991). 'The Relative Effectiveness of Projects in Teaching Entrepreneurship', *Journal of Small Business and Entrepreneurship*, 9, pp. 14-24.

McMullan, E., Chrisman, J.J. and Vesper, K. (2001). 'Some problems in using subjective measures of effectiveness to evaluate entrepreneurial assistance programs', *Entrepreneurship Theory and Practice*, 26: 1, pp. 37-54.

McMullan, W.E. and Long, W.A. (1987). 'Entrepreneurship Education in the Nineties', *Journal of Business Venturing*, 2: 3, pp. 61-275.

McNabb, A. (1996). 'What does Entrepreneurial Mean to the Small Business Owner?', *Proceedings of the 19th Institute of Small Business Affairs – National Small Firms Conference*, Birmingham, pp. 301-318.

Menger, C. (1950). *Principles of Economics*, translated by J Dingwall, B. F., Hoselitz, Free Press, Glencoe.

Meredith, G.G., Nelson, R.E., and Neck, P.A. (1982). 'The Practice of Entrepreneurship', International Labour Office, Geneva.

Miller, A. (1987). 'New Ventures: A Fresh Emphasis on Entrepreneurial Education', *Survey of Business*, 23: 1, pp. 4-9.

Mintzberg, H. (1973). 'Strategy Making in Three Modes', *California Management Review*, 16: 2, pp. 44-53.

Mintzberg, H. (1973). *The Nature of Managerial Work*, Harper Row: New York.

Mischel, W. (1973). 'Toward a Cognitive Social Learning and Reconceptualisation of Personality', *Psychology Review*, 80: 4, pp. 252-283.

Mohr, L.B. (1985). 'Causation and Case Study', cited in H.E. Klein (ed.), *Case Method Research and Application*, 1.5, WACRA: Boston.

Monroy, T.G. (1995). 'Getting Closer to a Descriptive Model of Entrepreneurship Education', in T.G. Monroy, J. Reichert and F. Hoy (eds), *The Art and Science of Entrepreneurship Education*, 3, Ballinger: Cambridge, Mass., pp. 205-217.

Morrison, A. (1997). *Entrepreneurship - An Introduction,* The Scottish Hotel School, University of Strathclyde.

Moss Kanter, R. (1983). *The Change Masters*, Thomas Publishing Inc: Boston, MA.

Mueller, S. L. and Thomas, A. S. (2001). 'Culture and Entrepreneurial Potential: a nine country study of locus of control and innovativeness', *Journal of Business Venturing*, 16: 1, pp. 51-75.

Mukthar, S.M., Oakey, R.P., and Kipling, M. (1998). 'Utilisation of Science and Technology Graduates by the Small and Medium Sized Enterprises Sector', *proceedings of the 6th Annual High Technology Small Firms Conference*, University of Twente.

Murray, J., and O'Donnel, N. (1982). 'Explorations in the Entrepreneurial Process', The Enterprise Centre, University College Dublin, Ireland.

Musson, G., and Cohen, L. (1996). 'Making Sense of Enterprise: Identity, Power and the Enterprise Culture'. *Proceedings of the 19th Institute of Small Business Affairs – National Small Firms Conference*, Birmingham, pp. 285-300.

Nahavandi, A. and Chesteen, S. (1988). 'The Impact of Consulting on Small Business: a further examination', *Entrepreneurship Theory and Practice*, Fall, pp. 29-40.

National Audit Office, Department of Employment/Training Commission. (1988). 'Assistance to Small Firms', Report to the Comptroller and Auditor General, HMSO: London.

Nulty, P. (1995). 'Serial Entrepreneur: tips from a man who started 28 businesses', (Courtland L. Logue), *Fortune Magazine*, 10th July, 132: 1, p. 182.

Nunnally, J. Jr. (1959). *Tests and Measurements: Assessment and Prediction*, McGraw-Hill: New York.

Oakey, R., Mukhtar, S.M., and Kipling, M. (1998). 'Student Perspectives on Entrepreneurship: observations on the propensity for entrepreneurial behaviour', *Proceedings of the Enterprise and Learning Conference*, University of Aberdeen.

O'Farrell, P. (1986). 'Entrepreneurs and Industrial Change', Irish Management Institute, Dublin.

O'Gorman, C. and Cunningham, J. (1997). *Enterprise in Action - An Introduction to Entrepreneurship in an Irish Context*, Oak Tree Press: Dublin.

Oldfield, C. (1999). 'Age Improves Entrepreneurs', *Sunday Times*, Business Supplement (UK), 24th January, p. 12.

Olson, P. (1985). 'Entrepreneurship: Opportunistic decision-Makers', *Journal of Small Business Management*, 11: 2, pp. 25-31.

O'Neill B. (2001). 'Chasing the Rainbow – the elusive consumer content value chain', Paper presented at the *Web Intellect – Advantage Seminar Series Online Survival Conference*, Dublin, 17th October.

Orser, B., Hogarth-Scott, S., and Wright, P. (1996). 'Enterprising Intention and Likelihood of Growth: a predictive model of firm performance', *Proceedings of the 19th Institute of Small Business Affairs – National Small Firms Conference*, Birmingham, pp. 728-747.

Osborne, R.L. (1995). 'The Essence of Entrepreneurial Success', *Management Decision*, 33: 7, pp. 4-9.

Ostermann, D. (2001). 'New Economy New Leadership', *Decision*, October/November issue, pp. 30-33.

Paul, P.C. & Joyner, T. (2000). 'New economy sprouting grey hair', *Atlanta Journal-Constitution*, 23rd November, p. G1.

Pelhamn, A. (1985). 'Should the SDBC Program be Dismantled?', *American Journal of Small Business*, 10: 2, pp. 41-51.

Peters, T. and Waterman, R. (1982). *In Search of Excellence*, Harper & Row: New York.

Pettigrew, A and Whipp, R. (1991). *Managing Change for Competitive Success*, Blackwell Business: Oxford.

Pinchot, G. III. (1986). *Intrapreneuring: Why You Don't Have to Leave the Organisation to Become an Entrepreneur*, Harper & Row: New York.

Ramachandran, K., Vyakarnam, S. and Handelberg, J. (1996). 'Entrepreneurial Types at the Start-up Stage'. *Proceedings of the 26th European Small Business Seminar*, Vaasa, Finland, pp. 393-406.

Roberts, E.B. (1968). 'A Basic Study of Innovators: how to keep and capitalise on their talents', *Research Management*, 11: 4, pp. 249-266.

Roberts, E. B. (1991). Entrepreneurs in High Technology, Oxford University Press: Oxford.

Roberts, E.B. and Wainer, H.A. (1968). 'New Enterprise on Route 128', *Science Journal*, 4: 12, pp. 78-83.

Roberts, E.B., and Wainer, H.A. (1996). 'Some Characteristics of Technical Entrepreneurs', Research Programme on the Management of Science and Technology, Massachusetts Institute of Technology, pp. 145-166.

Robichaud, Y., McGraw, E. and Roger, A. (2001). 'Toward the Development of a Measuring Instrument for Entrepreneurial Motivation', *Journal of Developmental Entrepreneurship*, 6: 2, pp. 189-201.

Ronstadt, R. (1984). *Entrepreneurship: Text, Cases and Notes*, Lord: Dover, MA.

Rotter, J.B. (1966). 'Generalised Expectancies for Internal versus External Control of Reinforcement', *Psychological Monographs*, 80: 609.

Saee, J. (1996). 'A Critical Evaluation of Australian Entrepreneurship Education and Training', *Proceedings of the Internationalising Entrepreneurship Education and Training Conference*, Arnhem.

Say, J.B. (1803). *A Treatise on Political Economy, or, the Production, Distribution and Consumption of Wealth*, Imprint, (1964), Sherwood, Neeley and Jones.: London.

SBA – Small Business Administration. (2001 and 2002). Background to the Small Business Administration, www.sba.gov.

Scaife, D. (2001). 'Online Survival', Paper presented at the *Web Intellect – Advantage Seminar Series Online Survival Conference*, Dublin, 17th October.

Scanlan, T. J. (1979). 'Self-employment as a Career Option: an investigation of entrepreneurs from the perspective of Hollands' theory of career development and Levenson's measures of locus of control', PhD Dissertation, University of Illinois.

Scanlan, T. J. (1984). 'Teaching Entrepreneurship at the Secondary Level', *Education Ireland*, 1: 3.

Scasse, R. (2000). 'The Enterprise Culture: the socio-economic context of small firms', in S. Carter and D. Jones-Evans (eds), *Enterprise and Small Business*, Pearson Education Limited: Essex.

Schollhammer, H. and Kuriloff, A. (1979). *Entrepreneurship and Small Business Management*, Wiley & Sons: Chichester.

Schrage, H. (1965). 'The R & D Entrepreneur: Profile of Success', *Harvard Business Review*, 43: 6, pp. 56-69.

Schumpeter, J.A. (1931). *Theorie der wirtschaftlichen entwicklung*, Duncker und Humblat: Munchen und Leipzig.

Schumpeter, J.A. (1934). *The Theory of Economic Development*, Cambridge, Harvard University: MA.

Schumpeter, J.A. (1965). 'Economic Theory and Entrepreneurial History', in Aitken, J.G. (ed.), *Exploration in Enterprise*, Harvard University Press: Cambridge, Mass.

Scottish Enterprise. (1993). 'Improving the Business Birth Rate: a strategy for Scotland', Scottish Enterprise, Glasgow.

Searchwebmanagement.com. (2001). 'Dotcom', 27th July.

Sexton, D. L. (1988). 'The Field of Entrepreneurship: Is it growing or just getting Bigger?'. *Journal of Small Business Management*, 26: 1, pp. 4-8.

Sexton, D.L., and Bowman-Upton, N.B. (1985). 'The Entrepreneur: a capable executive and more', *Journal of Business Venturing*, 1: 1, pp. 129-140.

Sexton, D.L. and Bowman-Upton, N.B. (1991). *Entrepreneurship: Creativity and Growth*, Macmillan: New York.

Sexton, D.L., Upton, N.B. Wacholtz, L.E. and McDougall, P.P. (1997). 'Learning Needs of Growth-Oriented Entrepreneurs', *Journal of Business Venturing*, 12, pp. 1-8.

Shapero, A. (1971). 'An Action Programme for Enterpreneurship', Multi-Disciplinary Research Inc; Austin, Texas.

Shapero, A. (1982). 'Social Dimensions of Entrepreneurship', in C. Kent, D. Sexton and K. Vesper (eds), *The Encyclopedia of Entrepreneurship*, pp. 72-90, Prentice Hall: Englewood Cliffs, N.J.

Sharma, P. and Chrisman, J. J. (1999). 'Toward a Reconciliation of the Definitional Issues in the Field of Corporate Entrepreneurship', Entrepreneurship Theory and Practice, 23: 3, pp. 11-27.

Shepherd, D. A., and Douglas, E. J. (1996). 'Is Management Education Developing or Killing the Entrepreneurial Spirit?', *Proceedings of the Internationalising Entrepreneurship Education and Training Conference*, Arnhem, June.

Simon, M., Houghton, S. M. and Aquino, K. (2000). 'Cognitive Biases, Risk Perception and Venture Formation: how individuals decide to start companies', *Journal of Business Venturing*, 15: 2, pp. 113-134.

Small Firms Enterprise Development Initiative. (1999). 'Building a Better Business', SFEDI, London.

Small Firms Lead Body. (1996). 'National Vocational Qualifications Standards: Owner-Management Planning/Business Management', Levels 3 and 4, Small Firms Lead Body/Small Firms Enterprise Initiative, London.

Smith, N.R. (1967). 'The Entrepreneur and his Firm: the relationship between type of man and type of company'. Michigan State University, Graduate School of Business Administration: East Lansing.

Sonnenfeld, J. (1988). *The Hero's Farewell*, Oxford University Press: New York.

Specht, P. H. (1993). 'Munificence and carrying capacity of the environment and organization formation', *Entrepreneurship Theory and Practice*, 17: 2, pp. 77-86.

Stake, R.E. (1980). 'Programme Evaluation, Particularly Responsive Evaluation', in Dockwell and Hamilton (eds.), *Rethinking Educational Research*, Hodder and Stoughton: London, pp. 72-87.

Stanworth, J., and Curran, J. (1971). *Management Motivation in the Smaller Business*, Gower Press: London.

Stanworth, J. and Gray, C. (1991). *Bolton 20 years on: the small firm in the 1990s*, Chapman: London.

Stewart, W. H., Watson, W. E., Carland, J. C. and Carland, J. W. (1999). 'A Proclivity for Entrepreneurship: A comparison of entrepreneurs, small business owners and corporate managers', *Journal of Business Venturing*, 14: 2, pp. 189-214.

Stigler, G. (1971). 'The Economic Theory of Regulation', *Bell Journal of Economics*, 2, pp. 3 21.

Storey, D.J. (1992). 'Should We Abandon the Support to Start-up Businesses?', paper no. 11, Warwick Business School, SME Centre.

Storey, D.J. (1994). *Understanding the Small Business Sector*, Routledge: London.

Storey, D.J. (2000). 'Six steps to heaven: evaluating the impact of public policies to support small business in developed economies', in D. Sexton and H. Landstrom (eds) *The Blackwell Handbook of Entrepreneurship*, pp. 176-193, Blackwell: Oxford.

Storey, D.J. and Johnson, S. (1986). 'Job Generation in Britain: A Review of Recent Studies'. *International Small Business Journal*, 4: 4, pp. 29-46.

Storey, D.J. and Johnson, S. (1987). 'Are Small Firms the Answer to Unemployment?', Employment Institute, London.

Storey, D.J. (2000). 'Public Policies to Assist Small and Medium Sized Enterprises in Developed Countries: rationales for intervention and a review of effectiveness', Warwick SME Centre, University of Warwick, Coventry.

Stumpf, S.S., Dunker, R.L.M. and Mullen, T.P. (1991). 'Developing Entrepreneurial Skills through the use of Behavioural Simulations', *Journal of Management Development*, 10: 5, pp. 32-45.

Smithson, S. (1991). 'Combining Different Approaches: discussant's comments', in H.E. Nissen, H.K. Klein and R.H. Hirschheim (eds), *Information Systems Research: contemporary approaches & emergent traditions*, pp. 365-369, Elsevier: Amsterdam.

Task Force on Small Business. (1994). 'Task Force on Small Business', Government Stationery Office, Dublin.

TechEncyclopedia.com. (2002). 'dot-com company', 20th March.

Telesis Consulting Group. (1982). 'The Telesis Report', Government Stationery Office, Dublin.

Terpstra, R., Ralston, D. and Bazen, S. (1993). 'Cultural Influences on the Risk-Taking Propensity of United States and Hong Kong Managers', *International Journal of Management*, 10: 2, pp. 183-93.

Tiernan, S.D., Morley, M.J. and Foley, E. (1996). *Modern Management: Theory and Practice for Irish Students*, Gill & MacMillan: Dublin.

Timmons, J.A. (1978). 'Characteristics and Role Demands of Entrepreneurship'. *American Journal of Small Business*, 3: 1, pp. 5-17.

Timmons, J.A. (1985). *New Venture Creation*, (2nd edition), Irwin: Homewood, Illinois.

Timmons, J.A. (1990). *New Venture Creation: Entrepreneurship in the 1990s*, 3rd edition, Irwin: Boston MA, cited in Stewart, W. H., Watson, W. E., Carland, J. C. and Carland, J. W. (1999), 'A Proclivity for Entrepreneurship: A comparison of entrepreneurs, small business owners and corporate managers', *Journal of Business Venturing*, 14: 2, pp. 189-214.

Timmons, J.A. (1994). *New Venture Creation* (4th edition), Irwin: Homewood, Illinois.

Timmons, J.A., Smollen, L.E., and Dingee, A.L. (1977). *New Venture Creation*, (1st edition), Irwin: Homewood, Illinois.

Timmons, J.A. and Stevenson, H.H. (1985). 'Entrepreneurship Education in the 1980s – What Entrepreneurs Say', in Kao. J. and Stevenson, H.H. (eds), *Entrepreneurship – What it is and How to Teach it*, Harvard Business School: Cambridge, Mass., pp. 115-134.

Timmons, J.A., Muzyka, D.F., Stevenson, H.M. and Bygrave, W.D. (1987). 'Opportunity Recognition: the core of Entrepreneurship', in Neill Churchill (ed.), *Frontiers of Entrepreneurial Research*, pp. 42-49, Babson College: Babson Park, Mass.

Ucbasaran, D. and Westhead, P. (2001). 'The focus of entrepreneurial research: contextual and process issues', *Entrepreneurship Theory and Practice*, 25: 4, pp. 57-80.

Van der Sijde, P., Van Tilburg, J., Henry, C., Sygne, J., Asplund, R. (1997). *UNISPIN Workbook*, UNISPIN Project Team, University of Twente, The Netherlands.

Van Slambrouck, P. (2000). 'Facing red ink, dotcoms temper their idealism', *The Christian Science Monitor*, 12th April, p. 3.

Van Voorhis, K.R.W., Stenhorn, G. and Hofer, M. (1996). 'B-17 Educational Plan - for new business start-ups', *Proceedings of the 26th European Small Business Seminar*, Finland, pp. 433-438.

Veciana, J.M. and Genesca, E. (1997). 'Entrepreneurship and Small Business Research in Spain', in H. Landstrom, H. Frank and J.M. Veciana (eds), *Entrepreneurship and Small Business Research in Europe – an ECSB survey*, Avebury: Aldershot, pp. 263-275.

Venkatraman (1996), as cited in Fiet (2000b), cited as personal correspondence.

Vento, I. (1998). 'Promoting Enterprise Culture Through Education', *Proceedings of the Enterprise and Learning Conference*, Aberdeen.

Vesper, K.H. (1982). 'Research on Education for Entrepreneurship', in Kent, C.A., Sexton, D.L. and Vesper, K.H. (eds), *Encyclopedia of Entrepreneurship*, pp. 321-343, Prentice Hall: Englewood Cliffs, NJ.

Wainer, H.A. and Rubin, I.M. (1969). 'Motivation of R & D Entrepreneurs: determinants of company success', *Journal of Applied Psychology*, 53: 3, pp. 178-184.

Walsham, G. (1995). 'Interpretative Case Studies in IS Research', *European Journal of Information Systems*, 4: 2, pp. 74-81.

Wan, V. (1989). 'The Enterprise Workshop Programme in Australia', *International Small Business Journal*, 7: 2, pp. 23-34.

Watkins, D. S. (1983). 'Development Training and Education for the Small Firm: a European Perspective', *European Small Business Journal*, 1: 3, pp. 29-44.

Watkins, D.S. (1976). 'Entry into Independent Entrepreneurship - Toward a Model of the Business Initiation Process', *Proceedings of the EIASM Joint Seminar on Entrepreneurship and Institution Building*, Copenhagen, May.

Watts, A.G. (1984). 'Education for Enterprise: the concept and the context', in A.G. Watts and Paul Moran (eds), *Education for Enterprise*, published by CRAC: Ballinger,Cambridge, UK:, pp. 3-6.

Weber, M. (1930). The Protestant Work Ethic and the Spirit of Capitalism, Allen and Unwin: London. Weber, M. (1958). *The Protestant Work Ethic and the Spirit of Capitalism*, translated by T. Parsons, C. Scribners and Sons: New York.

Weinreich, P. (1980). 'A Manual for Identity Exploration using Personal Constructs', Social Science Research Council (Economic and Social Research Council).

Westhead, P. and Birley, S. (1994). 'Environments for Business De-registrations in the UK, 1987-1990', *Entrepreneurship and Regional Development*, 6: 1, pp. 29-62.

Westhead, P., Storey, D.J. and Martin, F. (2001). 'Outcomes reported by students who participated in the 1994 Shell technology Enterprise Programme', *Entrepreneurship and Regional Development*, 13, pp. 163-185.

White Paper. (1994). 'White Paper: Competitiveness and Growth', HMSO: London.

White Paper. (1995). 'White Paper: Competitiveness, Forging Ahead', HMSO: London.

White Paper. (1999). 'Learning to Succeed', Department for Education and Employment, HMSO: London.

Wickham, P.A. (1998). *Strategic Entrepreneurship*, (1st edition), Pitman Publishing: London.

Wickham, P.A. (2001). *Strategic Entrepreneurship*, (2nd edition), Pitman Publishing: London.

Wiesner, F. von. (1927). *Social Economics*, translated by A.F. Hindrichs, Adelphi: New York.

Wright, P. (1996). 'Simulating Reality: the role of case incident in higher education', *Journal of Education and Training*, 38: 6, pp. 20-24.

Wyckham, R.G. (1989). 'Ventures Launched by Participants of an Entrepreneurial Education Program', *Journal of Small Business Management*, 27: 2, pp. 54-61.

Yin, R.K. (1981). 'The Case Study Crisis: some answers', *Administrative Science Quarterly*, 26: 1, pp. 28-65.

Yin, R.K. (1994). *Case Study Research - Design and Methods* (second edition), Applied Social Research Methods Series, 5, Sage Publications: London.

Yoffie, D.B. & Kwak, M. (2001). 'Lessons from dotcom days', *The Financial Times*, 2nd October.

Young, J.E. (1997). 'Entrepreneurship Education and Learning for University Students and Practicing Entrepreneurs', in Sexton, D.L. and Simlor, R.W., *Entrepreneurship 2000*, Upstart Publishing: Chicago.

Index